# Making a Difference in the Lives
# of Bilingual/Bicultural Children

# Studies in the
# Postmodern Theory of Education

Joe L. Kincheloe and Shirley R. Steinberg
*General Editors*

Vol. 134

PETER LANG
New York • Washington, D.C./Baltimore • Bern
Frankfurt am Main • Berlin • Brussels • Vienna • Oxford

# Making a Difference
# in the Lives of
# Bilingual/Bicultural Children

EDITED BY
## Lourdes Diaz Soto

PETER LANG
New York • Washington, D.C./Baltimore • Bern
Frankfurt am Main • Berlin • Brussels • Vienna • Oxford

#49757579

LIBRARY OF CONGRESS CATALOGING-IN-PUBLICATION DATA

Making a difference in the lives of bilingual/
bicultural children / edited by Lourdes Diaz Soto.
p. cm. — (Counterpoints; vol. 134)
Includes bibliographical references.
1. Education, Bilingual—Social aspects—United States. 2. Children
of minorities—Education—Social aspects—United States. 3. Multicultural
education—United States. 4. Educational change—United
States. I. Soto, Lourdes Diaz. II. Series.
LC3731 .M35    370.117'0973—dc21    99-057651
ISBN 0-8204-4892-3
ISSN 1058-1634


DIE DEUTSCHE BIBLIOTHEK-CIP-EINHEITSAUFNAHME

Making a difference in the lives of bilingual,
bicultural children / ed. by: Lourdes Diaz Soto.
–New York; Washington, D.C./Baltimore; Bern;
Frankfurt am Main; Berlin; Brussels; Vienna; Oxford: Lang.
(Counterpoints; Vol. 134)
ISBN 0-8204-4892-3

Cover design by Joni Holst

To the lovers of children,
teaching, advocacy, and social justice

*Only through the bringing together of head and heart intelligence and good-ness shall man(woman) rise to the fulfillment of his(her) true nature.*
MARTIN LUTHER KING, JR.

# CONTENTS

# FIGURES

# TABLES

# FOREWORD

PETER MCLAREN, UNIVERSITY OF CALIFORNIA, LOS ANGELES

Educators have been encouraged to be optimistic as they navigate their way through the first precarious stage of the new millennium. They are told that they are entering a new postindustrial, high-tech information era that will usher in a gilded age of prosperity for themselves and their students. As James Petras notes, however, this characterization of current economic conditions is patently false, since computer industries represent less than 3 percent of the economy. In this predominately financial-industrial economy, government leaders in league with privateers and laissez-faire evangelists like to hype the information age, because in doing so it is easier for them to generate false optimism about the future, and to draw attention away from the fact that prosperity is largely confined to speculative financial and real estate sectors of the capitalist class. By creating a façade of information-era utopianism, criticism can be siphoned away from the fact that we live in an era marked by monopolistic giants, greedy conglomerates, selective protectionism, massive state subsidies, the selling-off of public enterprises to private monopolies, welfare for the rich, domestic and overseas multibillion dollar money laundering, arms industry domination of the export sector, the placing of key state institutions under the influence of financial sectors of civil society—in short, a social order in which class warfare runs amok (Petras 2000).

Of course, the marketization, privatization, and neoliberalization of schooling is functionally advantageous to the conditions described above. That schooling has been reduced to a subsector of the economy and that it gives ballast to existing discourses and practices of class exploitation and white-supremacist patriarchy is no longer a secret. What is new is the resignation that has accompanied the news. When we learn that Latino students are twice as likely as African-Americans and three times as likely as whites to drop out of high school, or that in 1997, 25.3 percent of Latinos aged sixteen to twenty-four dropped out of high school compared with 13.4 percent of African-Americans and 7.6 percent of whites (McQueen 2000), the information registers but somehow ceases to enrage us. Part of the reason for this is that exploitation through the capitalist marketplace has been so naturalized that we have learned to accept a certain amount of exploitation and accompanying forms of racism, sexism, and homophobia that we feel are an inevitable part of living in a developed capitalist democracy. What we fail to grasp is that capitalism and democracy actually work against each other and the familiar coupling of the two words is really just a form of linguistic— hence ideological—mystification. I guess the rationale is that if we keep hearing the term "capitalist democracy" frequently enough, we will begin to believe that the two terms are inseparable. In fact, the two terms need to be torn apart, not yoked together. Maybe another adjective needs to precede the term "democracy." Maybe "socialist democracy" is a more appropriate coupling. But since we have been programmed throughout the cold war to get a headache even at the mere mention of the word "socialism," it is unlikely we will ever see "socialist democracy" appear in the journals devoted to educational reform, at least not anytime soon.

California is often a precursor to the dominant scenarios of US futurity. It is the state that passes propositions (i.e., 187, 209, 227) that routinely are given birth through a marriage of political Monday-morning quarterbacks in the form of rich businessmen like Ron Unz, and manic, mean-spirited, right-wing populists such as Pat Buchanan, Pat Robertson, and their ilk. California's political initiatives often serve as political harbingers for a politics that will eventually spread throughout other states like a runaway contagion, mixing racism, sexism, bourgeois historical amnesia, class arrogance, and homophobia into a political cocktail as dangerous as any biological weapon invented by the US military. California is a state that generates a lot of tension around educational reform—a tension that can be traced largely to Latinophobia. This is not hard to understand in an agonistic geopolitical arena where scapegoating immigrants from Mexico is a commonplace and accepted practice. California is also where the English-only movement is gaining momentum.

Donaldo Macedo captures the absurdity of the English-only proponents who argue that English is the most effective language for citizens of the United States, and that it is the language that will best guarantee a successful future:

> First, if English is the most effective educational language, how can we explain why over 60 million Americans are illiterate or functionally illiterate? Second, if English-Only education can guarantee linguistic minorities a better future, as educators like William Bennett promise, why do the majority of Black Americans, whose ancestors have been speaking English for over two hundred years, find themselves still relegated to the ghettos? (in press, 2).

In the midst of the widening scenario of immigrant bashing, it is not difficult to make the case that democracy has fallen into disfavor, even been rendered obsolete. Two types of reactions predominate. The first is to engage in a half-revolution through "reformist" efforts, underwritten by a teleological belief in the evolution of democracy through the free market. The second is to engage in political activism that cuts to the heart of neoliberalism, corporate control of the schooling process, and capitalist relations of exploitation. While the former beggars the praxis of critical struggle, the latter lacks a coherent national and international strategy.

Opposition to neoliberalism has been muted, thanks to the polished statecraft of Clinton and his successful cheerleading for an unfettered free market (under cover, I might add, of a Third Way détente between Keynesian economics and ultracapitalism). Opposition has also been blunted through the efforts and cagey triumphalism of New Right apologists of the free market. The colonial apotheosis of New Right heroes such as Pat Buchanan, Donald Trump, Jesse Ventura, and George W. Bush and the brain-stunting banality of their political platforms have met with a lack of any real spirited opposition among the left. Spurred on by this lack of opposition, multiculturalism continues to defang its most emancipatory possibilities by calling for diversity in isolation from an interrogation of its center of sameness known as the hegemony of whiteness. It is this sameness that is the distillate of colonialism and the ether of white lies that spikes the very air we breathe. We need to join Noel Ignatiev, David Roediger, and others in calling for the abolition of whiteness. We need to recognize (as I have tried to make clear in my work over the years) that there is no positive value that can be given to the social position known as whiteness. The term cannot be recovered, or given a positive spin. White people need to disidentify entirely with the white race. To seek any kind of identity with a white race—or political détente—is ill-conceived at best. But along with efforts to abolish the white race (not white people; there is a distinct difference), we must support efforts to abolish capital.

Educators are fed up with white lies. They see through them. They are beginning to attach a language to them and are starting to theorize the issues more completely, and more deeply, thanks to the efforts of Lourdes Díaz Soto and others contributors to *Making a Difference in the Lives of Bilingual/Bicultural Children.*

Are decorous shifts toward decentralization, rigorous academic standards, teacher accountability, and parental choice supposed to fool anyone? Have recent attempts to camouflage the deep assumptions of terms such as "accountability," so frequently bandied about by neoliberal pundits these days, really blinded teachers to the protofascist elements of the New Right gospellers and free-market evangelists? Are teachers fooled by such aerosol terms as "empowerment" that are shouted as much in the board rooms of corporations as they are in teacher education programs? Teachers are no fools, and they are not to be fooled with. While we might inhabit a period of political defeat at the ballot box, we find ourselves on the cusp of a moral victory as teachers begin to exercise their voices of dissent.

One promising sign on the horizon is that the political fade-out of Marx has been temporary; the old bearded devil is coming back with a vengeance, having been summoned by those who both recognize and rage against the fact that "the inexorable march of privatization [is] leading England (and a good part of the Western world) forward to the social hierarchy of the 17th century" (Morris 2000, 67).

While Marx might not have anticipated the specific trajectory capitalism would take at this particular moment in history, his work was most certainly premonitory of the current crisis of capitalism. What is so significant about Marx's analysis is that it stressed above all the underlying systemic dynamics of capitalism in all of its capillary detail. No doubt Marx would have recognized the current crisis of capitalism as implicated in the global capitalist economy as a whole, inextricably tied to the laws of motion of capital and the ways in which capital and wage labor reproduce themselves (McNally 1999). Marxist theory is congruent with leftist multiculturalists and bilingual educators who recognize the relationship between the exploitation of human labor and systems of classification and mythologies linked to the demonization of certain groups on the basis of race, ethnicity, phenotype, etc. (McLaren 1997; McLaren 2000). It is also congruent with attempts by multiculturalists to tease out the labyrinthine and arabesque complexities that scaffold race, class, gender, and sexual antagonisms and their co-constitutivity.

The articles in this book reflect a powerful recognition of the relationship among capital, exploitation, and systems of representation. What is especially compelling about this volume is that the authors recognize and address new conditions that face the current generation of educational reformers.

Perry Anderson summarizes these changes:

> First, there has been a massive displacement of dominance from verbal to visual codes, with the primacy of television over every preceding means of communication, followed by the rise of subsequent electronic media in which the same shift has been technologically replicated. This pattern has, of course, defined the arrival of postmodern forms at large. Secondly—another hallmark of the latter—most of the tension between deviant or insurgent impulses from below and the established order above has been absorbed, as the market has appropriated and institutionalized youth culture in much the same way it earlier encapsulated avant-garde practices: but—this being a mass market—much more thoroughly (2000, 8).

The authors of *Making a Difference in the Lives of Bilingual/Bicultural Education* call attention to the impact that new media technologies have made on the politics of educational reform. And they recognize the importance of making structural changes in the larger social system while fighting the ability of capital to reabsorb reform efforts within its own commodity logic. Consequently, many of the authors see the need for a direct-action politics centered around equality, antiracism, and a politics of difference. This is decidedly not a politics of piecemeal increments. It is a praxis for the present.

Faced with the uncertainty of the present, some look to religion to save us from ourselves. It has been said that religion is for those who fear hell; but it could also be said that educational activism is for those of us who have already been there. The educational activists of today are those who are not afraid to recognize the type of social evil that we see all around us and to name it as such. They are committed to fight the racist, sexist, and corporate evil that still envelopes us even as we move with confidence into the new millennium. In such a struggle we could not ask for better compañero/as than Lourdes Díaz Soto and her band of courageous contributors. Hasta la victoria siempre!

# NOTE

Some sections of this Foreword have been expanded into several articles by Peter McLaren and Ramin Farahmandpur. See *Multicultural Education and Educational Policy*, forthcoming.

# ACKNOWLEDGMENTS

We would like to acknowledge the struggles of bilingual children, families, and teachers who are rarely rewarded for their wisdom. Our deepest gratitude is expressed to our friends, families, students, and colleagues who have seen the value of our work. I am personally indebted to Barbara Apaliski for formatting the pieces and to Judy Nastase for her support. We are all ever so grateful to the courageous editors and publishers at Peter Lang, especially Shirley Steinberg, Joe Kincheloe, and Chris Myers whose encouragement and support have helped to provide "voice" to the needs of bilingual/bicultural children.

# INTRODUCTION

## THE POLITICAL, THE DIALOGIC, AND THE CRITICAL

LOURDES DÍAZ SOTO, THE PENNSYLVANIA STATE UNIVERSITY

> *More than loving*
> *living means giving*
> *Like homegrown food*
> *from the eternal harvest within*
> SANDRA MARÍA ESTEVES

Growing up bilingual and bicultural in the new millennium is complex and ultimately related to sociopolitical, sociohistorical, and power relations. Bakhtin (Holquist 1981) wrote about the effects of other people's words in our lives. The main point of his analysis relates to the importance of our perceptions of ourselves through the lenses of others' words. Linguistically and culturally diverse children face daunting challenges in educational settings that not only disregard their home language and culture but the wisdom of previous generations.

This book asks the reader to first view the continued need for critical understanding by exploring selected issues of power, linguicism, racism, grand theories, and critical literacy. The second part of the book provides examples of the daily realities bilingual/bicultural children face and the need to ultimately uncover and deconstruct multiple issues. The third part of the book highlights promising educational practices as well as how educators can address ethical responsibilities. The examples of practices in this book are as valuable as the theoretical, the critical, and the daily realities because in spite of draconian conservative stances against bilingual education, educators and

classroom teachers are still faced with providing for the needs of bilin-
gual/bicultural children on a daily basis.

How do children make sense of existing educational and cultural practices? How can educators provide for the educational needs of children in
ways that can "make a difference" in their lives? The paradox for us as educators is to understand that young bilingual/bicultural children can, in spite
of their colonized existence, express love for "the other." Children interviewed elsewhere (Soto 1999) shed light on how learners shape and negotiate their identities as bilingual/biliterate subjects in postmodern America.
Cne of the themes that emerged from a slice of the research project included
descriptions of helping compassionate love relations for the "other." Bilingual children's collages, drawings, and interviews continually illustrated love
in the form of helping relations and altruistic behaviors.

While the bilingual/bicultural children I interviewed in Steeltown
demonstrated "love for the other," their own schools have rejected them in
many ways (Soto 1997). The school district's reliance on language domination has established subordinate social relations whereby the possibility for
critical literacy by bicultural subjects has been denied. Language domination
by the "bilingual education abolitionists" constitutes hegemonic forces of
class oppression and cultural invasion.

Colonized children in America have been systematically stripped of their
integrity, independence, freedom, and voice. This form of educational violence and slaying of the soul has functioned to perpetrate social control.
Children have been stripped of their ability to participate in school and community life. Their voices are silenced, and they are unable to enter into dialogue or reflect on their daily realities and lived experiences. Ultimately this
marginalization leads to multiple and complex issues for children, including
issues of identity. As the privileged assert their superiority, bicultural children
continue to lead an oppressed existence while continually reaching out to
the "other" with love and compassion.

Freire (1970) pointed out

> For cultural invasion to succeed, it is essential that those invaded become
> convinced of their intrinsic inferiority ... The more invasion is accentuated
> and those invaded are alienated from the spirit of their own culture and
> from themselves, the more the latter want to be like the invaders: to walk
> like them, dress like them, talk like them (151). Ultimately the oppressed
> instead of striving for liberation, tend themselves to become the oppressors
> ... the very structure of their thought has been conditioned by contradic-
> tions of the concrete, existential situation by which they were shaped ... this
> phenomenon derives from the fact that the oppressed, at a certain moment

in their experience, adopt an attitude of adhesion to the oppressor ... the oppressed find the oppressor their model (29–30).

Cummins (1996) refers to the "enemy within":

the politics of greed and exploitation that is willing to jeopardize not only the lives of individual children but also the coherence of entire societies for its own coercive ends ... coercive relations of power operate to manufacture consent for programs and policies ... the scapegoating of immigrants and cultural diversity since the 1980's has reignited Us versus Them divisions and fears in order to obscure and distract attention from the increasingly obvious redistribution of wealth in North American societies. Indoctrination and disinformation are the tools whereby consent is manufactured for this process (220).

The study conducted by Poplin and Weeres (1992) focused on four urban California schools. The children's experiences showed a sense of despair and were summed up by one student who said, "This place hurts my spirit."

*Tendran nuestros niños que dejar sus almas en la puerta de la escuela?* Will our children have to leave their souls at the schoolhouse door? How do we liberate our children when they are receiving a toxic education against their will? Freire (1970) indicated that "it would be extremely naive to expect the dominant classes to develop a type of education that would enable subordinate classes to perceive social injustices critically (102)."

What are these children telling us? Their example is one of love and altruism. What is our collective and ethical responsibility?

Moraes's (1996) vision for dialogic-critical pedagogy that incorporates both Bakhtin's and Freire's works calls for a dialogue of social "multivoicedness." Morales sees the Freirian perspective as providing the impetus "from the margins to the center," while the Bakhtinian movement exemplifies a move "from the margins and from the center." In light of bicultural children's daily realities the question remains—will the oppressive forces travel in any direction other than toward cultural invasion? An important point for educators in particular to address is that as we chart experimental and newly evolving paradigms we must not fall victims to the standard models in education. Instead, we can move toward a deeper understanding of the multiple dimensions that permeate children's daily lives.

Freire (1970) described the potency of love: "Love is an act of courage, not of fear, love is commitment to others ... As an act of bravery, love cannot be sentimental: as an act of freedom, it must not serve as a pretext for manipulation" (71).

This book will guide you (the reader) in critically examining how to best make a difference in bilingual/bicultural children's postmodern lives. The contributors have selected areas that are close to their hearts representing multiple and complex issues. The authors themselves have multiple experiences that have led them to share powerful personal experiences, scholarship, theoretical perspectives, and research endeavors.

In the first part of the book you will examine the need for a *critical understanding* of the field.

In chapter 1, Kharem and Villaverde ask teachers to become allies and coworkers with the oppressed ones. These newly emerging scholars take issue with the current school curriculum and call on educators to change institutions that they may become sites representing altruism, justice, and democracy.

In chapter 2, Moser draws a chilling and convincing comparison of the German-only ideology of the Nazi era with America's English-only movement.

In chapter 3, Bryzzheva examines how Vygotsky's and Bakhtin's work can be useful to the classroom teacher in her/his daily teaching. Bryzzheva notes that the "soul of language" is not considered by those who find it difficult to view language as a social construct.

Lankshear and Knobel uncover a teacher's misconception about her one "nonmainstream" learner's capabilities in chapter 4. They also provide selected readings to benefit teachers.

Semali, in chapter 5, reflects on how linguistic repression affects students. Reflecting on his own teaching in Kenya and the United States, he depicts colonial "cargo" as cultural invasion.

In chapter 6, De Gourville takes up the home language policy issue impacting black children in American schools.

The second portion of the book, "Becoming Aware of Children's Daily Realities," begins with (chapter 7) Itsa-Lichii's kindergarten struggle in a Texas school. Gutierrez-Gomez retells her son's struggle with a school that forbade his long hair (like his Apache fathers).

In chapter 8, Espinosa-Dulanto, a passionate Peruvian educator, uses American Latino/a stories and fiction to relate social agency. She relates her fears, her search for the families' empathy (in spite of her differing from them), and how the schools and the research grant dealt with the children.

In chapter 9, Pabon describes her own evolution as a Puerto Rican woman when confronted with a critical examination of the colonizer/colonized depictions described by Villenas (1996).

Yamuna in chapter 10 relates his early childhood memories in Papua New Guinea, the intergenerational practices and wisdom as well as the cost of a formal education leading to his own biculturalism.

In chapter 11, Blum-Martínez argues that language minority parents (recently arrived Mexicano and American Indian, Pueblo) are involved in their children's lives and schooling contrary to stereotypical notions. She also includes a personal vignette about her son's bar mitzvah.

Part 3 titled "Promising Practices" begins with Reyes and Costanzo's piece (chapter 12). These scholars debunk the narrow interpretations of Cummin's hypothesis as they recount a first grader's personal journey toward biliteracy.

In chapter 13, Han and Ernst-Slavit describe the actions and interactions of six recently arriving Chinese kindergartners in their classroom and their pullout ESL program.

In chapter 14, Smrekar calls on early childhood educators to critically analyze their own beliefs, pratices, and education that will benefit young bilingual/bicultural learners.

In chapter 15, Fránquiz offers a piece that describes her ethnographic fieldwork in an alternative high school where literate activities draw connections between in-school and out-of-school daily living.

In the last chapter (16), Cummins interjects ethical concerns by noting the rights and responsibilities of educators of bilingual/bicultural children. He describes three programs where collaborative power relations exist (New Zealand, USA, and Belgium).

We hope that these pieces taken together will add insights new perspectives, wisdom, a place for reflection, an opportunity for dialogue, and the courage to make a difference in the lives of bilingual/bicultural children.

As educators it has become increasingly evident that we need to summon our courageous collective selves. We can continue to teach children and families to recognize not only how communities victimize and oppress them but how school policies, school procedures, and school programs operate. We can overcome the prevailing forces of domination, cultural invasion, racism, classism, and sexism. This is no easy task, but just as the Steeltown children who demonstrated so much courage and love, so must we summon a path that has heart, a path that cares, a path that nourishes our very souls.

The rest of the journey in this book will lead the reader to examine the political, the dialogic, and the critical. Only when we dare to examine the complexity of the issues while acting in an ethical manner will we reach our dreamspace of equity, social justice, and liberation. Our very best role models are the very children whose loving hearts reach for the "others."

# PART ONE

# THE NEED
# FOR CRITICAL
# UNDERSTANDING

# CHAPTER ONE

# TEACHER

# ALLIES

## THE PROBLEM OF THE COLOR LINE

HAROON KHAREM, BROOKLYN COLLEGE

LEILA E. VILLAVERDE, DEPAUL UNIVERSITY

Teachers who are or will be involved in bilingual/bicultural education can fully comprehend the oppression, history, culture, and political movements of the students they intend to teach. Teachers can understand that the disregard of native tongues is not a benign act. There is a renewed movement of Anglo-Protestant nativism that believes any form of bilingual and/or multicultural education is a menace to American society. The aim of this renewed nativism in public schools is to guarantee the cultural domination of Anglo-Protestant culture and language in the United States. Throughout the history of the United States, schools have always been sites and agencies of "Americanism" whereby children of color have been segregated and isolated and forced to speak only English and learn a curriculum and use textbooks that reflect only an Anglo-Protestant culture. Bilingual students of color are acculturated and conformed to follow the patterns of "Americanization" in the quest for a homogeneous white society (Carlson 2000). Native, African- and Hispanic-American children have not been allowed to express their culture or religion as white teachers represent the Anglo-Protestant norm which is very important to the maintenance of white supremacy (Spring 1994 and 1997; Asante 1990).

During the 1960s and the early 1970s, as the Civil Rights Movement achieved some degree of success and reformed some of the nation's racial apartheid system, the movement came immediately under attack by right-wing and conservative alliances (Omni and Winant 1994). The federal government, along with other societal leaders, from this nation's inception was determined to use public schools to create and secure a national culture that would be unified around Anglo-Protestantism. Public schools became the defenders of Anglo-Protestant cultural values that were allegedly challenged by Catholicism and Native and African-American culture (Spring 1997). Since the beginning of the United States, government and other public figures decided to Americanize Native Americans and acquire their lands, while at the same time Hispanics and African-Americans were sent to school to be deculturalized and forced to accept Anglo-Protestant culture as their own (Macedo 1994; Spring 1994).

Bilingual education has aroused issues of political power and social status that are far removed from the classroom and have given many citizens in the United States the perception to redefine school knowledge and challenge the principles of Western ideology, its concepts of race, and its economic and educational hegemony that is being challenged by people of color to bring about a more equitable society. Educators can become critical researchers and produce knowledge leading to freedom from the dominant forces of society that will be emancipatory for curriculum development and teacher preparation. In this chapter, we will delineate how teachers can grasp and impart these concepts through relevant and productive curricular changes.

Curriculum change also involves the way a teacher teaches; that is, their particular style of teaching that is usually permeated by their philosophy of education, beliefs, and values. Teaching is not a neutral activity. It is not devoid of our innermost thoughts and ideals. In order to effectively infuse our teaching with critical awareness and consciousness, we must put ourselves under the same microscope to which we put the content of curriculum. Consequently, we expand that which we deem necessary to include, challenge, and revisit in the construction of curriculum. In this chapter we will address the issue of race, consciousness, teacher identity, and curriculum through the larger issue of bilingual education. We will offer numerous books as resources for the bilingual educator.

In 1900, W. E. B. Du Bois prophecied that

> the problem of the twentieth century is the problem of the color-line, the question as to how our differences of race—which show themselves chiefly in the color of skin and the texture of the hair—will hereafter be made the basis of denying to over half the world the right of sharing to their utmost ability the opportunities and privileges of modern civilization (Du Bois 1963, 20).

Du Bois understood that the struggles of people of color for position, credibility, and respectability within Western society would have global implications. The controversy over who will educate children of color and what the nature of that education will be, whose vision will be imparted to them, and whose language they will speak is crucial to the debate in education today. He came to the conclusion that if people of color in the United States, South America, Asia, and Africa were going to maintain their culture, then they must liberate themselves from Europe and the United States' political, economic, and cultural exploitation, subordination, and dominating colonial system (Aptheker 1973).

Educators who teach children of color must not only become allies to people of color, they must organize themselves, cultivate their critical thinking and their educational practice, and rethink their curriculum and school organization. These teacher-allies can become coworkers with people of color to see and understand the perspectives of the oppressed. They can learn to respect the knowledge and language that people of color bring to bear on culture and society, and assist them in tearing down the walls of oppression, which will allow the human spirit reach its potential.

Theoretical paradigms grounded in Eurocentric, white supremacist ideology construct a pedagogy of classroom practices and instructional materials that silence the voices, languages, and perspectives of nonwhite people and students of color. Anglo-Protestant paradigms essentially validate only the dominant white, upper-class male voices as the "standard" knowledge and language that students must know. They disregard all other interpretations and perspectives or ostracize people of color. Knowledge that is produced by people of color is erased from mainstream scholarship and made to appear pathologically dangerous to the public eye.

Bilingual education in the United States is seen as antagonistic, as it disrupts established patterns in the curriculum. Money spent on immigrant, alien children is viewed as wasteful. Instead, children's home language and culture must be replaced by English, because they must be assimilated into Anglo-Protestant culture. Any knowledge that does not reflect Anglo-Protestant culture must be Americanized and rearticulated to look patriotic and loyal to the United States.

We need to ask for what purposes are the children of color educated and what the consequences will be if their disenfranchisement continues to prevail in Western society. Bilingual teachers and administrators must confront public policies that continue to discriminate against Native Americans, Puerto Ricans, Mexicans, Asian-Americans, and immigrant children of African descent. They must prepare their students politically as well as economically to survive in a land that devalues their worldview. Those within curriculum circles must ask themselves how education might help children of color in confronting the societal structures that preserve and reproduce white supremacy and inequality. These investigations are not meant to displace the English language or marginalize the culture and history of white upper-class male epistemologies. Rather, this critique of European ideology seeks to raise questions that have the possibility to transform this dominant and patriarchal alignment so as to place it in a context that demands the inclusion of accurate portraiture of all cultures and groups of people.

The massive migration of nonwhite people into industrial countries is replacing unionized workers and is filling the need for cheap labor. Nonwhite people have created a new multiethnic and multiracial society, especially in the United States. Nonwhite migrations have always caused racial tensions, as corporate America deceives displaced, mostly white, workers to look for scapegoats to blame not only for the loss of their jobs, but also for the nation's economic and moral decline (Perlmutter 1992; Omni and Winant 1994). Over the next few years the majority of children in public schools will be children of color, struggling through a system that has inherently built in their lack of success and an almost automatic stigmatization. In order for educators to be adequately prepared, their educational courses must not be pathologically oriented. By this we mean that these courses cannot continue to belittle, essentialize, misunderstand, or neglect minority populations. Curricular knowledge and college teacher preparation courses can and should create and utilize cultural models and theories that support the experiences of people of color. Throughout this chapter, we intend to focus on the oppression of people of color in the American educational system.

Thousands of potential teachers and administrators, including students of color, graduate every semester with a four-year degree without ever hearing about or studying classic works by scholars such as Carter G. Woodson's *The Mis-Education of the Negro* (1933), James D. Anderson's *The Education of Blacks in the South* (1988), or Horace Man Bond's *The Education of the Negro in the American Social Order* (1934) and *Negro Education in Alabama: A Study in Cotton and Steel* (1937). Nor are students ever exposed to recent works by Harding, Yeo, Willie, Shujaa, Macedo, Zinn, Perry and Fraser, Sleeter and Grant, McCarthy and Chrichlow, Bigelow et al., Adams, Shobat and Stam, Kincheloe and Steinbeg, Gordon and Newfield, Soto, and Leistyna.

This is only a partial list of numerous scholars whose works address issues of equity in the preparation of teachers and administrators. Not only should present and future teachers and administrators read these resources; they should incorporate them into their curricula, as well as research more resources that may directly speak to the populations they are serving. Critiques of mainstream educational issues are not readily acknowledged or examined by college faculty, students, teachers, or administrators throughout the nation. Rather than make a paradigm shift in the curricular, language, and literacy arena, compensatory images of people of color are inserted into the curriculum to supposedly absolve educational inequities and protect the maintenance of Western thought (Sleeter and Grant 1988; Swartz 1992). Therefore, the school curriculum remains as a powerful symbol of social control and a resistance to the heterogeneity that has always constituted the United States.

According to people like Allan Bloom, William Bennett, Chester Finn, and Diane Ravitch, the only knowledge worth knowing is that of ancient Greece and Rome. The knowledge produced in textbooks challenges neither students nor teachers. Conservative interest groups have succeeded in the continual marginalization of a true multicultural society, and continue to suppress the history, tongues, and identities of people of color. Conservatives promote an "us against them" ideology that includes feelings of a loss of control of economic and personal security. They want an English-only curriculum, ensuring that the knowledge they perceive as important will be passed on to all children. They want to decide what are the sacred texts, preaching that middle-class white people are the only hardworking, virtuous, and homogeneous citizens in the United States. They have articulated that people of color are lazy, immoral, permissive, heterogeneous, undeserving and getting something for nothing (Omni and Winant 1994).

Conservatives want to emphasize test scores and comprehension of isolated irrelevant information, which diminishes the skills of students. These notions are so pervasive that national reports and school reform assume that increasing the measurable outcomes of the "basic" subjects of reading, writing, and mathematics will rectify the social and economic problems of children of color. Conservative school reformers want to prohibit teachers and students from speaking their native tongues. They want to keep students from analyzing and thinking about literature or raising questions about race, gender, or power relations. Conservatives interpret these as not being rigorous and supposedly lowering test scores. Qualitatively studying these issues is not considered rigorous within the academe, either. In fact, it is sometimes deemed controversial, militant, and agenda-driven. As far as allowing students and faculty to use their native tongues, some claim that the English language will be lost and their culture will change if people are allowed to do so. Others argue that bilingual and critical multicultural education is a menace to the national well-being of the United States (Bloom 1987; Stotsky 1999). The result has led to a pedagogy that encourages competition, linear progress, empiricism, English-only movements, statistical measurement, dehumanized instruction, and segregated educational experiences. The idea of having concern for a student's enjoyment of learning has become secondary to the anxiety of quantifiable grades and comprehension test scores. Students in this classroom environment learn to become passive receptors of particular bits of information instead of becoming independent and critical thinkers (Freire 1970; Kincheloe 1991; Apple 1993).

The current school curriculum not only validates European traditional values as the norm for the world, but it also validates certain black leaders as role models for African-Americans who project the beliefs of the dominant Anglo-Protestant society. While allegedly democratizing curriculum textbooks, conservatives have created a small list of worthy black men and women who are nonconfrontational and have appropriated the behavior and social mores of the dominant white society. However, their voices are still silenced to maintain the historical falsifications that are embedded in Anglo-Protestant cultural perspectives (Crichlow 1990). These sanitized heroes, such as Booker T. Washington or Martin Luther King, Jr. have in one way or another embraced the values of the dominant society. They love to highlight Dr. King for his faith and labor with white people and have created pleasing stories to be read on his holiday; yet King's critique and denouncements against the racial policy of apartheid that is upheld by the United States are silenced. On the other hand, black heroes such as Malcolm X, W. E. B. Dubois, and Marcus Garvey are identified as having challenged and critiqued the values of the United States and are therefore excluded.

For example: Why has Frederick Douglass, who has been inserted into the mainstream textbooks, been silenced? One of his most powerful speeches, the famous *Fourth of July Oration*, condemns those celebrating the Fourth of July while over four million black people were in chains. Because Douglass criticized this cherished holiday, this speech is excluded from the textbooks. His critical pedagogy of white supremacy reflects a long, continuing struggle against domination, colonialism, and hegemony. Douglass reminded those who were listening that the Fourth of July was not a holiday black people wanted to honor. He stated that the Fourth of July

> is yours, not mine. You may rejoice, I must mourn. To drag a man in fetters into the grand illuminated temple of liberty, and call upon him to join you in joyous anthems, were inhuman mockery and sacrilegious irony. Do you

mean, citizens, to mock me by asking me to speak today? (McFeely 1991, 172–173).

Through classroom discussion teachers would begin to understand the anger, pain, and hate of marginalized students who see clearly how this society is constructed out of the neglect and greed of a democratic capitalist society. Teachers would reflect and begin to question what purpose is there for a society as prosperous and philanthropic as the United States to consistently abandon children to poverty and squalor year after year with very little public indignation (McLaren 1989; Kozol 1991). They would begin to understand and have compassion as to why students of color reject our passive education of "too much schooling and very little education" and want no part in Anglo-Protestant society.

Bilingual teachers can become researchers, take curriculum courses, and ask why movements against tyranny and domination are not presented in a critical pedagogical sense and fail to catch the eye and heart of the dominant society. Teacher preparation courses can grapple with questions like: What precisely is teaching? What is the historical, political, and rational purpose behind curricular courses in universities and public schools? Why are particular books chosen? Who are the teachers? Who is being taught and for whose benefit? Those who want to maintain the status quo understand that teachers are dangerous because teachers can liberate the minds and hearts of society. The bilingual teacher who engages his or her students in emancipatory knowledge that is gained through activity and political struggle will always find him or herself at odds with the bureaucratic regulations linked to the hegemonic corporate and political infrastructure of the United States.

Teacher preparation courses can prepare teachers to become emancipatory in their approach to teaching and strengthen their research skills. They can be taught to critically redefine school knowledge from the perspectives of people of color and the disadvantaged. This style of teaching must go beyond the language of inclusion. Teacher education must not only be emancipatory, it must be effective in transcending the Eurocentric school curriculum in today's public schools. There must be a radical rethinking of the nature of school knowledge that fundamentally reflects today's heterogeneous student population (Kincheloe 1991). Bilingual teachers must begin to examine white privilege and rethink their understanding of how it refuses to acknowledge any form of liberating multicultural curriculum. Teachers who are truly critical pedagogues involve themselves and their students in discussions about race, gender, patriarchy, and the socioeconomic advantages and disadvantages of people. Teachers who have critically researched the scholarship of people of color will bring to the classroom not only what they have learned from those works, but their life experience as well (Sleeter 1993).

Progressive curricular changes in education textbooks do mention various aspects of people of color but fail to reconceptualize the content and continue to articulate a hierarchy of power that validates a Western patriarchal culture as the dominant epistemology. Students are given selective access to ideas and information that predisposes them to think and act a certain way. The dominant curricular ideology does not encourage or ask students to critically analyze and consider other possibilities, questions, or actions. Therefore, the curriculum serves as a means of social control, legitimizing the existing social mores and the status of those who dominate. It does so in a way that suggests that there are no other versions of the world, and that the interpretation taught in schools is the unquestionable truth (Sleeter and Grant 1991). Scholars and students alike can examine and debate why scholars of color are marginalized from mainstream discourse on college campuses. Inquiries need to be raised on how the scholarship of people of color challenges and critiques the dominant perspectives.

Hegemony is a powerful idea, but a very evasive one. Many white and some black teachers seem to understand; they can critique journal articles and engage in various graduate-level dialogue, yet are stymied when they try to understand the power of hegemony and how it affects the curriculum and their classrooms. They tenaciously hold on to various presumptions about the student population. In order to comply with multicultural and diversity requirements, school districts hold one day in-service programs, and hold nonchallenging programs that expect participants to critically analyze their belief systems. Twenty or thirty years of socially assimilated beliefs cannot be altered by one- or two-day in-service programs or in one college-level course when curricula and ideology support and maintain hegemony and Eurocentric power relations. Scholarship presented by people of color like *Multicultural Education: Towards Good Practice* (1986), edited by Ranjit Arora and Carlton Duncan, deals with the insidious nature of racism that is an integral ingredient of Western society. By analyzing these essays, teachers, administrators, and curriculum developers can see how racism is constructed and reflected in the miseducation and de-skilling of African-American and Hispanic children. Curriculum and teacher preparation courses can use fundamental shifts in their frameworks so that students can begin to see their culture as opposed to the Western paradigms that validate white supremacy.

Today, educators are realizing that they must respond to the challenges of educating various ethnic and racial groups and confront issues of racism, classism, and sexism that have been largely ignored by society. Paradigm shifts can occur in curriculum courses when professors, school administrators, teachers, and students alike discuss the endemic loss of students of color in education, or debate why standardized tests and memorization cause so many students of color to become disinterested in school. They can research and examine the continuous role hegemony is playing in the social, economic, and political constructs of difference, race, class, and gender with little regard to the lives of students of color (Kincheloe and Steinberg 1996). Professors can encourage potential teachers and educators to critically research why the United States ranks at the top of the list of industrialized nations in poverty, or why 80 percent of its children live in ghettos. Why is there callousness among public sentiment and politicians that breeds a meanness dominating the majority of citizens in the United States? Why do people refuse to lend a hand to the disadvantaged (Omni and Winant 1986; Marable 1992)? They can ask questions why Western nations refuse to listen to and/or understand the societies of nonwhite people who do not contribute or assist in furthering hegemony and subjugation.

Most curriculum and teacher preparation courses in the West do not critically investigate their nation's past or present policies or its relationships with its oppressed populations and the rest of the world. One begins to see and understand how the curriculum becomes a racial text that defines the national identity of the United States, but do we really understand the meaning of race? The concept of race is very complex and dynamic and changes according to the political circumstances of the time. Before the 1860s, southern Europeans, Jews, and the Irish were considered nonwhite. When these various ethnic groups stepped ashore onto the North American continent they sought to define themselves white in order to separate themselves from black people (Omni and Winant 1986; Perlmutter 1992).

Curriculum courses examine not only the meaning of race, but also how race is expressed through the construction of difference, and how it is negotiated in the public arena. Professors, teachers, and administrators can debate how our national identity, history, and culture have been shaped and deformed by the absences, denials, and fragmentation of the text. Debates can be held in classrooms as to why women, Native Americans, Hispanics, Africans, African-Americans, and the poor are reconstructed as being deviant and inferior. These groups are both marked as stereotypes and made invisible. In public schools they are forced to internalize the experience, history, values, goals, and achievements of Western thought. Only after discussing these issues will it become clear why there is a reluctance in education to make any appropriate curricular changes to empower children of color.

College courses can offer teachers, administrators, and curriculum developers a chance to investigate and respect the vast knowledge that oppressed people bring to bear in critiquing the dominant curriculum. They can learn how not to view nonwhite culture and knowledge as inferior, and to appreciate the culture and literature of African-Americans, Hispanics, and other people of color. White teachers and some teachers of color who feel threatened and who express displeasure in their students' attitudes and behaviors by their use of African-American and Hispanic dialects will become aware that their students are not resisting them personally. Rather, these students are responding to what the teachers represent, and are refusing to identify with a white society that does not accept them for who they are. Instead of trying to domesticate students of color through colonizing their minds, anesthetizing their critical abilities, and trying to maintain the social order, teachers can emphasize critical theory and self-knowledge, encouraging students to become producers of a knowledge that is liberatory and emancipating (Lee 1992).

In light of the fact that the majority of teachers in the United States are white, the question that needs to be addressed is whether we understand that an essentially white Anglo-Protestant education is being compelled upon African-American, Hispanic, and other children of color. Do we really recognize that the most serious blow to these children is that they are consistently being removed from their history, culture, and community? African-American, Hispanic, and other children of color are forced to incorporate the values of the dominant culture at the price of devaluing their culture. The cultural traditions of African-Americans, Hispanics, and other minority groups have virtually disappeared in a welter of statistical rhetoric, technocracy, pervasive corporate consumerism, and the fearful alienation of a ritualized individualistic conformity. Education has increasingly come to play a major role in the maintenance of the Anglo-Protestant paradigm (Kincheloe 1991).

Teachers must personally assist every student in their struggle to achieve a compassionate and equitable system that includes every human being. As teachers we must engage our students in their cultural heritage and those of others to bring about freedom and social justice. We must help change educational institutions to become sites for legitimate expressions of diverse opinions and truths, while at the same time being compassionate in the relationships of race, gender, class, and age. Our goal is to denounce racism and inequality in all of its constructs, and demand that the United States live up to its rhetoric of altruism, justice, and democracy.

# CHAPTER TWO

# BILINGUAL

# ABOLITIONISTS

## SHADOWS OF FASCISM—PROPAGANDA
## OF THE THIRD REICH AND THE
## ENGLISH-ONLY MOVEMENT

RYAN MOSER, THE PENNSYLVANIA STATE UNIVERSITY

*Propaganda tries to force a doctrine on the whole people; the organization embraces within its scope only those who do not threaten on psychological grounds to become a brake on the further dissemination of the idea.*
HITLER (1925/1943, 582)

*America is being invaded by hordes of dusty third world peoples, and with each passing hour our economic well-being, cultural heritage, freedom, and racial roots are being battered into oblivion.*
BARTOLOMEO (1997, 230)

On January 30, 1933, Adolf Hitler seized the office of German Chancellor. With him came viciously racist Nazi politics and an eliminationist program that resulted in the extermination of over six million Jewish people. Nazi rule of Germany endured little more than a decade, but in that time both the face of modern history and our understanding of the nature of humanity were shaken to their foundations. How could such an atrocity come to pass? How could that type of hatred become so ingrained in a national conscience?

Contemporary American media is permeated with the politics of "bilingual education abolitionists," a name given by the Center for Equal Opportunity to a group that includes prominent statesmen, lobbyist organizations, conservative celebrities, and private citizens (Soto 1998, 155–156). Bilingual abolitionists warn about the dangers of bilingual and multicultural education, the growing language minority, and illegal immigration. More than passive voices, they are pursuing a substantive goal—an amendment to the constitution declaring English as the official language of the United States, and an affirmation of national unity and heritage through the English language. Critics of the movement have called it nationalistic and xenophobic. They accuse it of being a thinly veiled racist agenda that endangers minority rights. Who is right?

A critical understanding of the controversy increasingly depends on our ability to reflect on the past and find analogous situations. As historians study Hitler's Germany, they have uncovered frightening images that reveal a clearer picture of the Nazi rise to power. Perhaps the most frightening of these are the parallels to our own society. Language and culture politics played a central role in the legitimization of anti-Semitism in Germany. Attempts to purify the German language were supported by racist ideologies very similar to the xenophobic views of bilingual abolitionists. Searching for common threads that connect the ideologies can provide a historical perspective on the illegitimacy of the English-only movement.

# A QUESTION OF WHO BELONGS

*The Jews are our misfortune ... Year by year, our eastern boundary is penetrated by a stream of ambitious, trouser-selling youngsters from the inexhaustible Polish cradle.*

GERHARD (1998, 85)

*... regarding the illegal invasion of Mexicans and Central Americans across our porous, poorly guarded border. This is intolerable and an end must be put to this now. Illegal aliens already here need to be ferreted out, rounded up, permanently ejected, and prevented from re-entering the country.*

COMMENT POSTED ON THE FREE REPUBLIC WEB SITE

The ideologies of anti-Semitism in Germany before World War II and of bilingual abolitionists in the United States are similar in both structure and content. Both focus on the creation and protection of a national identity and use that identity to define and attack an excluded group. In *Mein Kampf*, Hitler divides the inhabitants of the *volkisch* state into three classes: citizens, subjects, and foreigners. The foreigner is considered an inferior who was not educated to be a patriotic nationalist. The subject was born in Germany, but is not a productive member of the national community and has not taken a solemn oath to the state. After taking oath, the subject can become a citizen and stands at the top of the social hierarchy, "privileged as against the foreigner" and "the lord of the Reich" (Hitler 1925/1943, 440–441).

The bilingual abolitionist view of national identity is structurally parallel to Hitler's *volkish* state. Residents of the United States are divided into three groups: American citizens, immigrants, and illegal immigrants. At the bottom of the social hierarchy stands the illegal immigrant. Like the foreigner in Hitler's classification, the illegal immigrant is not considered a member of the national community and is therefore not entitled to the rights of the citizen. The legal immigrant status is similar to that of the subject, a "second-class citizen." He or she is a part of the national community, but has not taken an oath of allegiance and is entitled to only limited societal benefits. The highest platform is given to the American citizen, and the welfare of the American citizen is the primary concern of the state.

Hitler also said that the "man without honor or character, the common criminal, the traitor to the fatherland, etc., can at any time be divested of this honor [citizenship]" (441). In Germany, ethnicity, language, and the positive aspects of German character defined the group worthy of citizenship, the *Volk* (the people). Goldhagen explains that implicit in the creation of the *Volk* was the creation of an excluded group:

> The foundational concept for German popular political thought, the *Volk,* was conceptually linked to, and partly dependent upon, a definition of Jews as the *Volk's* antithesis. Built into the concept of *Volk* was a deprecation of Jews, who embodied all the negative qualities which were absent from the *Volk,* including moral ones (1996, 77–78).

Clearly, the Jews did not fit the national character of Germany, and this was used to justify the removal of citizenship, rights, and finally, the extermination of the Jewish people.

The bilingual abolitionist support for Official English legislation uses a similar character-based justification based on language proficiency. The argument states that the English language is the binding force of the United States as well as its heritage. This "National Unity Argument," as termed by Wiley and Lukes, rests on the assumption that the "perpetuation of a minority language is a potentially divisive factor in maintaining national unity.

Therefore, the host receiving society should require linguistic assimilation and a surrender of language minority rights" (1996, 521). This argument assumes that the ability to speak English is the responsibility of every American citizen and naturalization candidate. Wiley and Lukes critique the argument, saying, "In many instances in which language minorities have been accused of lack of national loyalty, their perceived disloyalty has been caused by overt discrimination and a denial of language minority rights" (1996, 521).

Hitler once praised a nation's immigration policy, saying:

> By refusing immigration on principle to elements poor in health, by simply excluding certain races from naturalization, it professes in slow beginnings a view which is peculiar to the volkisch state concept (1925/1943, 440).

Surprisingly, Hitler was not speaking about the German immigration policy. He was referring to the American system.

# THE GERMAN-ONLY MOVEMENT REVISITED

> *By the early twentieth century, Germany had become an economic magnet for immigrants, especially Poles, working in heavy industry, mining, and commercial agriculture. As migration increased, the Pan German League's concern for the "preservation of German Volkstum" (nationhood) enveloped virtually all of Wilhelmine Germany's political parties.*
> KVISTAD (1998, 51)

> *Since 1970, the United States has absorbed 27 million immigrants from foreign lands. This year, 1.3 million, 90% from the Third World, will pour into the United States, 400,000 of them will be illegal aliens—many smuggled in by organized crime and Chinese Communists.*
> BUCHANAN (1999)

It is important to understand that anti-Semitism in Germany did not appear overnight. It was a rather slow-building ideology that can be traced back many years. With this in mind, the anti-Semitic politics and legislation of Germany in the years prior to the Third Reich can be understood not only as isolated events, but also as a part of a progression toward the Holocaust. Some of the most striking comparisons between the English-only movement and anti-Semitism appear in this progression. Parallels can be seen in the move to purify, protect, and enhance the German language and dominant culture at the expense of minority languages, cultures, and rights.

Assimilation was the first step in the German-only movement. This can be seen by the profusion of the conceptual *Kulturnation* during the time period. The *Kulturnation* represented the idea that "the German language, German nation, and German Spirit were manifestations of one and the same thing" (Bering 1998, 259). Language was considered the central unifying force of these three ideas. William Humbolt commented frankly on the role of language when he wrote, "The language is, basically and above all, the nation" (259).

Ironically, the English-only politics of assimilation has similar roots in American history. One of the nation's presidents, Theodore Roosevelt, was a strong proponent of language assimilation. The official U.S. English home-page posts this quote from Roosevelt to support their case: "We have room for but one language here, and that is the English language, for we intend to see that the crucible turns our people out as Americans" (U.S. English 1999a). Two decades ago the popularity of these views was revived by Senator S. I. Hayakawa under the rallying cry, "One official language and one only, so that we can unite as a nation" (1992, 100).

According to Dietz Bering, German language laws can be found in the legal code as early as the 1739 Jewish emancipation edict which obligated Jews to keep business records and sign their names in German. By 1812 Jewish rights had been reduced and a ban on the use of Hebrew characters for signatures carried with it a maximum penalty of deportation. An 1847 law prohibited the use of Hebrew to draft contracts and levied a penalty of fifty talers or six weeks in jail (1998, 266–271).

Although citizenship in the United States cannot be revoked as a result of foreign language usage, English language proficiency is required for naturalization. Bilingual abolitionists have also enforced legislation that penalizes the use of a foreign language in business signs. Recently in Atlanta, Georgia, fines of $115 were given to business owners for signs in Spanish (*El Norte* 1998, 23).

Bilingual abolitionists claim that English-only legislation is justified by majority vote even in the face of judgments of unconstitutionality (Francis 1999). One of the first indicators of the increasing tide of anti-Semitism in Germany during the late nineteenth century was a Bavarian petition drive calling for the rescission of Jewish rights that garnered 265,000 signatures in 1880 (Goldhagen 1996, 62). The populist movement was not effective immediately, but as support continued to grow the protection of Jewish rights by the government was weakened.

California Proposition 227, an English-only measure that passed a referendum vote in June 1998, effectively foreclosed on bilingual schools statewide. One of the most surprising results of the polls was the large percentage of language minority votes in favor of the legislation. However, this type of minority support was also prevalent in Germany when Jewish language schools were targeted (Bering 1998, 269). Bering attributed Jewish support of assimilation to an underdeveloped sense of identity as a population in an anti-Semitic nation. It is possible that the language minority support of English-only has similar roots.

Anti-Semitism continued to grow and with the arrival of Hitler, Jewish rights moved from endangered to extinct. In *Hitler's Willing Executioners*, Goldhagen explains the process of the social death of the Jewish people. "The progress of the gradual, systematic exclusion of the Jews from all spheres of society—the political, social, economic, and cultural—was as grinding as the hardship that it created for the Jews was punishing" (1996, 137). One of the tragic symbols of this process was the yellow Star of David armband that the Jews were required to wear, a symbol of separation and social exclusion. Lourdes Díaz Soto describes a chilling radio hoax called the "Blue E" that was perpetrated in a town embroiled in an English-only controversy:

> The "Blue E" referred to a proposed city ordinance encouraging local merchants to post a "Blue E" on their doorways to signify their support for the English-only ordinance. The ordinance provided storeowners with the ability to price goods based on the English language proficiency of their prospective buyer ... Supporters of this ordinance called the radio talk show, expressing views such as: "Send all the spics back to their country," [and] "This is America ... for whites only ..." (1997, 65)

Other terrifying ideas surfaced as the Jewish people were forced into social death. The scientific mind-set of the Nazi party produced a eugenic theory which stated that inferior races should be sterilized in order to prevent the contamination of the Aryan race. Sadly, eugenics is also reflected in the Bilingual Abolitionist movement. A controversial drug called Quinacrine is a contraception drug that induces irreversible sterility. Its use is opposed by the World Health Organization and banned in the United States because it causes menstrual bleeding, backaches, fever, abdominal pain, headaches, and possibly cancer. Two independent American citizens working under their own authority out of a basement distributed the sterilization pellets to over 100,000 women in third-world countries and as of March 1999 had no intention of stopping. As the only known distributors in the world, the two men justified their actions as a necessary part of curbing immigration saying, "The explosion in human numbers, which after 2050 will come entirely from immigrants and the offspring of immigrants, will dominate our lives. There will be chaos and anarchy" (*St. Louis Post-Dispatch* 1998, B6).

Nazi activists in Germany said that the German-only movement was a necessary part of the beneficial process of establishing a national identity. Bilingual abolitionists support the English-only movement with the same claim.

# IMAGES OF HATRED: JUSTIFYING RACISM

*Taxpaying citizens are not being given access to these welfare and health services that they deserve and desire, but if you're an illegal immigrant and cross the border, you get everything you want.*
STEVEN (1995, 7)

Justification of both the bilingual abolitionist movement and the anti-Semitic movement rely heavily upon demonization of an excluded group. Hugh Rank, drawing on the field of media literacy, created a framework for the analysis of propaganda. His intensification pattern of propaganda utilizes repetition, association, and composition to convey the desired statement (Rank 1978, 20). Each of these themes can be seen in the rhetoric of the anti-Semitic and Bilingual Abolitionist movements. Three themes of the anti-Semitic movement that are particularly telling are the conceptions of the Jew as a parasite, the Jewish monopolization of the economy, and the Jew as a conspirator bent on destroying Germany. Clear reflections of these images are evident in the bilingual abolitionist characterization of the immigrant as a parasité, a colonizer of the American economy, and a conspirator seeking to dismember the United States along ethnic lines.

The image of the parasite was prolific in Nazi propaganda. Hitler illustrated the Jews in one of his speeches accordingly: "The Jew is a parasite. As such, he lives off the work of others and he has attempted to falsify our image of it" (Mendelsohn 1982, 90). He wrote that the Jewish people "can sneak their way into the rest of mankind like drones, to make other men work for them under all sorts of pretexts ..." (Hitler 1925/1943, 150). Alexander Hardy, a prosecutor at Nuremberg, describes *German Weekly Service* reports that portrayed the Jewish people as a criminal class of cheats, profiteers, swindlers, and defrauders (Hardy 1967, 296). The fact that these claims about the character of Jewish people were unfounded is now commonly accepted, but at the time a large segment of the German population was convinced of their truth. The idea of Jewish work-shirking parasitism was a primary justification for internment in labor camps (Goldhagen 1996, 402).

This segment of a fundraising letter distributed by English First in 1986 holds many of the same parasitic images:

> Tragically, many immigrants these days refuse to learn English! They never become productive members of society, they remain stuck in a linguistic and economic ghetto, many living off welfare and costing working Americans millions of tax dollars every year (Crawford 1999c).

The quote works to justify the dichotomy between the American citizen and the other. The immigrant is presented as an obstinate, separatist, unproductive member of society that is sponging off of the hard-working American citizen. This image is used to justify the termination of language-minority programs such as bilingual education and affirmative action for immigrants.

The second theme, closely related to the first, is the conception of the minority monopolization of social institutions and of the economy. In *Mein Kampf*, Hitler portrays the Jewish people as opportunists who use their parasitic qualities to dominate the German economy:

> He begins to lend money and as always at usurious interest ... He regards commerce as well as all financial transactions as his own special privilege which he ruthlessly exploits ... Finance and commerce have become his complete monopoly (1925/1943, 309).

The anti-Semitic claims that the Jew monopolizes the economy resonate with the fear that the American workforce is being colonized. Research such as the Center for Immigration Studies 1986 paper, "Illegal Immigration and the Colonization of the American Labor Market," is often cited by bilingual abolitionists to support the claims that immigrants steal work from Americans and have a disastrous effect on the economy:

> He [Dr. Martin] documents the displacement of American workers by illegal immigrants in agriculture, food processing, services and construction, analyzing the process of network recruiting and subcontracting that lead ultimately to the exclusion of American citizens and legal residents from many work places (Martin 1996, 6).

The Center for Immigration Studies has been funneled over $100,000 by an umbrella organization for U.S. English and the Federation for American Immigration Reform. This conflict of interests is often ignored, as are many other economic trends such as the role of immigration in the current economic boom. Helle Bering said of the Center for Immigration Studies, "It seems that by studying immigrants the folks at the Center have conceived a hearty dislike of their chosen subject ... for every negative statistic produced by the Center, many positive ones can be found" (Bering 1999, A17).

The image of economic domination in Germany was expanded to include social institutions, the government, and the press. "Goebbels's rabble-rousing newspaper *Der Angriff* ... stated in 1928 that one could correspond with the Berlin police headquarters only in Yiddish, because that was the only language understood there" (Bering 1998, 279). Majority exclusion from local affairs is commonly exploited in English-only conflicts like the one in Monterey Park, California. The early leader of the drive, Frank Acuri, commented on Asian business signs, saying, "Monterey Park has turned into a segregated city, a Chinese-Only city" (Crawford 1992a).

The final theme of the demonization of Jewish and immigrant peoples works to promote the position that the minority is destroying the national culture or is a threat to national security. The Jewish presence in Germany was represented with terms such as "infestation," "swarm," "flood," and "inundation" (Gerhard 1998, 91). Propaganda pamphlets depicted the Jews as desiring to destroy Germany as a part of World Jewry. The Jewish desire to tear down the nation and rebuild it in its own image was a leitmotiv of *Mein Kampf*. The term "Jewification" was used to describe the Jewish degradation of many aspects of Jewish society, ranging from the work ethic to the mating instinct. It was associated with the negative images of disease, bacilli, rape, murder, and laziness. A translated portion of one such leaflet, published in 1935, reads "German Citizen do you know that the Jew: oppresses your child, rapes your wife ... murders your parents, steals your property, ridicules your honor ... spoils your culture, corrupts your race" (Mendelsohn 1983, 116).

Bilingual abolitionists use the themes of national security and the destruction of American culture as ammunition for the English-only cannons. Euphemisms for immigrants include the "immigration invasion," *la reconquista*, "the flood of immigration," and "the alien invasion." These negative images are accompanied by warnings about the threats that language minorities and immigrants pose as language segregationists and secessionists. FAIR posts this quote by Thomas Fleming on its web site under the topic "Immigration and Ethnic Separation": "In any major city, the peace is disturbed by Latino, Black, and Asian nationalist gangs, which in some cases are only the shock troops of ethnic movements seeking the racial dismemberment of the United States" (Federation for American Immigration Reform 1999a).

U.S. English portrays Mexican immigration as a symptom of the radical movement called Aztlan saying, "The goal of the Aztlan movement is to 'liberate' the southwestern states and form an independent homeland" (U.S. English 1999b). The statement is similar in content to one published by a group called the American Patrol only a few days after the United States started bombing Serbia in an attempt to end ethnic cleansing of ethnic Albanians:

> Over time ... the Albanians moved into Kosovo until the Serbs became a 10 percent minority ... We could rewrite it slightly to read: ... Over time ... the Mexicans moved into the American Southwest until the Americans became a 10 percent minority. Then NATO intervened (and joined the INS and the Congress) to stop the Americans from retaking their home (American Patrol 1999a).

The concept of the Latinization of America is used by bilingual abolitionists in the same way that the Nazis used the Jewification of Germany. On the web site of the anti-immigration group American Patrol, immigration invasion images are posted alongside notices of individual instances of criminal activity including murder, child abuse, drugs, teenage pregnancy, and prostitution. On April 6, 1999, the page contained the proclamations "L.A. School System-Mexican Coach Assaults Little Kids," and "California Prisons to Be Full," as well as links to past postings such as "American Dream? Immigrant Rips Off Customers and Kills Competition," and "Tucson Girl Raped by Mexican" (American Patrol 1999b). This type of association is a very effective manner of demonizing immigrants and language minorities.

# UNSETTLING CONNECTIONS

*If fascism came to America, it would be on a program of Americanism.*
BELLANT (1991, XII)

U.S. English posts a list of Official English movement supporters. The American Latvian Association of the USA, The Bulgarian National Front in the USA, The Heritage Foundation, The Lithuanian American Council, and the Ukranian Congress Committee of America were listed (U.S. English 1999c). All five of these groups have been linked either in the present or in their origins to right-wing, Nazi-affiliated groups (Bellant 1991, 6, 63–4,

71–4, 77–80). FAIR has received over one million dollars from the eugenics foundation of the Pioneer Fund (Crawford 1989, 79). Larry Pratt, the founder of English First, has been linked to white supremacist groups including Aryan Nation (1996).

The mention of these connections is not intended to imply that all bilingual abolitionists or their supporters are Nazis and white supremacists. They are mentioned to show that the historic gulf that separates our society from Nazi Germany is not as wide as some people believe. Certain aspects of the English-only movement are frightening reflections of fascist ideologies. The United States' sense of national pride (not unhealthy by itself) combines with a xenophobic current of thought to create a climate where language minorities become the targets of symbolic and legislative attacks.

As educators, we need to cultivate more than simple awareness. We must challenge xenophobic views and propaganda on a daily basis in an effort to expand critical consciousness. We can do this by becoming informed advocates for bilingual education and minority language rights in our schools and communities and by integrating authentic multicultural education into our lessons. Above all, we must make a personal commitment not to allow fear and prejudice to guide our classrooms, because in the end it is clear that equality does not provide for itself. It must be defended.

# APPENDIX

## Comparison Chart:
## German-Only vs. English-Only Movements

| | German Only | English Only |
|---|---|---|
| **Ideology Structure** | Citizen<br>Subject<br>Foreigner | Citizen<br>Legal Alien<br>Illegal Alien |
| **Propaganda Pattern** | Reinforcement of the dichotomy between dominant German class and excluded Jewish minority | Reinforcement of the dichotomy between the dominant class and the excluded language minority |
| **Justification of the Ideology** | The Jew as a parasite<br><br>The Jew as a monopolist<br><br>The Jew as a conspirator | The language minority as a parasite<br>The language minority as a monopolist<br>The language minority as a conspirator |
| **Mode of Operation** | Assimilate Jews into dominant culture<br>Attack minority rights through legislation and political pressure<br>Force Jews into social death<br>Extermination | Assimilate language into dominant culture<br>Attack minority rights through legislation and political pressure<br>Force language minority out of social institution |

# FROM VYGOTSKY

# TO BAKHTIN

## GRAND THEORIES AND TEACHING PRACTICES

LYUDMILA BRYZZHEVA, THE PENNSYLVANIA STATE UNIVERSITY

This chapter highlights the main ideas drawn from Lev Vygotsky's (1962, 1978) sociocultural theory of development and Mikhail Bakhtin's (1935; Voloshinov[1] 1973) philosophy of language. Both Vygotsky and Bakhtin talk about language as a social construct. They also give a detailed account of the sociohistorical roots of human language and human relationships, in general, that involve the use of language as a means of communication. Both scholars lived and worked in the Soviet era and were therefore influenced by Karl Marx's dialectical materialism. Vygotsky (1896–1934) approached language as a psychologist who is interested in the role of a language in the development of higher mental functions in humans, whereas Bakhtin (1895–1975) looked at it from a philosophical standpoint. The purpose of this chapter is to bring these two grand theories that had a significant impact on the field of bilingual education closer to teachers and practitioners, and make them useful for everyday teaching practice.

For a long time linguists have played with language like a toy: taking it apart, analyzing parts, putting them back together, rearranging them, and so on. This approach does not provide the full picture. The soul of a language is not taken into consideration. It is still hard for many of us to think of a language as a  social construct that "reflects and refracts existence" (Voloshinov 1973,19). I argue that language has a soul, and this soul is the culture where it is born and utilized. This culture can be characterized by its unique socioeconomic conditions, political structure, social relationships, beliefs, and values. All of these elements are reflected in its language. Language has human history reflected in it, but it also influences human history. According to Voloshinov (1973), the word is viewed as "the most sensitive index of social changes" (19).

The relationship between language and culture that is central to teaching is taken into consideration in Vygotsky's sociocultural theory of development. Lev Vygotsky recognized the importance of biological factors at an early stage of human development. However, he found that since humans are social beings, ignoring the social element in their development would be an artificial exclusion.

There are two main themes in Vygotsky's theoretical framework that are important for my analysis. First of all, he claims that higher mental functions in the individual have their origin in social processes (Vygotsky 1978). Thinking and speech are considered higher mental processes; therefore, it is legitimate to claim that the peculiarities of sociocultural and historical factors are responsible for the unique development of thinking and speech in individuals. Thus, understanding the unique properties of any given culture helps us embrace the differences and similarities in the development of each individual's social identity or "speaking personality" (Voloshinov 1973). If you have a culturally or linguistically diverse student in your class, do not assume that you understand why he or she behaves a certain way: Vygostky suggests that two students may engage in a seemingly similar activity for two different reasons, which automatically changes the meaning of activity. We may say that these two students engage in two different activities. Learn more about your student's home culture—socioeconomic conditions of the society, in general, and the student's family, in particular; social conventions, and traditions, the ways people relate to each other (pay special attention to how teachers and students communicate in that culture), differences in learning styles, and so on. Remember that your student, depending on how long she lived in her home culture, is likely to have learned particular ways of relating to people that are different from what is familiar to you.

I once had to help an American elementary school teacher who could not understand why a Russian boy in her class was so much more disruptive than other children. It was an eye-opener to her when I mentioned that most Russian children are not used to having a lot of freedom in the classroom. In a teacher-centered classroom, children are expected to follow instructions. In most public schools permission should be asked to move around the classroom. A teacher is an authority figure. I was hoping that this explanation helped my colleague to better understand her student and not label him as "a problem child." It does not mean that she should treat this student differently. It means that now she has the power of knowledge to collaborate with his parents and other teachers to make his school experience into a positive one.

Secondly, Vygotsky (1978) argues that to understand the development of mental processes we need to understand the "tools and signs that mediate them." By "tools and signs" Vygotsky primarily means "language." Language plays a very important role in the development of thinking, speech, and memory. It originates in a community of people who use it to mediate their communication. A community's language will reflect its specific view of the world.

As both Bakhtin and Vygotsky would argue, learning a language has a significant impact on the development of sociocultural identity. Voloshinov (1973) suggests that "the speaking personality, its subjective designs and intentions ... do not exist outside their material objectification in language. Without a way of revealing itself in language, be it only in inner speech, personality does not exist either for itself or for others ..." (152). I would like to extend this argument by relating it to the English-only movement. It seems that if we concentrate our efforts on teaching a second language prior to the development of literacy in the first language, we deny our bilingual student a chance to develop an important part of his or her identity that finds expression in the native language.

In their discussion of human language, both Vygotsky and the members of the Bakhtin Circle argue that a language will be inscribed with the unique meanings provided by a given social context with its unique economic, historical, and social relationships. Voloshinov (1973) extends Vygotsky's approach by addressing the relationship between the development of language and social institutional phenomena. The argument is that the language reflects social relationships and social relationships in turn are affected by socioeconomic conditions and the power structure of a society. Thus, the socioeconomic and power structures begin to be reflected in the language we utilize. Stop and think for a moment about the meaning of the word "hunger." What does it mean to a person who lives in a society with a stable economy, where food is often taken for granted? How about a person who lives in a society with an underdeveloped economy, where all people think about is how and where to get food? Obviously, the meaning of this word would be very different for these two people. Even within the same language community, people of different classes will interpret the meaning of the word "hunger" differently. If we think about it, people of different classes initially belong to different strata/cultures. In the above example, it becomes obvious that sociocultural context should always be taken into account when talking about language. Bakhtin's philosophy of language sheds some light on how a word acquires meaning. Voloshinov (1973) views language as a social phenomenon, in which the social relations and history of a given society are reflected in the meaning of a word. A word or a physical object becomes a sign only when it acquires meaning:

> Signs are particular, material things; and, as we have seen, any item of nature, technology, or consumption can become a sign, acquiring in the process a meaning that goes beyond its given particularity. A sign does not simply exist as a given part of reality—it reflects and refracts another reality. Therefore, it may distort that reality or be true to it, or may perceive it from a special point of view, and so forth. Every sign is subject to the criteria of ideological evaluation (i.e., whether it is true, false, correct, fair, good, etc.). The domain of ideology coincides with the domain of signs. They equate with one another. Whenever a sign is present, ideology is present too (Voloshinov 1973, 10).

In order to understand how ideology and signs are connected, we need to define the notion of ideology. Unfortunately, we cannot borrow Bakhtin's definition of ideology because he never explicitly defines it. Plenty has been written about ideology; therefore, I will attempt to come up with a definition that will explain and possibly extend what was originally meant by Bakhtin.

Although widely criticized for not being inclusive, Marxist understanding of the notion of ideology should be addressed, for it was widely used at the time when Bakhtin developed his theory. Marx views ideology as the system of the ideas and representations that dominate the minds of a social group. To extend this approach, I will borrow another definition from Macedo (1999), who suggests that "'ideology' refers to the framework of thought that is used by members of a society to justify or rationalize an existing social (dis)order" (141). Thus, ideology has to do with consciousness, subjective representations, beliefs, and ideas that are introduced by the elite of the society in order for them to be able to control people's beliefs and ideas, which, consequently, lets them (the elite) maintain their power. "Ideologies are reproduced and maintain the best in language"(van Dijk 1998, 141); that is, language is a social manifestation that "represents and masks ideologies" (Moraes 1996, 15)

When we speak about dominance of one language in the classroom and conscious repression of other languages, we may be concerned with new and unwanted ideologies (ways of thinking, etc.) that may be introduced by other languages. Hence, the classroom discourse (power structure) represents a hierarchy in which one language has power and so do its speakers, whereas other languages and their speakers are oppressed.

So far, we observed that as social beings we cannot stay free from the influence of ideologies that are inscribed in the language. They are responsible for shaping our thinking and speech, and, consequently, our "speaking personalities." In the process of our development we are able to internalize the representations that become available to us by virtue of being a part of a community:

> Every function in the child's cultural development appears twice: first, on the social level, and later, on the individual level; first, between people (interpsychological), and then inside the child (intrapsychological) (Vygotsky 1978, 57).

However, we are also able to externalize what we have learned and in this way give back to the community what we have taken from it with the necessary introduction of an individual element that is informed by our unique histories. In this respect, teaching a diverse class is a unique learning opportunity for all the participants (any class can be diverse once we dig into the wealth of experiences). Imagine that somebody initiates a discussion about racism. Some participants in the discussion may have had firsthand experience with racial discrimination, some not, but everybody's understanding of the concept is very unique, and, therefore, has a potential to expand the meaning of the word "racism" beyond the meaning it was given originally. This is an example of a dialogue of accents (or unique ideological meanings) as introduced by Voloshinov (1973) and Bakhtin (1935). It is also an illustration of how learning occurs in what Vygotsky (1978) refers to as "zone of proximal development" (ZPD). ZPD is defined as "the difference between the child's developmental level as determined by the independent problem solving and the higher level of potential development as determined through problem solving under adult guidance or in collaboration with more capable peers" (86). The above example illustrates the construction of group ZPD. Every member of the group becomes a teacher and a learner at the same time. Through dialogue, every group member contributes to the development of the other. Teachers must recognize that everybody's experience is valuable. All voices contain the wealth of knowledge.

In conclusion, I would like to reemphasize one of the main issues discussed in this chapter. As suggested by Bakhtin, a crucial moment in a true dialogue is that we must recognize in our utterances who we are speaking after and anticipate who will speak after us. Our English language learners are not "clean slates" extracted out of social environment. As teachers we must recognize and respect a student's history; by doing so we become aware of those who spoke before us and must give credit to these people, for they are the ones who helped our student become who she or he is now. By remembering that our student will interact with other people outside the classroom, we recognize those who will speak after us. Sometimes these interactions may support the values and knowledge that we, as teachers, share with our students; at times, however, students may disregard, contradict, or negate what we have taught. Teachers need to be constantly aware of this potential conflict and use this awareness as a resource to inform our teaching: What we share and how we share it may give freedom and voice to our students, or it may contribute to the inner conflict and potentially silence them.

# NOTE

1.  Valentin Voloshinov was one of the principal members of the Bakhtin Circle during the 1920s. Some scholars believe that Mikhail Bakhtin published some of his works under Voloshinov's name.

# CHAPTER FOUR

# DOOM OR
# MORTAL KOMBAT?

## BILINGUAL LITERACY IN
## THE "MAINSTREAM" CLASSROOM

COLIN LANKSHEAR, NATIONAL AUTONOMOUS UNIVERSITY OF MEXICO

MICHELE KNOBEL, CENTRAL QUEENSLAND UNIVERSITY IN AUSTRALIA

*Although technology and world culture progressed rapidly throughout the twentieth century, their advancements paled in comparison to the seemingly reckless leaps that were to follow.*

STARCRAFT THORAN HISTORY (1998, OPENING LINE)

## GETTING STARTED

It has become almost a cliché that in postindustrial economies and so-called information societies, being literate is more important than ever before (Levett and Lankshear 1994; Rassool 1999). This increased significance is associated partly with the idea that the capacity to manipulate symbols is fundamental to practically all forms of contemporary work and, increasingly, of leisure as well. It is also, however, associated with implications of the move from big to small government, from a welfare state to a more "minimal" one. Many previously existing personnel, public sector social services, and forms of welfare provision for individuals, families, and targeted groups have disappeared in the wake of neoliberal policies of fiscal restraint and a rampaging cult of performativity. In the context of a reduced welfare safety net, individuals have to become more self-sufficient and conform to an ethos of "responsibilization" (de Alba et al. 2000). Achieving self-sufficiency and "responsibilization"—where governments make individuals responsible for health care, welfare, and education—requires people to negotiate diverse and often complex and sophisticated uses of language, texts, information displays, images, and other kinds of symbols and semiotic systems involved in the everyday practices they encounter. In this context the importance of ensuring that *all* learners achieve effective literacy has enjoyed increased emphasis and centrality within education policy demands on schools and in public perceptions of school accountability.

If the contemporary importance of literacy is practically a cliché so far as school-based language education is concerned, the meaning, significance, and implications of the cliché are nowhere near as straightforward as they may seem at first glance. School-based literacy education faces complex questions. Two questions are of particular interest in this chapter.

First, what is an appropriate conception of literacy on which to base literacy education? What sorts of things are involved in best realizing this conception of literacy within classroom pedagogies?

The second question is complicated by the presence of learners from diverse linguistic and cultural groups in "postmodern" classrooms. These groups are impacted by a burgeoning transnationalism which produces global "flows" of persons as well as of data and information (Castells 1996). Under current conditions, literacy education in any given classroom may have to be shaped in accordance with the very different needs, experiences, and backgrounds of learners from diverse cultural and social groups.

This chapter will address two intersecting aspects of the broad problematic surrounding these questions. First, how must literacy education responds to an extended conception of literacy that includes and accounts for characteristically contemporary forms of linguistic experience? And second, what kinds of factors have to be taken into account within mainstream classrooms when developing literacy programs for linguistically and culturally diverse learners?

# TECHNICAL SUPPORT

Traditionally, literacy has been thought of as "a largely *psychological* ability—something true to do with our heads" (Gee, Hull, and Lankshear 1996).

That is, to become literate is to have something done to our brains, so that we achieve a special kind of cognitive "faculty" or inner capacity. This view reflects the domination of psychology in educational theory and research throughout this century. Being literate has been seen as a matter of cracking the alphabetic code, word-formation skills, phonics, grammar, and comprehension skills. According to this view, encoding and decoding skills serve as building blocks for doing other things and for accessing meanings. For instance, once people are literate, they can get on with learning through the medium of texts—by studying subjects in a curriculum, or by other print-mediated means. When people are literate, they can use "it" (the skill repertoire, the ability) as a tool to pursue all sorts of goods (employment, knowledge, recreational pleasure, personal development, economic growth, innovation). But to "get literate" in the first place is seen from this perspective as a matter of inserting the necessary skills into people's heads. There are debates about how best to achieve this—for example, phonics, letter recognition, "letter chunking"—but at the end of the day, those debating the most effective way all share the idea of literacy as basically a "head thing," a psychological ability.

Recently, however, this long-dominant view has been challenged from two main (and increasingly related) directions. The first involves a broad trend in theory and research within social sciences and humanities dating from the 1970s, which Gee (1998) calls "the social turn." This was a turn "away from focusing on individuals and their 'private' minds and towards interaction and social practice" (1). Gee maps more than a dozen of the myriad discernible movements that collectively made up the "social turn." These movements included an emerging sociocultural approach to literacy and several which strongly influenced and were subsequently taken into the "new" literacy studies: notably, ethnomethodology, conversation analysis, and interactional sociolinguistics; ethnography of communication; work in poststructuralism and postmodern social theory centered on discourse; sociohistorical psychology based on the work of Vygotsky and his associates and Bakhtin; situated cognition; and cultural models theory.

From the sociocultural viewpoint, then, any acceptable concept of literacy has to make sense of reading, writing, imaging, and other modes of meaning-making as integral elements of social practices. Such a definition is provided by Gee (1996), who defines literacy in relation to Discourses. Discourses are socially recognized ways of using language (reading, writing, speaking, listening), gestures and other semiotics (images, sounds, graphics, signs, codes), as well as ways of thinking, believing, feeling, valuing, acting/doing, and interacting in relation to people and things, such that we can be identified and recognized as being a member of a socially meaningful group, or as playing a socially meaningful role (Gee 1991, 1996, 1998). To be in, or part of, a Discourse means that others can recognize us as being a "this" or a "that" (a pupil, a mother, a computer or video gamer, a researcher, a teacher, and so on) by virtue of how we are using language, believing, feeling, acting, dressing, doing, and so on. Language is a dimension of Discourse, but only one dimension, and Gee uses discourse (with a small "d") to mark this relationship: "discourse" referring to the language "bits" in Discourses—stretches of language, images, signs, etc., that make sense within particular contexts of social practice.

Gee distinguishes our *primary* Discourse from our various *secondary* Discourses. Our primary Discourse is how we learn to do and be (including speaking and expressing) within our family (or face-to-face intimate) group during our early life. It (we each have only one primary Discourse, although there are many different primary Discourses) comprises our first notions of who "people like us" are, and what "people like us" do, think, value, and so on. Our secondary Discourses (and we each have many of these, although they differ from person to person) are those we are recruited to through participation in outside groups and institutions, such as schools, clubs, workplaces, churches, political organizations, and so on. These all draw upon and extend our resources from our primary Discourse, and may be nearer to or further away from our primary Discourse. The further away a secondary Discourse is from our primary Discourse and our other secondary Discourses—as in the case of children from marginal social groups who struggle to get a handle on the culture of school classrooms—the more we have to stretch our discursive resources to perform within that Discourse. Often in such cases we simply are unable to operate the Discourse at the level of fluent performance.

These ideas have important implications for literacy. Because our particular uses of language and other kinds of meaning-making signs and symbols can only be understood and only make sense in relation to the larger social practices in which they are embedded, and because there are many such practices, we should think in terms of *literacies*, rather than literacy. There are many literacies, since there are many Discourses. Moreover, these literacies are never ends in themselves, but are always parts of larger purposes. Hence, at times we may appear to get the language and literacy bits right, but to little effect—because of failures to get other aspects of the social practice right. For example, we may produce our texts tidily, with accurate grammar and spelling and clear images, yet fail to meet our goals because the register of the text is inappropriate for its context and purpose, or because we have misconstrued the nature and mood of the audience, or because we have pre-sented our (written) texts verbally in awkward or unconvincing ways, and so on.

In addition, the sociocultural view of literacy denies the idea that literacy is linked in linear ways to larger social practices. It is not as if we "learn the text stuff" and can then go on and apply it in straightforward ways within various Discourses. Likewise, this view emphasizes the need for literacies to be acquired whole. The language bits need to be acquired and mastered in conjunction with the other components of the Discourses they belong to. It also provides a basis for questioning the way some discourses and Discourses are privileged over others within school-based language and literacy educa-tion. Finally, from a sociocultural perspective, learning focuses not on chil-dren or schools, but on human lives seen as trajectories through numerous social practices across a range of social institutions. For learning to be effica-cious, what a person does now as a learner must be connected in meaningful and motivating ways with mature versions of related social practices as prac-ticed by "insiders" (Gee, Hull, and Lankshear 1996, 4). Schools usually are not ideal settings for efficacious learning in this sense; partly because they build activities around inadequate notions of children and their needs and capabilities, and partly because they are cut off from the "real world" of mature versions of social practices. Schools create their own versions of social practices, which are often very different from mature versions of social prac-tices to which they are supposedly related.

The second direction from which the established view of literacy has faced strong challenges recently is from the rapid development and mass adoption of new electronic and digital communications and information technologies (CITs). Today, as much as in any other historical period, the development of new technologies has implications for changing forms and practices of literacy. We need to attend to the reality of new and emerging lit-eracies and new modes of human practice and ways of experiencing the world that have accompanied the emergence and adoption of new CITs (Green and Bigum 1993). Whether we are conscious of it or not, "the cre-ation of new technologies continues to change society's concept of literacy, just as it has always done" (Durrant and Green 1998, 3).

Today, print is just one medium of literate practice within an entire range of available media, and the center of gravity is shifting. We are currently see-ing "a broad-based shift from Print to Digital-Electronics as the organising context for literate-textual practice and for learning and teaching" (Durrant and Green 1998, 1). This does not mean the end of print as the paradigm lit-eracy medium, or the death of the book as the text paradigm. It does, however, mean that educators need more flexible and expansive views of literacy than hitherto.

Since the invention of the printing press, the printed word has been the main carrier of (what is presented as) truth. Mass schooling has evolved under the regime of print, and print has more generally "facilitated the literate foundation of culture" (Heim 1999). Of course, various kinds of images or graphics have been used in printed texts to help carry truth (e.g., tables, charts, graphs, photographic plates, illustrations). However, web technology merges pictures and print (not to mention sound) much more intricately and easily than has ever been possible before. As Heim puts it

> The word now shares Web space with the image, and text appears inextricably tied to pictures. The pictures are dynamic, animated, and continually updated. The unprecedented speed and ease of digital production mounts photographs, movies, and video on the Web. Cyberspace becomes visualized data, and meaning arrives in spatial as well as in verbal expressions (Heim 1999).

Hence, practices of reading and writing undergo profound changes as ideas and information are communicated in nonlinear (as well as linear) ways through the use of hyperlinks, and as scanning and scrolling and following links become standard procedures for reading online. Writing is radically transformed as graphics, images, hyperlinks, cutting and pasting, downloading, web-page building, compiling archives, emailing, chatting, MOOing, and the like become common practices.

All this is associated with the emergence of new Discourses and their more or less distinctive embedded discourses (language uses). Young people are party to the creation of myriad new and revamped genres which are often more immediately available, authentic, and significant in their development as persons than established ones which have long been associated with school-based language and literacy education.

# TROUBLESHOOTING (1)

While the ideas presented in the previous section apply to all learners, they have particular significance in relation to nonmainstream learners in mainstream classrooms.

The term "mainstream" is problematic to the extent that it runs the risk of totalizing contexts and experiences. On the other hand, it can be a useful concept for talking about some of the issues generated when ESL (English as a Second Language) or NESB (Non English-Speaking Background) learners are members of English-only classrooms without access to first-language education or ESL tutoring during the course of a normal school day. In this chapter, "mainstream classroom" refers to classrooms that define learners in terms of having English as a first and only language, and assumes all learners share a common historical and cultural heritage (cf. Vale, Scarino, and McKay 1991). By definition, all learners for whom English is not a first and only language, and whose cultural and historical heritages vary from learners for whom English is a first and only language, are "nonmainstream." (This definition, of course, elides the fact that learners for whom English is a first and only language do not share a common historical and cultural heritage— since they come from a range of social class, race-ethnic, religious, etc., backgrounds. For reasons of space, we must live with this shortcoming here.)

In the case of nonmainstream bi/multilingual learners in mainstream classrooms, the sociocultural approach to literacy and learning and the recognition that technological changes impact strongly on social practices and their associated literacies have far-reaching and constructive implications for literacy education. They also provide a valuable troubleshooting perspective, from which we can identify strengths and weaknesses in existing pedagogical approaches to literacy education and advance ideas and recommendations designed to enhance classroom practices.

Our argument builds on an illuminating case of a nonmainstream learner in a mainstream classroom. The case of Tony is by no means typical of all learners. It is, however, a case which, with some variations at the level of detail, is increasingly common within sizable cities throughout the English-speaking First World. With minor modifications to detail, it could be generalized much more widely.

## Main Screen

Tony is 13 years old. He is in Year 7, the final year of primary school in the Australian state where he has lived since his parents migrated from Taiwan six years previously. He is tall in comparison with other boys in the class, and his jet-black hair is cut in a heavy fringe which he often seems to hide behind. Tony is the only student of Asian origin in the class of more than thirty. Indeed, he is the sole ESL student.

Tony sits at a group of six desks toward the front of a cramped and congested classroom. A rapidly growing student population combined with restrained government spending on education means that resources and space are stretched to the limit in the school. Notwithstanding the pressure on space and the chaos of furniture and bodies in the tiny classroom, the teacher (Ms. Bryant) has made space for a "Writer's Center" in one corner of the room, where students can produce narrative texts during free writing time. She has equipped the center with paper of different kinds and colors, glue, scissors, tape, staples, and cardboard (for covers), and on the walls she has posted guidelines for writing in a range of genres on large sheets of card-board. The center reflects Ms. Bryant's commitment to "process writing" approaches to literacy education (cf. Graves 1983).

It is important to recognize that this is *not* a context of literacy educa-tion constrained by any kind of mechanistic, basics-oriented view of literacy grounded in psychological theories and applications alone. The state's Eng-lish syllabus aims to develop students' ability to compose and comprehend spoken and written English fluently, appropriately, effectively, and critically, for a wide range of personal and social purposes" (Department of Educa-tion, Queensland 1994, iii). It is based on a text-context model of language, according to which texts are structured in conventional ways to realize peo-ple's purposes within particular social and cultural settings. The syllabus is based on five organizing principles, known as growth and development, skills, cultural heritage, genre, and critical literacy—the latter three principles being derived explicitly from a sociocultural view of language, literacy, and learning. Key assumptions underlying the principle are that knowing and understanding genres enables members of all cultural groups to operate effectively and usefully in society, and that "people who understand how genres work can be powerful instruments of critical review and change in any culture." (Department of Education, Queensland 1994, 5).

Ms. Bryant's approach to her Year 7 program, in accordance with the syllabus requirements and guidelines, emphasized and integrated genres and process writing. She took the idea of drafting, conferencing, and publishing phases of text production from process writing and wove them into the genre model of teaching and learning. She would give examples of a partic-ular genre—e.g., expository argument—and model it using an overhead pro-jector. She would then give the class a pro forma example which set out the main structural features of the genre—e.g., Thesis, Argument 1, Argument 2, Restate the Thesis—and a text from which to produce their own sample of the genre working in pairs or small groups. After this (scaffolded) modeling and guided practice phase, the students would work individually to produce drafts of their own texts within the same genre. Students would then confer-ence their drafts once or twice (if necessary) with the teacher before publish-ing their final versions.

The genres officially designated to be covered in the Year 7 English program include literary and nonliterary genres. The former include *narrative*—which covers text types such as stories (yarn, parable, adventure story), story board, biography, ballads, personal diary entry, and plays—and *non-narrative* text types—including caricature, personal journal entry, lyric poem, formula verse (e.g., cinquain, tarquain, limerick), and public speech. Nonliterary genres to be covered include *transactional genre*—such as apology, interview, display advertisement, film poster, and letter of application—*procedures*—such as meeting agenda and instructions—*reports*—including graphs/tables, learning log entry, information report, and newspaper/television news report—and *expositions*—including explanation and complaint. Covering these genres is a cross-curriculum endeavor rather than work confined to the English timetable slot alone.

## Snapshot

In class, Tony's group of five students—two girls and three boys—are putting the finishing touches to their project about India, which takes the generic form of an information report. "Countries of the World" is the current theme for the class. Tony's main task appears to be designing and producing the graphics for the project report. During the two weeks of classroom observations (thirty hours) in the final term of the school year, he works carefully on a bubble-font title page. The other group members show visible pride in his contribution. During this time he rarely speaks in class. He is a noticeably silent participant. The only time he speaks to the class as a whole is when presenting a segment of the oral component of the report, and the only students he is observed talking with are the four at his table. On the occasions he does speak, he is easily understood, although he speaks quietly and hides shyly behind his fringe. He interacts particularly well with the two girls in his group.

Ms. Bryant, who has ten years of teaching experience, agreed with our suspicion that Tony's silence reflects his doubts about the quality of his English. She explains that there is no teacher aide support for ESL students in the school, that she has never previously had ESL students in her class before, and as a result does not know how to meet his needs. She is not sure of Tony's immigration history, and seems to know little about him at all. She observes that NESB immigrants have access to a migrant center and free English lessons in the city, but that they prefer to enroll their children in ordinary school—for what Ms. Bryant calls "status reasons." She says she cannot do everything for every student, and in the absence of specialist support and sufficient time to tailor lessons to meet his language needs and provide him with additional English tutoring, she has to let Tony find his own way in the class. When probed to talk more about having Tony in her class, she shrugs and declares, almost defensively, that she really doesn't know what to do with him. In light of her highly conscientious approach to teaching, and the visible efforts she made to scaffold learning for the class as a whole, this response signaled frustration about lack of wider school support for students like Tony, and a sense of being out of her depth in this, her first time teaching Year 7.

At this point she ruffles through some files near her desk and pulls out a fat wad of A4-sized paper, covered in handwriting and stapled in one corner. She throws it down on the desk, heaves an exasperated sigh, and asks rhetorically: "What do you do with that? It doesn't even make sense!"

Tony had been working on this text—a narrative—for more than a month at the time he handed it in. Ms. Bryant explained that by the time she first saw it as a draft it was far too long for her to "conference" properly (i.e., to give him feedback about his text, identify its strengths, and suggest how to improve it as a basis for subsequent work in class). She had filed it in his assessment portfolio, and said she was not going to mark it because it was too long and the time was now too close to the end of the year to find time for marking it and giving feedback. She felt she just didn't have time to correct his English and explain what was wrong with his turn of phrase.

## The Text: A Fragment

We made a copy of Tony's narrative and took it home for analysis. The following fragment, which is representative of the quality and character of the text as a whole, comprises the Orientation to his narrative: Orientation, Conflict, Resolution, and Coda being the four main generic structural features of narrative as defined in the syllabus.

---

### DOOM: PART 1

In the dark Ages, Europe was broke into many different countries.

In the *Kingdom* of Khimmur, King Little, the ruler of Khimmur gave a mission to one of the brave warriors, Jake Simpson.

His mission was to defeat Shang-Tsung. Shang-Tsung was an evil person. He tried to rule the whole china, but he never did it, so he went to Europe. Now he is planning to take over the whole Europe. And he has three warriors.

Kung-Lao, before he was a dragon, then Shang-Tsung made him \into a/ human Raiden, God of Thunder.

Gora, a 2000 year old giant with four hands.

Shang-Tsung also took control of lots of things. He has a vast number of soldiers.

Snow Witch, Lizard King and Baron Sukumvit were also Shang-Tsung's helpers, because Shang-Tsung promised to Share the power with them.

And the Warlock of Firetop Mountain, was the guard for Shang-Tsung's Rich.

"So, I will send you to attack Shang-Tsung" said King Little.

"Isn't there anyone going with me?" asked Jake.

"Oh, I nearly forgot to tell you about this" said King Little "There will be two Martial Arts Master from the great Empire of Han, Chung-Hi-San-Wu and Lee-Quan-Lin will go with you. They were send by the Emperor of China."

## The Game Play

This excerpt from Tony's narrative reveals much about his literacy proficiency. At the surface level it is evident that he has an excellent grasp of a range of important writing conventions. These include compiling lists, paragraphing, direct speech conventions, punctuation, and controlling the genre structure of a narrative. His use of "\ /" marks show that he has mastered the convention for inserting text into a sentence already handwritten. Likewise, a word he was not sure how to spell is underlined—another school writing practice. Tony's vocabulary belied our interpretation of Ms. Bryant's description of his command of English, which we had taken to indicate that he had very little grasp of English in his writing. The fragment presented here and his text as a whole contain some more or less systematic errors in tense, with plurals and some prepositions, etc. By the same token, our observations of the class and our collected artifacts of student work suggest that in terms of conventional print literacy indicators—e.g., ability to produced sustained text, accuracy of spelling and grammar, fluidity, clarity, and sense—Tony's literacy "competence" is *considerably* greater than a number of his native English-speaking classmates (cf. Knobel 1997, 1999; Lankshear 1998).

Things become even more interesting and significant  when we look beyond the surface features of school literacy performance. Even the most perfunctory glance at Tony's text reveals *to anyone with relevant insider knowledge* what a complex intertextual narrative he has produced. Taking the excerpt provided above, we can readily identify a range of other texts woven into his narrative.

The characters Shang-Tsung, Raiden, and Kung-Lao are all characters in *Mortal Kombat*, an adventure game from the early 1990s produced originally by Nintendo, and now available as a computer game as well. Kung-Lao is described on the *Mortal Kombat* official web site as "a troubled young warrior from the Order of Light Temple. He is a skilled *Mortal Kombat* fighter with incomparable focus and strength. Kung-Lao was raised alongside other children from the temple and trained from birth to fight in the *Mortal Kombat* wars…" (www.mortalkombat.com). Similarly, the character Gora-Gora can be found in the Nintendo game, *The Ultimate Evil*. Subsequent references to a skeleton army echoes skeleton armies found in a range of Nintendo games including *Dungeon Keeper II*. Later in the text, characters from the Nintendo (and computer) *DOOM* games appear in the adventure, such as Demon Queen and Barons of Hell. The Warlock of Firetop Mountain who makes an early appearance as a character is actually the title of the first Fighting Fantasy Gamebook produced in the 1980s by Steve Jackson and Ian Livingstone. The reference to Snow Witch echoes another Fighting Fantasy Gamebook by Ian Livingstone (1984) called *Caverns of the Snow*. This series of books—60 in all—were "quest games" that came with dice and maps and required role-playing and a large amount of reading to plot and navigate the adventures written into them. The books were *extremely* popular in the 1980s and were distributed in English—in England, Australia, and Canada—and in Japanese—in Japan. (As is common with narratives written by boys in upper primary school—cf. Gilbert and Rowe 1989—Tony's narrative also contains the names of two boys in his class.)

Tony's text builds on his membership in the "Video Action Games" Discourse (for present purposes we have left aside issues of violence and constructed masculinity associated with the narrative, although these are important matters for a different focus). He is an "insider." The knowledge of characters evident in his work comes *only* from commitment and proficiency as a game player and, of course, from having adequate command of the considerable textual requirements for playing the games successfully. These games are *saturated* in text. In addition, entire genres and "libraries" of *print* texts (books, magazines, comics, "cheats," manuals, etc.) circulate around the games Discourse. The Fighting Fantasy Gamebooks are one instance. Tony's narrative suggests close familiarity with these texts as well as with the text-mediated electronic games themselves.

In terms discussed above, the games Discourse has its own demanding and sophisticated discourse. Tony has written his narrative out of the very kind of membership and participation in mature ("insider") versions of Discourses that are increasingly identified as hallmarks of authentic learning and effective social practice (Heath and McLaughlin 1994; Rogoff 1990, 1995; Lave and Wenger 1991; see Gee, Hull, and Lankshear 1996 for a larger discussion). Effective literacy is precisely about having fluent mastery of the language uses of Discourses (Gee 1991, 1996). *Powerful* literacy is about having fluent mastery of the language uses of Discourses that carry high status in social settings. Mastery of the kind of literacy inchoate in Tony's narrative undoubtedly carries high status and attracts attention (Goldhaber 1997) as well as other social rewards in a range of social contexts within youth/popular culture and the (adult) work world alike (Bennahum 1998; Rushkoff 1996a, 1996b). The brute fact is that school generally, and Tony's classroom specifically, are not among these contexts! It is arguable how far this may be problematic given present and foreseeable social practices and priorities within societies like our own.

From the perspective we have adopted in this chapter, Tony seems to us to have signaled very clearly that he understands what his teacher requires in terms of creative writing—a strong plot line, acceptable narrative structure, dialogue, interesting characters, a range of adjectives, and the like. However, we were well aware (as we believe Tony was as well) that Ms. Bryant was not picking up these signals or recognizing his work as literate practice (Davies and Monroe 1987).

# TROUBLESHOOTING AND TECHNICAL SUPPORT (2)

In many ways, this is a sobering case. We have a diligent, energetic, competent teacher working with a potentially expansive mandated syllabus. Yet the outcomes for Tony were far from satisfactory. In this section, we will briefly troubleshoot some features of the classroom practice and then, on the basis of the theory and practice described above, advance some suggestions (technical support) intended to contribute to enhanced practice under similar sorts of conditions.

## Troubleshooting

First, it seems that by constructing Tony as an ESL learner—who thus needs special ESL support which is not available—Ms. Bryant is unwittingly distorting Tony's base of relevant prior experiences, his actual capabilities, and the options available pedagogically for optimizing his literacy education. The teacher is working in objectively difficult conditions—cramped space, a large class, no prior experience with ESL learners, in her first year teaching this level. In this context the simple (and seemingly reasonable) act of constructing Tony in this way helps make sense of a trying situation and provides some relief for the teacher from feeling guilty or inadequate about not being able to do as much as she might like for the student. By doing so, however, Ms. Bryant is prevented from recognizing Tony's existing English language and literacy strengths and how these could be readily built on.

Second, this problem is compounded by the normal circumstances of school literacy, whereby social practices in classrooms take on distinctive *school* forms and are systematically distanced from social practices in the world beyond the school (including those to which they are supposed to relate). The need to locate learning *within* the classroom militates against acquiring literacies whole since it is difficult, and often impossible, to import into the classroom many of the elements of authentic social practices in which literacies are embedded. Putting literal walls around classroom literacies has the further effect of marginalizing learners' out-of-school practices. Literacy becomes defined in terms of what belongs to and can be done in classrooms, and an entire lore, tradition, and actor network (Bigum 1997) exist here which teachers can and do draw upon, reproduce, and otherwise contribute to shoring up. These norms typically get incorporated into teacher education, producing a closed shop and a closed loop of practice. Learners like Tony (for a further example from the same classroom, see Knobel 1997, 1999; Lankshear 1998) are effectively constrained from bringing their out-of-school literacies to bear on classroom learning. This in turn makes it difficult for teachers to act on what are otherwise acknowledged as sound principles of effective learning: building on learners' existing interests and strengths, taking learners from where they are to where they want or need to go, etc. The further consequence is that school-based learning is denied the possibility of maximum authenticity (Heath and McLaughlin 1994). School literacies become increasingly school-like and "for school only." Learners who are well grounded in Discourses and discourses from their everyday discursive worlds are unable in school to develop, build upon, expand, and diversify from things they do well and that are actually valued and practiced in their out-of-school lives (present and future).

Third, Ms. Bryant has construed issues and difficulties of Tony's learning in terms of inadequate time and lack of specialist support. There is no question that teachers are working under increasingly difficult conditions, and that previously available resources of time and specialist support have been reduced in recent years. Yet, what seems more obviously to be lacking in the case described here are forms of theoretical understanding, knowledge of students' worlds beyond school and of changes in the world more generally, and prior training in possible strategies for building students more actively into the pedagogy in ways that can free up teacher time and energy without compromising the quality of learning. Leading-edge theory and research in literacy and pedagogy alike emphasize the importance of embedding learning as far as possible in roles and procedures of acquiring expertise in authentic social practices. Learners enact a range of roles along the expert-novice continuum and consolidate their knowledge and understanding by experiencing these roles within such processes and relationships as cultural apprenticeship, guided participation, and participatory appropriation (Heath and McLaughlin 1994; Rogoff 1995). Being able to act on such theory will often call for shifts in educator mind-sets (Lankshear and Bigum 2000) and broader and more up-to-date knowledge of contemporary social, economic, and cultural practices beyond the school.

## Technical Support

Space limitations confine us to just four of the many points that could be made here. Readers will, however, easily be able to generate further ideas by drawing on their own existing knowledge and experience in conjunction with the theoretical resources and the snapshot provided here, and the wider research base to which we have referred.

First, it is interesting to consider the ways in which Tony's insider knowledge of the games Discourse could have been exploited and built upon in teaching and learning a range of the genres set down in the Queensland English syllabus for Year 7 (DEQ 1994). (Other students with similar and related experiences could have further enriched the pedagogical possibilities here.) For example, texts such as the guides to the "cheats" in a video game could have been enlisted in teaching, learning about, and producing *procedural* texts. In terms of our present case, Ms. Bryant could have introduced Tony—and interested others in the class—to writing cheat guides by means of an activity-based learning center (for activity ideas see Millard 1994). Learning centers have fallen out of favour in many classrooms but lend themselves to busy schedules by enabling students to become self-sufficient learners.

Likewise, Ms. Bryant could have put the current classroom practice of producing "learning log" text type (within the report genre and comprising a few sentences each day that record what the student feels s/he has learned that day) to use, tailoring it to include Tony's reflections on what he actually set out to learn and understand in terms of the various video game moves he learned in a given week, and so on. At other year levels, text types like reviews (within the exposition genre category) could be linked with a learner's or group of learners' active interest in a range of video or computer games and the like that appear in magazines (e.g., *Nintendo*, *PC Gamer*). And, as an extension, the reviews produced by the students make effective material for student-generated web pages. Writing biographies, another text type addressed in Year 7 in Queensland schools, could be linked to exploring the lives of key characters in a video game (e.g., Shang-Tsung, Kung-Lao from *Mortal Kombat*), and the limits to which good biographies can be produced from information obtained in magazines and on the Internet can be examined and critiqued. This is not to say that the teacher should produce a separate curriculum for Tony (which would be impossible), or that all Tony's learning should be held hostage to his interest in video games. But to miss the kinds of opportunities identified here is educationally unfortunate: not least, since what holds true for Tony will hold for other learners regardless of their particular linguistic and cultural backgrounds.

Second, a range of theoretically-grounded strategies that could have been usefully applied to Tony's situation spring readily to mind, none of which depend upon specialized second language learning theory or specialist training in teaching ESL students. Most obviously, perhaps—even if Ms. Bryant felt the need to deal sufficiently with Tony's *entire* text—any part of it could have generated rich material for conferencing, given a sound grasp of the syllabus organizing principles (e.g., skills, critical literacy, genre theory), the generic and grammatical features of the narrative genre, and so on. Less obviously—but very importantly—techniques and processes such as the use of editing circles which make use of carefully selected and planned small groups to discuss each other's "writing-in-process," instead of the laborious one-to-one conferencing of the process-writing approach, free up teachers and enable them to spend more time with students who need close attention. Likewise, including visual literacy into classroom practices in the form of storyboards, political cartoons, cartoon strips (all text types listed in the Queensland English syllabus) also builds on theory and research in literacy and pedagogy.

The kinds of literacy research and teaching strategies that mainstream classroom teachers can—and do—use make effective use of literacy theory and research. For example, Barbara Rogoff's take on Vygotsky's concepts of "scaffolding" and "zone of proximal development" is very useful for teachers (Rogoff 1995). Rogoff proposes three dimensions of effective learning: apprenticeship, guided participation, and participatory appropriation (Rogoff 1990). In a nutshell, apprenticeship refers to a group of peers and experts working together in some sort of social activity (e.g., writing a picture book, designing and building a web page). Guided participation refers to the process of the experts letting go, but still providing learners with guides and supports that contribute to successful completion of the activity (e.g., editing circles, cloze activities aimed at helping students master a new genre, helping a group of students innovate on an existing text to produce a new one). Participatory appropriation is that dimension of learning where the student begins to be able to engage in the activity independently, and may even end up transforming the activity in some way (e.g., a group of students are asked to produce a school web page, but instead produce a web page comprising narratives about issues in the school; see Bigum et al. 1999).

Third, we need to problematize the notion of linguistic and cultural difference in ways that may at first seem confronting to teachers. Given the massive changes that have occurred beyond schools, not to mention developments in electronic communication, information technologies, and new social practices surrounding them, it is increasingly likely that the "alien" in the classroom may be the teacher (Green and Bigum 1993). To a large extent, teachers speak a different language from learners who have grown up in electronically saturated environments. Learners from different linguistic backgrounds may well speak common languages—discourses—associated with common or shared Discourses (e.g., games, various online practices, popular cultural forms) that are not known to teachers, administrators, curriculum planners, etc. It is nothing for young people who are wired to computer networks to communicate with ease across linguistic, cultural, and geographic borders. This burgeoning "transculturation" suggests important ways in which conventional school literacies may have increasingly little to do with effective communication in a postmodern world, and that—to para-phrase Marx—it may be the "literator" herself who needs "literating." At the pedagogical level, this will require a sea change in teacher education, con-ceptions of and approaches to professional development, and a willingness to actively seek ways of school-based teaching and learning that contract closer links to mature versions of social practices that have genuine currency in the contemporary world.

Finally, educators need to get closely in touch with the world of current times and with the kinds of issues raised in the previous paragraph. This is not something teachers should be expected to undertake individually and on their own initiative. It calls for a combination of well-conceived school-based professional development organized on a regular basis and factored into the formal life of the school staff, backed up by informed work by teacher pro-fessional associations, and revitalized and reoriented preservice and inservice teacher education programs. Professional development initiatives aimed at getting to grips with the cultural worlds of the learners in their classrooms and the changed and rapidly changing world beyond the school gate can be assisted by focused and challenging reading programs built around dis-cussing, interpreting, and considering potential applications of ideas from helpful texts. Some of those we have found most useful are appended below (see also Lankshear and Snyder 2000, Chapter 6 for more detailed discussion).

# GAME OVER

Literacy education must respond to an extended conception of literacy that includes and accounts for characteristically contemporary forms of linguistic experience (including those mediated by new technologies) and up-to-date understandings of the relationship between Discourses and discourses (Gee 1991, 1996). Even more importantly, educators must pursue and respond to expanded views of literacy that include and account for characteristically con-temporary forms of experience. Often, differences in linguistic experience—perceived and actual—are *not* the key factor to be taken into account in learning situations. It may be much more important to take into account new modes of communicating and new forms of shared D/discourses, to recognize the importance of building on insider knowledge and experiences, and to be willing and able to integrate learner expertise and prior experience more actively into pedagogy along the kinds of lines suggested by people like Barbara Rogoff and Jean Lave (among many others). What may be most at issue under postmodern conditions of learning and teaching may be differences in *mind-sets* that have little or nothing to do with conventional constructions of linguistic and cultural difference.

# APPENDIX

## Some Professional Reading Suggestions

### Type 1: Texts That Emphasize Life
### and Practices in an Electronic World

Bennahum, D. *Extra Life: Coming of Age in Cyberspace.* New York: Basic Books, 1998.

Digitarts homepage. *<http://digitarts.va.com.au>.* June 1999.

GRRROWL. <http://digitarts.va.com.au/frames.html>, <http://digitarts.va.com.au/grrrowl>. June 1999.

Howard, S., ed. *Wired Up: Young People and the Electronic Media.* London: Taylor and Francis, 1997.

Howe, N., and B. Strauss. *13th Gen: Abort, Retry, Ignore, Fail?* New York: Vintage Books, 1993.

McCloud, S. *Understanding Comics.* New York: Harper-Perennial, 1994.

Rushkoff, D., ed. *The GenX Reader.* New York: Ballantine Books, 1994.

———. *Playing the Future: How Kids' Culture Can Teach Us to Thrive in an Age of Chaos.* New York: Harper Collins, 1996.

Tunbridge, N. "The Cyberspace Cowboy." *Australian Personal Computer,* September 1995.

### Type 2: Texts That Focus on Global Change
### and Their Associated Issues

Castells, M. *The Rise of the Network Society.* Oxford: Blackwell, 1996.

———. *The Power of Identity.* Oxford: Blackwell, 1997.

Goldhaber, M. "The Attention Economy and the Net." *<http://firstmonday. dk/issues/issue2_4/goldhaber/>* 1998.

Heim, M. "Transmogrification." <http://www.mheim.com/transmog/>. 1999.

Lyotard, J. F. *The Postmodern Condition: A Report on Knowledge.* Translated by Geoff Bennington and Brian Massumi. Foreword by Fredric Jameson. Minneapolis: University of Minnesota Press, 1984.

Robertson, H. J. *No More Teachers, No More Books: The Commercialization of Canada's Schools.* Toronto: McClelland & Stewart, 1998.

Roszak, T. *The Cult of Information*. Berkeley: University of California Press, 1994.

Shenk, D. *Data Smog*. San Francisco: HarperEdge, 1998.

### Type 3: Texts That Deal with Contemporary Social Practices

Hafner, K., and J. Markoff. *Cyberpunk: Outlaws and Hackers on the Computer Frontier*. New York: Ballantine Books, 1994.

Hafner, K., and M. Lyon. *Where Wizards Stay Up Late: The Origins of the Internet*. New York: Touchstone Books, 1996.

Johnson, S. *Interface Culture: How New Technology Transforms the Way We Create and Communicate*. San Francisco: HarperEdge, 1997.

Rushkoff, D. *Cyberia: Life in the Trenches of Hyperspace*. San Francisco: Harper, 1994.

———. *Media Virus: Hidden Agendas in Popular Culture*, 2d ed. New York: Ballantine Books, 1996.

Stone, A. *The War of Desire and Technology at the Close of the Mechanical Age*. Cambridge, Mass.: MIT Press, 1996.

# CHAPTER FIVE

# THE CASE OF

# REPRESSED NATIVE

# OR INDIGENOUS

# LANGUAGES

LADISLAUS M. SEMALI, THE PENNSYLVANIA STATE UNIVERSITY

*The ideal of biculturation helps explain how people learn and practice both mainstream culture and ethnic culture at the same time. Much intragroup socialization is conditioned by ethnically distinct experience, ranging from linguistic and other expressive patterns.*

VALENTINE (1971, 143)

*Languages do not exist independently from the people, families and communities that use them. In other words, language and ethnocultural identity and existence are inextricably linked...when people lose their native language to English; they do not become Anglos and obtain social acceptance. They lose the language as a tool for accessing the help that their families and communities can give them.*

FISHMAN (1994, 69)

*Learning to listen to different voices, hearing different speech challenges the notion that we must all assimilate—share a single similar talk—in educational institutions. Language reflects the culture from which we emerge. To deny ourselves daily use of speech patterns that are common and familiar, that embody the unique and distinctive aspect of our self is one of the ways we become*

*estranged and alienated from our past.*
HOOKS (1989, 79–80)

Language reflects the culture from which we emerge. As illustrated in the above quotations, the premise that languages do not exist independently from people, families, and communities that use them is well established and accepted by sociolinguists. But a suggestion that indigenous languages are valid, effective, and worthy as the dominant dialogue (say Standard English) is often enough to send the self-ordained guardians of language and mainstream culture or a faculty member of the English department into apoplectic fits. What accounts for this language-related confusion and bias? Why is local language literacy such an explosive issue? Why do contradictions and confusion persist in the USA amid pluralistic and multicultural attempts to diversify the school curriculum? Unfortunately, the excellent scholarship that has focused on dialects and language bias has done little to reverse the general nature of judgment and discrimination that operates in US society, where issues of dialect and indigenous languages are of paramount concern.

# AIMS OF CHAPTER

In this chapter, my task is to examine the biased assumptions and contradictions that are played out on the lives of bilingual/bicultural children. What roles do schools and teachers play as they mold the lives of indigenous children? It is significant to note in this essay that when students lose their indigenous language or local language literacy to English, they do not become Anglos or Europeans. No matter how well African students can speak the new language, for example, they do not obtain social acceptance. Instead, they experience an irreversible loss. They must adopt complex bilingual/bicultural or dual ways of knowing to learn and practice mainstream culture and ethnic or indigenous culture at the same time. Why, then, is such dualism allowed to continue? Who benefits? What arguments sustain a pedagogical practice that ignores years of research that supports mother-tongue and first-language instruction?

One of the underlying difficulties with promoting minority or indigenous languages in schools is that teachers are either unprepared, uncomfortable, or simply prefer to hold tightly to their language biases. These problems usually stem from a lack of familiarity with the life experiences of indigenous people.

Because of such unfamiliarity and social distance, even well-intentioned teachers may be unable to satisfy the intent of indigenous languages.

Although few studies have examined the case of repressed native or indigenous languages or even documented the consequences of a sustained repression of local language literacy, a plethora of studies have investigated bilingual education in the United States and the attendant dual ways of knowing necessary for minority children to function in mainstream society. This phenomenon of dual ways of knowing has been studied by social theorists and educators since the early 1900s. Overall, social theorists acknowledge the existence of a form of a dual or separate socialization process involving indigenous or nonmainstream populations in the USA. They refer to a variety of constructs used in these studies to describe the personality development, identity, or traits of nonwhite children. These constructs include concepts such *double consciousness* (Du Bois 1903); *double vision* (Wright 1953); *bicultural* (Valentine 1971; de Anda 1984; Ramirez and Castaneda 1974; Red Horse et al. 1981; Rashid 1981); *diunital* (Dixon and Foster 1971); *multidimensional* (Cross 1978); and other references that closely resemble notions of *duality* and *twoness* (Memmi 1965; Fanon 1967; Kitano 1969; Hsu 1971; Sue and Sue 1978).

Even though there exists little consensus on the dual ways of knowing of bicultural children, or a glimmer of reversal of years of language bias, these studies seem to acknowledge that in the nonwhite populations of Africans, African-Americans, Latinos, Asians, and Native Americans, the phenomenon of intragroup socialization is conditioned by ethnically distinct experiences ranging from linguistic and other expressive patterns to historical and cultural experiences.

The inability of the dominant American culture to accept the reality of people of color (non-European) as legitimate is intensified by the repressed contradictions that have existed since the advent of American society. In this vein, not all educators are convinced that children from indigenous communities need special consideration. Some of these educators see the examination of indigenous discourse systems as a crazed, politically correct argument for eliminating the use of clear organization and logic in the development of well-written essays. They see no reason to make excuses just because some Chinese, Chicanos, or African-Americans think and develop narratives differently or speak counter to the grammatical rules of print (Courts 1997, 1). Even though it is simplistic to think that utilizing a student's primary language (e.g., Spanish, Ebonics, Swahili, etc.) guarantees that a student's emancipatory interests are being met, it is significant to know that there is more damage evidenced in the underlying bias and discrimination that seem to surface when authorities in dominant mainstream institutions make judgments about intelligence and the quality of students' speaking and writing abilities based on misinformation, prejudice, and often ignorance of important aspects of socio- and applied linguistics played out in the field of language (Courts 1997, 35).

As will be shown later in this chapter, what is overlooked in these arguments is that English is the language of people who represent the dominant power structure—within the nation or the language of powerful nations in global geopolitics. In the USA, for example, English is most commonly associated with the language spoken by educated, upper middle-class whites. In contrast, dialects, patois, and indigenous languages are seen as languages of poor people, natives, or primitive people, or simply a sign of being illiterate or uneducated. When it comes to debates about dialects of English, some people equate "standard" English with "Network English"—the use of correct language associated with what newscasters are taught to use, which has uniform features of grammar and similar pronunciation features from coast to coast. The existence of Network English causes most Americans mistakenly to feel there is a national norm of English usage (Courts 1997, 39).

While the study of bilingual/bicultural children is significant to understand the plight of indigenous children, my focus in this chapter is on repressed indigenous languages. My task and interest aim to explore the contexts in which local language literacy has been repressed or is disappearing and being forgotten due to changes in knowledge-power relations inherent in the looming global techno-industrial culture, resulting in the devaluing or erasure of indigenous knowledge. What is the role of schools and teachers in this process? It is important to emphasize at this juncture that historically the phenomenon of denying students the use of indigenous languages is not new. It has been the main thrust of educational strategies of assimilation not only in recent times, but also central to the systematic geopolitical and economic domination characteristic of colonial penetration.

# KEY QUESTIONS ABOUT LANGUAGE BIAS

Besides the lingering of colonial vestiges of domination in our schools, perhaps even more significant in the discussion of language bias against bilingual/bicultural students is the deep psychological effect of denying students the use of indigenous languages. This kind of repression not only impacts students and their learning directly but also precludes their parents and other adult members of their communities from participating in the school educational experience. For example, when parents do not speak English, the language of school, they cannot confer with school administrators or help their children with homework and other school-related projects (Delgado-Gaitan 1990). Students from non-English-speaking families are therefore left to fend for themselves without much help or guidance, something their Anglo peers take for granted. Furthermore, language minority students suffer psychologically from a persisting language bias in public school classrooms. Andrienne Rich (1979) understood the complexity of this situation when she lamented: "When someone of the authority of teacher describes the world and you are not in it, there is a moment of psychic disequilibrium, as if you looked into a mirror and saw nothing" (29). This feeling of emptiness sums up the memories of students from repressed indigenous language environments. Usually, these students learn to speak and function in two or more distinct languages and sociocultural environments: the indigenous language/culture, and the dominant/mainstream culture of the society in which they live.

The psychic disequilibrium Rich is talking about is often experienced by children who, for no fault of their own, find themselves in classrooms where the language of school is different from that of home; the language of play is not the language of the textbook; the pictures in the books they read are not the images they see out the window of their school; the language teachers speak at home is not the language these teachers use in classrooms. When these teachers describe or paint the world of school prescribed in the basal reader and the student is not in it, there is a moment of confusion, wonderment, and amazement as students gaze into the empty fountain of knowledge in front of their tiny desks.

As cited earlier, bell hooks warns educators that to deny students the use of the language that embodies a unique and distinctive aspect of themselves is partly responsible for estranging and alienating them from their past. Such alienation is likely to cause deep psychological imbalance and disequilibrium. Ramirez and Castaneda (1974) found such alienation quite disturbing to Mexican-American children. When the Mexican-American child had been raised during his (or her) preschool years in the sociocultural system characteristic of the traditional Mexican-American community, the socialization practices pertaining to (1) language and heritage, (2) cultural values, and (3) teaching (and cognitive) styles were unique to that system, and the child developed a communication, learning, and motivational style which was appropriate to it. At the same time, when the child began his experience in the public schools, he (she) was required to relate to a sociocultural system whose socialization practices pertaining to language and heritage, cultural values, and teaching (and cognitive) styles were different from those experienced during his (her) preschool years. In effect, it was a new cultural world that he (she) had to explore and understand (29).

Given such a learning environment of double consciousness or double vision, critical educators are left to wonder: How can teachers make a difference in the lives of bicultural/bilingual children? How might the classroom teacher help? Where could schools and teacher training institutions begin to address this phenomenon? Which arguments support the reversal of this situation or unravel years of repression and bias that have fomented much of the devaluing and ignoring of local language literacy in school performance? These rhetorical questions form the core theme of this chapter in my attempt to examine the dilemmas and contradictions facing educators the world over, but more especially educators in charge of immigrant education, migrant worker's education, or remote area and reservation education systems.

# CULTURAL INVASION VERSUS LOCAL LANGUAGE LITERACY

To begin to unravel the underlying assumptions that justify the repression of local language literacy, it is necessary to uncover the contexts that underscore the dynamics of cultural invasion. To accomplish this task, one must look beyond school to see how mainstream or powerful cultures and their institutions repress indigenous languages to assimilate the indigenous culture into the mainstream culture. While teaching in Tanzania in the early years of the postindependence era, I struggled like many teachers in African schools to develop relevant and meaningful lessons that met the local needs of students, drawing on examples of the history and wisdom of local people, parents, and grandparents. Unfortunately, many of the examples I used in Tanzanian classrooms were not found in textbooks available at the time. We read, for example, Shakespeare's *Julius Caesar*, *Adventures of Huckleberry Finn*, *Gulliver's Travels*, Greek mythologies, and the famous Arabian stories of *Alfu-Lela-Ulela* and *Ali Baba and His Seven Sons*. My students, for no fault of their own, had to struggle with the English language, the metaphors, and the English idiom to understand some of these works. Missing were examples of local imagery, history, folklore, and African beliefs. Instead, students were taught to value and admire the beliefs, stories, histories, and myths of other societies. The language used by the characters in these stories did not match the everyday language these students spoke. Their African languages had been suppressed and made illegal to be spoken on the school grounds. In addition, their indigenous knowledge and local language literacy had no place in their school experience.

For my students, indigenous knowledge was unofficial knowledge—essentially anecdotal memories of customary law, inheritance rights, and beliefs about witchcraft, taboos, and rituals. This body of knowledge formed the wisdom of how things were done in the villages where the majority of students came from. Such indigenous knowledge—the local knowledge that is unique to a given culture or society—contrasts with the knowledge of other nations or international systems, which is generated through the global network of universities, research laboratories, and institutes. Contrary to today's expectations, this body of knowledge was not part of what students ordinarily learned at school. The distinction between indigenous/African and Western/European education and the attendant languages was clear. The dichotomy between these knowledge systems did not glorify the similarities. Instead, Africans had to find a way to accommodate and make sense of both systems and, as a result, the two systems competed for attention.

Even though indigenous or community languages formed the primary means of communication and discourse that was vital in the socialization of children and crucial to the survival of a cultural community, it was muted or relegated to second place at school. English, as a foreign language, was believed without question to be superior and more efficient in academic work. What was quickly forgotten, though temporarily, was that within the community's native language was contained "the codification of lived experiences that provided the avenues for adults and children to express their own realities and to question the wider social order" (Darder 1991, 37). Thus, as stated in the above quotations, language, indigenous or not, reflects the culture from which we come (hooks 1989).

Although some parents and teachers were willing to accept the apparent repression or language domination exercised during the preindependence era in return for a "good" education, they became ambivalent when it came to the psychological damage manifested by students. It was acknowledged and widely known that colonial education silenced student voices and seriously curtailed their active participation in school life. There was little to comment about Shakespearean language or the metaphors used in these works of literature. With few opportunities to enter into dialogue and reflect on their reality and lived experiences in terms of political and historical contexts, my students who spoke indigenous languages (or non-European languages) were caught between two worlds: Swahili versus English, local versus global (foreign) language. To master schoolwork and pass the national examinations, my students had to use rote memorization and reproduction techniques that they had learned to value and were good at doing. After taking the examinations, whatever materials were learned were quickly forgotten. Little applied to their local reality. Students soon returned to speaking indigenous languages and doing things the way their community has always done.

This phenomenon of local language literacy repression represents a process by which individuals mediate the different strategies of survival in response to the dynamics of living in constant tension between conflicting cultural values and conditions of cultural subordination. They must also address the dominant discourse of educational institutions and the realities that they must face as members of indigenous or remote area cultures. Denying the native language and its potential benefits in the development of the student's voice constitutes a form of psychological violence and functions to perpetuate social control over subordinate language groups through various linguistic forces of cultural invasion. Nowhere is there a more poignant example of cultural invasion than the history of Native American children, who have been forced to leave their families and their cultural community on the reservation to attend government schools.

In many schools indigenous students are not only discouraged but also actively prevented from speaking their native languages (e.g., Spanish, Japanese, Chinese, Ebonics, Swahili or other African languages). Educators justify these silencing practices with Eurocentric theories and paradigms which claim that the native language will interfere with student's intellectual and emotional development (Ramirez and Castaneda 1974). Even where bilingual programs exist, these Eurocentric values and beliefs are reflected strongly in school policies that encourage the rapid mainstreaming of bicultural students into English-only environments or provide only English as a Second Language (ESL) instruction to students who are limited English speakers. Students from these subordinate groups rarely read their own history of oppression (e.g., slavery, the Japanese retention camps, etc.) and are seldom given the opportunity to critically evaluate it, or to rethink what it means to enter the ever-changing multilingual and multicultural world of the twenty-first century.

When it comes to supporting minority or subordinate languages in education, some critical educators and researchers affirm the privileged mainstream and conservative positions which claim that local language literacy in public schools is misplaced and doomed. Macedo (1994), for example, observes that during the past decade conservative educators such as the former Secretary of Education, William Bennett, and Diane Ravitch, among others, have mounted attacks on bilingual and bicultural education. They use the "melting pot theory" and common cultural assumptions as their basic arguments, primarily to maintain the status quo—a cultural reproduction model that systematically does not allow nonwhite individuals who are considered outside of the mainstream to be present in history. These conservative positions are often uncritical and tend to ignore, and for the most part falsify, the well-documented empirical evidence in support of bilingual education. It is no longer unthinkable that institutionalized concepts, theories, and paradigms of local language bias tend to privilege mainstream students and disadvantage low-income students, students of color, and indigenous/native students. These knowledge systems and paradigms are often used to justify the educational neglect of disparate and needy students, to privilege groups who are advantaged, and to legitimize and justify discriminatory educational policies and practices (Banks 1998).

# COLONIAL "CARGO" AS CULTURAL INVASION

When colonialism is examined in the broader contest of cultural domination, the examples mentioned above are neither isolated phenomena experiences limited to one region of the world. It is significant to note that cultural invasion through the repression of indigenous languages was spread throughout the world during the European colonization period before World War II. In his essay on the colonization of Papua New Guinea, Nicholas Faraclas (1997) captures the dynamics of cultural invasion as they underlie the educational practices of the colonial governments imported into their colonies. Faraclas sees much of the literacy education and religious conversions that followed the conquest of the colonies to be a form of cultural invasion "cargo." Through this cargo metaphor, a critical educator will understand, for example, what happened to the languages of colonial Africa or what might have triggered the English-only movement in America. These contexts illustrate how African languages share a history of extinction and cultural invasion. The legacies of cultural invasion in this period still remain in force in many countries, particularly in former colonies in Africa, Asia, and Latin America. For example, there are over eight thousand African languages spoken on the continent. In general terms, you would find no single ethnic group is large enough to constitute a significant section of the population. Consequently, there is no concentration of power in the hands of any particular group to exert a continental language.

These African languages are distinguished from the colonial European languages that were imposed on Africans in the colonial period by the British, French, Spanish, and Portuguese governments. As colonial languages, these tongues were introduced to schools and have been constitutionally recognized either as official or national languages. Oftentimes, the distinction between official and national languages is not clear. In this confusion, however, lies the contradictions, politics, and ideologies that surround native or indigenous languages in many of the fifty-four countries of Africa. In South Africa, for instance, after the fall of apartheid, eleven languages were selected among the many indigenous languages found in the country to become official languages and languages of instruction in lower primary grades.

The politics of language bias—Swahili versus English, Bambara versus French, indigenous versus European languages—embody many of the dilemmas and contradictions underlying local language literacy and cultural invasion legacies. For many politicians in African countries, both in English-speaking East Africa and French-speaking West Africa, the questions of local language literacy and the case of repressed indigenous languages are better left alone than addressed. Nevertheless, within the national language politics lie the tension between assumptions of being "educated," "literate," or "civilized" and the impetus for promoting local language literacy, dialects, and indigenous languages, rather than English or French. The historical events outlined above partly help to explain how indigenous people came to learn and practice both European (Anglo) culture and ethnic culture at the same time. Thus, the suppression of local knowledge or local languages and the replacement of print literacy in English (or other European languages) have done more to destroy critical literacies in non-European populations than any other force. How can teachers make a difference in the lives of linguistic minority children? What must teachers do for students who don't talk and write the way "we" do? How might the classroom teacher come to grips with the predicament bilingual/bicultural children find themselves in and begin to help? The rationale and legacies of colonial penetration into people of colors' knowledges and cultures represent in large part much of the rationalization that continues to justify the abandonment of local language literacy in public schools today where language minority children attend.

To overcome language bias and to counteract cultural invasion legacies in education, critical educators look to constructive and multiple intelligence approaches to confront diverse classrooms of students of color: Mexican-Americans, African-Americans, Puerto Ricans, and so on. These teachers understand that constructivist and multiple intelligence theories ask different sets of questions that direct their attention toward multiple ways of knowing and reflective approaches. They realize that attempts to institute proper and more effective methods of educating non-English-speaking students cannot be reduced to issues of language but rest on a full understanding of the ideological elements that generate and sustain linguistic, racial, and sex discrimination. That is, these educators know that they must strive to develop, as Henry Giroux (1992) has suggested, "a politics and pedagogy around a new language capable of acknowledging the multiple, contradictory, and complex subject positions people occupy within different social, cultural, and economic locations" (235). These critical educators ask: How do children from indigenous communities produce knowledge? How might their local history, the environment, local languages, and traditions help to shape their indigenous literacy? How can teachers make a difference in the lives of linguistic-minority children? How can classroom teachers help?

# EXPLORING INDIGENOUS PEDAGOGIES

How might one respond to these questions and those posed earlier? In sum, how might indigenous pedagogies become important to today's educators—say bilingual educators in the USA or, even more particularly, African educators? Recent literature on cultural difference, multilateralism, critical literacy, postcolonial theories, and poststructuralist approaches reveals a growing interest in understanding the educational needs of learners from other cultures and a growing awareness that methods to help learners from non-European cultures should be anchored to indigenous critical ethnographic research (Thomas 1993). In multicultural education, for example, Western educators are encouraged to holistically and comparatively understand not only indigenous cultural psychologies, but also how other cultures view "self."

In North America, the works of James Banks (1998), Christine Sleeter and C. A. Grant (1991), Joanna Posey (1998), and others have urged educators to reevaluate their instructional methods in pluralistic societies at different levels. First, how non-Western cultures teach their children involves understanding non-Western groups' complex worldviews and teaching, and learning systems that are centered around specific cultural values. Second, in trying to understand what academic skills were indigenously taught prior to European intervention brings to focus skills that incorporate several cultural lifeway patterns. These skills emphasize group management, motivation, social organization, beliefs, values, problem-solving approaches, time use, space use, maintaining relationships, sharing knowledge, education, and communication techniques, learning patterns, and instructional techniques. Third, why this knowledge is important to today's educators emphasizes educators' need to reevaluate the effectiveness of their instructional methods and recognize that many non-Western groups have value systems and teaching and learning methods different from their own.

# CONCLUSION

In this chapter, I presented the case of repressed native or indigenous languages and suggested ways classroom teachers can come to grips with the predicament linguistic-minority children find themselves in mainstream schools. I acknowledge the complexity that underscores the dilemmas and contradictions driving language bias against these bilingual and bicultural minorities. I have also observed that there exist strong ties and connections between language and a community's historical past. Because of this connection it is important for educators to recognize local language literacy. In the past, local language literacy attempts have been ignored, falsified, and repressed by school authorities primarily because of an underlying bias which has not been overcome in spite of years of research and well-documented empirical evidence. Historical legacies supported by conservative ideological positions have fueled much of the debate in this field of language study.

In English-speaking Africa, these legacies date back to the 1925 Phelps-Stokes Commission report on African education. Even though the commission mandated the localizing of education, teaching practical skills, Africanizing the curriculum, using local languages for instruction, and adapting education to suit the local environment, the reversal of the legacies has eluded politicians and policymakers until today. The achievement of the goals of African education has been marred by colonial dependence, teachers' attitudes, half-hearted policymakers, and a fervor for literary education divorced from the local context (Ssekamwa 1997, 212).

In the field of education, authors from different parts of the world have challenged many of the arguments held by conservative and traditional educators by introducing multicultural education and by acknowledging the growing diversity of the student population that continues to flow into American classrooms nationwide (Giroux 1992; McLaren 1989). These critical theorists insist that the successful usage of the students' cultural universe requires respect and legitimation of students' discourse, that is, their own linguistic codes, which are different but never inferior. They urge educators to respect and understand students' dreams and expectations.

It is therefore impossible to consider any form of education—or even human existence—without first considering the impact of language on our lives. I have argued that language must be recognized as one of the most significant human resources; it functions in a multitude of ways to affirm, contradict, negotiate, challenge, transform, and empower particular cultural and ideological beliefs and practices. I am convinced and I concur with many scholars that language constitutes one of the most powerful media for transmitting our personal histories and social realities, as well as for thinking and shaping the world (e.g., Cole and Scribner 1974). Language is essential to the process of dialogue, to the development of meaning, and to the production of knowledge. It must be respected in order to make learning meaningful and lifelong. I strongly believe, therefore, that *indigenous literacies* provide an important database for any follow-up to collateral learning. Through indigenous literacies students bring to the classrooms abilities which span their lifetime. These might include employing their indigenous language to relating their history, epistemology, and all that goes to make up the necessary skills and how they make pragmatic adaptations to communicate complex matters among themselves and with others outside their communities.

Teachers can build on these indigenous literacies in public schools by incorporating activities based on the languages their students bring into the classroom. In this way, the familiar language can function as significant portions of the required curriculum. An example of how teachers might do this with younger students is to develop language instruction and activities with their students that give them the opportunity to bring the home language into the context of the classroom. This can be done by having students and parents introduce their language through songs, stories, games, and other such activities. Giving attention to the home language raises it to a place of dignity and respect, rather than permitting it to become a source of humiliation and shame for indigenous students.

Furthermore, it should also be noted that the introduction of different languages must also be accompanied by critical dialogues that help students examine prevailing social attitudes and biases about language differences. These discussions can assist students to consider typical discriminatory responses to such situations as when people speak with foreign accents, or when people do not understand the language being spoken. In addition, students from similar cultural and language communities can be encouraged and made to feel comfortable when they converse together in their primary language as part of the classroom experience. Such opportunities support the development of voice, as well as affirm the bilingual/bicultural experience of students of color.

# CHAPTER SIX

# WHAT'S POLICY GOTTA DO WIT DIS?

RICHARD DE GOURVILLE, THE PENNSYLVANIA STATE UNIVERSITY

It seems almost inconceivable that despite an accumulation of national studies highlighting the underachievement of black children in America's schools spanning more than four decades (since Brown v. Board of Education 1954), there has been little if any political will on the part of educational policymakers to initiate a national dialogue on the issue. Given this "crisis of leadership," the federal courts have sought to impose such legal prescriptions as "desegregation" and civil rights to stem the tide of failure for African-American children overrepresented in predominantly urban educational environments. While new educational reform initiatives have come into being in the mid-1990s seeking to address this concern for the academic success of minority children in inner cities (e.g., Superintendent Hornbeck's Children Achieving Agenda in Philadelphia), scant, if any, attention has been given to the role of the black child's primary language as a possible factor in redressing their record of underachievement in the nation's schools. Moreover, the role of educational policy in negatively shaping the attitudes of the mainstream teaching establishment toward African-American Vernacular English (henceforth known as AAVE) ensures that generations of teachers working with predominantly African-American student populations will, in all likelihood, imbibe many of the prejudices and deficit views of their profession expressed toward nonstandard English speakers. It is therefore incumbent upon beginning as well as established teachers to understand that language teaching is a "political act," since the academic and economic fortunes of minority students are inherently tied into their mastery of the discourses of a monolingual-Anglocentric educational system. Thus, teachers will need to understand how educational policy functions to either restrict or expand the range of possibilities open to them with respect to the kinds of instructional decisions they make regarding English language learners.

Foregrounding our discussions on the Oakland controversy of 1996–1997, this paper will therefore seek to problematize the continued marginalization of the "primary home language" of a majority of African-American children by educational policymakers through a systematic analysis of deficit theories and the mind-set of all pertinent policy actors (general public, black middle class, educators, and politicians) in the educational policy domain. We will also review several pedagogical models that have been implemented with varying degrees of success in diverse metropolitan educational settings which comprise largely African-American student populations. Finally, we will examine some possible policy implications for the recognition of AAVE as the primary language of urban-based African-American children.

# LIBERAL VERSUS CONSERVATIVE MODES OF DISCOURSE

Given that most of the ideological debates surrounding the role and function of education in American society have largely gravitated between conservative and liberal thought positions, in order to adequately comprehend the causes underlying this long history of underachievement among African-American students (when compared with their Anglo-European counterparts), we must examine the basic premises and educational impact of these two philosophical positions.

While both ideological camps essentially uphold the notion that "the object of education is the free, enterprising, independent individual, and that students should be educated in order to adapt to the existing configurations of power that make up the dominant society" (Darder 1991, 4), there are nevertheless significant differences between these two positions.

Central to the very nature of a conservative educational discourse is "the implicit purpose of conserving the social and economic status quo through the perpetuation of institutional values and relationships that safeguard dominant power structures" (4). Through the allocation of "cultural capital," the dominant culture strives to systematically control the structure of schooling and to ensure that its children are clearly placed in secure positions of power to enter controlling roles in American society. Thus, African-American students, who make up a disproportionately larger number of the lower classes represented in urban educational settings, are also disproportionately tracked into remedial programs in accordance with the inherent beliefs of school personnel regarding their distinct language and culture. Worse, their apparent failure to appropriate the normative behaviors and language of the dominant monolingual school culture is viewed by the conservative camp as an "individual failing" rather than the result of an inequitable and racist society.

Liberals, on the other hand, while holding to the view that inequities do exist in the system and that there is a need for change, nevertheless affirm their belief that the American capitalist system is fundamentally superior and that it can function effectively with a few modifications by way of compensatory programs and reform policies. A fitting example of the liberal deficit view is the environmental interpretation of "cognitive development theory"—a view traditionally utilized by liberal educators to explain the underachievement of bicultural students. This view encompasses the assumption that inequality of social standing reflects inequality of individual capability. Thus, those environmental forces that are considered significant to the cognitive development of mainstream Anglo-American values are examined to determine what could be the problem. Studies based on this view invariably determine that bicultural students (e.g., African-American students) "do not receive enough verbal and social stimulation in their homes; consequently— it is concluded—the children develop low verbal ability, which hinders their school performance" (Darder, 9). However, as numerous studies of language and socialization and uses in African-American communities attest, by the time they enter kindergarten, African-American children are likely to have formed a sense of identity and self-efficacy strongly linked to their ability to use oral language in highly sophisticated and stylized ways (Hale-Benson 1982; Brice-Heath 1983; Goodwin 1990; Labov 1972; Taylor and Dorsey-Gaines 1988; Vernon-Feagans 1996).

Consequently, by espousing such liberal theories of cultural and verbal deprivation, educational institutions have been permitted to function within a conceptual framework that serves to absolve schools from responsibility for the widespread underachievement of African-American and other bicultural students. Hence, according to Darder (1991), "it has permitted the dynamics of victim-blaming to overshadow the necessity for systemic change and to distract attention from the basic causes of inequality while leaving the primary social injustices untouched"(10). Even the language used to frame federally-funded programs which target ethnic minorities connotes deficit theory: "compensatory," "remedial," "enrichment," or "corrective."

Negative attitudes toward AAVE or Ebonics abound in contemporary American society as both laypersons as well as language guardians refer to the prevalence of its usage among black working class and poor in both urban and rural settings as "broken speech," "broken English," "backward," "underprivileged," "illiterate," "street language," "intellectually deficient," "genetically deprived," "slang"—all of which function as signifiers of the denigrated and lowly status of AAVE vis-à-vis the unofficial Standard American English dialect variety, as well as the low socioeconomic position enjoyed by African-Americans in American society.

# THE POLICYMAKERS' MIND-SET

In order for us to comprehend the failure of AAVE to be officially recognized by the federal government as the "True Language of Black Folks" (a book title by Robert L. Williams), as well as its almost universal disregard by the educational establishment as a teaching tool to move African-American students toward competence in Standard American English, we will need to analyze the mind-set of the educational policymakers.

According to Knoke and Laumann (1982), policymakers function within what is known as a policy domain, which is distinguished by: (1) a substantive issue of mutual relevance and (2) a set of consequential actors concerned with articulating various policy options intended to resolve the issue in question (256). With respect to policy actors who operate within national policy domains, the focus is on formal organizations and not individual persons since the former possess the resources necessary for individuals to coordinate their actions in attempting to affect the outcome of a policy decision, thereby "magnifying their strength manifold" (Knoke et al., 1996, 11–12).

Thus, within the domain of language policy specific to AAVE, several significant policy actors can be identified among a host of many: the English-only movement (i.e., an umbrella group of English advocacy groups); Teaching English to Speakers of Other Languages; the Linguistic Society of America; the conservative print and electronic media; various congressional and senate committees on education; conservative think tanks; the US Department of Education; and state and local education agencies.

## Views from the Policy Domain

The case of the Oakland Unified School District's (OUSD's) decision to recognize Ebonics as the primary language of black inner city school children
on December 18, 1996, and the national furor evoked by such a resolution,
provides us with a unique opportunity to enter the mind-set of policy agents.

Many policy agents (e.g., politicians) are often driven by deficit theories
as they seek to influence policymaking on controversial issues relating to language. Senate Republican Whip Raymond N. Haynes (R-Riverside), in
attempting to rationalize a bill that would block the use of state funds for any
Ebonics instruction, summed up his ideology in the January 24, 1997, edition of the *Los Angeles Times*: "I believe that this whole concept of Ebonics
is institutionalizing bad communication skills." If passed, Haynes's bill,
called the "Equality in English Instruction Act," would have effectively put
an end to the Proficiency in Standard English for Speakers of Black Language Program (SEP)—a culturally and linguistically sensitive instructional
program that had been in use in three hundred schools in the OUSD since
1981.

One of Haynes's colleagues, Senator Lauch Faircloth (R-N.C.), who had
made up his mind on the issue even before the first speaker took the micro-
phone to testify before the US Senate Appropriations Subcommittee on
Labor, Health and Human Services and Education, was quoted in the same
article: "I think Ebonics is absurd. This is political correctness that has gone
out of control."

Thus, willful ignorance and prejudice toward Ebonics rather than openness and well-informed judgment based on the most current research in the
field of linguistics, seem to be the order of the day in the nation's capital.

Such blatant ignorance and prejudice are not restricted to congressmen
and high-ranking senators, but can also be found among the ranks of educational policy agents. Under the headline "Ebonics Isn't a Language" in the
Dec. 25, 1996, edition of the *Examiner,* the nation's top education officer,
Secretary Richard Riley, is reported as warning about the dangers of "elevat-
ing black English to the status of a language." Even Delaine Eastin, the
superintendent of public education for the State of California, echoed the
stereotypical view of Ebonics held by a majority of educators in the country.
In the following statement, quoted from the January 14, 1997, edition of
*The Chicago Tribune*, Ms. Eastin dogmatically declared: "This will not help
the students become doctors or lawyers or help them get into the University
of California. We have no research to show this is beneficial for students.
This will do a disservice to students."

Policymakers also pay keen attention to the signals emanating from the public sphere. In the case of Ebonics policy and their subsequent decision not to either recognize Ebonics as a legitimate language of urban black children or provide funding for instruction in it, the Washington-based policymakers took their cue from several sources. Firstly, the almost unprecedented solidarity demonstrated by both the black middle and lower classes in their determination that Ebonics not be taught to their children, albeit for very different reasons. While the black middle class (including the intelligentsia) has historically rejected the linkage of Ebonics with its class or group identity (i.e., identity politics), the Black lower class, on the other hand, was adamant in its belief that this was just another white conspiracy to destroy the life chances of its children. The prominent Democrat and political activist, Reverend Jesse Jackson, when asked for his initial reaction to the Oakland Board's decision that "black English, Ebonics, should be taught as an official language" (Tim Russert's wording!) on an NBC "Meet the Press" program, unthinkingly lashed out: "in Oakland, some madness has erupted over making slang talk a second language. You don't have to go to school to learn to talk garbage."

Ward Connerly, a prominent black Republican ally of California Governor Pete Wilson, businessman and member of the Board of Regents for the California State University System, echoing the "victim-blaming," "deficit" perspective of his respective political ideology, gave perhaps the most stunning judgment on the Ebonics controversy: "These kids that have had every opportunity to acclimate themselves to American society, and they have gotten themselves into this trap of speaking this language ... this slang, really ... that people can't understand. Now we're going to legitimize it."

Secondly, negative views expressed toward Ebonics by such a key education figure as Secretary Richard Riley, as well as opposing viewpoints held within the educational establishment itself, have predisposed policymakers within the language policy domain to adopt a "hands-off" position with respect to declaring Ebonics to be a legitimate language of a majority of urban black students. On such a nationally divisive issue, it is better to "keep one's seat" than "lose one's head."

Another major factor which greatly influences policy agents within the domain of language policy centers around myths of American identity and culture held in common by policymakers, the majority of whom are white Anglo-Saxon males. Such questions as, Who is an American and What is his or her culture, have traditionally been defined by the dominant culture group within American society, i.e., the WASP culture. Inherent in this monolithic belief structure is the ideology that the English language ought to be the sole language of currency in American culture and society.

In his book titled *To Renew America*, former House Speaker Newt Gingrich warns of the imminent dissolution of American civilization if immigrants and native ethnic minorities (e.g., African-Americans, Chicanos, Native Americans, Puerto Ricans, etc.) refuse to assimilate and adopt the English language as the common language of all Americans:

> "If people are encouraged to resist assimilation, the very fabric of American society will eventually break down ... The only viable alternative for the American underclass is American civilization ... Without English as a common language there is no such civilization" (Gingrich, 1995, 162).

Most policymakers, therefore, equate the acquisition of Standard American English with the profession of allegiance to a mythical American cultural identity. Such ideological myths as "English is the common language of all Americans" fly in the face of historical fact. Early American colonial history amply documents the existence of multiple languages utilized by the colonists to conduct business, government, and education. According to Crawford (1992), "fluency in more than one language was commonplace in eighteenth century America, especially in the cosmopolitan 'middle colonies'"(36). Noted anthropologist and sociolinguist Shirley Brice-Heath (1983) points to a "hidden agenda" underlying the attempt to impose Standard American English as the official language of all Americans:

> Throughout the history of the United States, whenever speakers of varieties of English or other languages [Ebonics] have been viewed as politically, socially, or economically threatening, their language has become a focus for arguments in favor of both restrictions of their use and imposition of Standard English (10).

Thus, Official English language legislation or anti-Ebonics legislation (in this case) has been wielded as a "technology of power" to deny the legitimate linguistic aspirations of those whose primary language is not English.

# REAL CHILDREN, REAL CHALLENGES

In all of the emotional debate surrounding the validation of Ebonics as a language peculiar to African-American children existing in the highly segregated urban cities of America, it seems as though very little attention has been paid to the pedagogical challenges faced by urban educators in places such as Oakland. According to Theresa Perry (1998), there were evidently stark and painful realities regarding the overwhelming and sustained failure of African-American children in the Oakland Unified School District (OUSD) that created a moral and ethical compulsion for the OUSD to unanimously approve the Black Language/Ebonics resolution. From statistics collated from the OUSD in 1996, African-American children, though making up only 53 percent of the district's enrollment, accounted for 80 percent of the school system's suspensions, 71 percent of those placed in special education programs while their average grade point was a D+ (i.e., 1.80 compared with the district average of 2.40) (Perry and Delpit 1998, 3). Interestingly enough, the majority of referrals made by teachers and administrators (white and black) for placement into special education services were disproportionately because of "language deficiency" (Perry and Delpit 1998, 173).

Given the driving pedagogical imperative to confront such urban academic underachievement and easy accessibility to a thirty-year database on successful reading strategies for AAVE speakers (Chall 1967; Hoover, Dabney, and Lewis 1990; Foorman 1997), it is morally and ethically irresponsible for policymakers to have consistently ignored the research evidence to support the use of AAVE as a pedagogically sound instructional approach. What does such research reveal about the pedagogic possibilities of AAVE?

# EXEMPLARY AAVE PROGRAMS

Stanford linguistics professor John Rickford, in written testimony to Senator Arlen Specter, chairman of the Subcommittee on Labor, Health and Human Services, and Education, submitted into the record of the Ebonics panel on January 23, 1997, cited several national and international innovative instructional approaches which highlighted the role of vernacular varieties in school success. For purposes of brevity, we will examine only a few of the major English-language development programs used in the United States since 1973.

In his written testimony, Rickford makes mention of the effectiveness of SEP (Standard English Proficiency), a program currently used in a minority of schools within the OUSD. Using contrastive analysis, students are explicitly taught to recognize the difference between vernacular and standard features and schooled in the standard variety through identification, translation, and response drills. Some of the English-language development guiding principles for SEP educators can be described as follows:

1.  A child's language represents the norm of his or her family and community.

2.  If a child can express a concept in any language, he or she possesses the concept.

3.  The teacher must provide as realistic a context for language experiences as possible, using materials from the child's culture.

4.  The child's self-identity must be supported at all times.

5.  The history of the social isolation (de facto and de jure) of Africans in diaspora has served to preserve African-language patterns of speech.

African-American language is a complete, well-ordered language system with rules for forming sounds, words, sentences, and nonverbal elements (Perry and Delpit 1998, 154–155).

The Piestrup (1973) study of 208 African-American first grade children in Oakland, California, showed that teachers who constantly interrupted Ebonics-speaking children to correct them produced the lowest-scoring and most apathetic readers, while teachers who built artfully on the children's language produced the highest-scoring and most enthusiastic readers.

Another major dialect awareness program was that of the Bridge readers, coauthored by Gary Simkins, Grace Holt, and Charlesetta Simpkins in 1977. These provided reading materials in Ebonics, a transitional variety, and Standard English. The 417 students across the United States taught with Bridge showed an average reading gain of 6.2 months over 4 months of instruction, while the 123 taught by regular methods gained only 1.6 months—showing the same below-par progress which leads African-American and other dialect speakers to fall further and further behind. Despite their dramatic success, the Bridge readers were discontinued because of hostile, uninformed reactions to the recognition of the vernacular in the classroom.

Hanni Taylor, in a 1989 book titled *Standard English, Black English, and Bidialectalism*, reported that she tried to improve the Standard English writing of inner city Aurora University students from Chicago using two different methods. The experimental group who were taught with contrastive analysis techniques showed a 59 percent reduction in the use of Ebonics features in their Standard English writing, whereas students taught by traditional methods, i.e., the control group, showed an 8.5 percent increase in the use of such features.

The bidialectal approach, similar to that of Taylor's and California's SEP program, has likewise produced excellent results. Doug Cummins, writing in *The Atlantic Constitution* on January 9, 1997 (B1), reported on the ten-year-old program in DeKalb County, Georgia, in which fifth and sixth grade students in eight schools were taught to switch from their "home speech" to "school speech" at appropriate times and places. According to Cummins, "The program has won a 'center of excellence' designation from the National Council for Teachers of English. Last year, students who had taken the course had improved verbal test scores at every school. At Cary-Reynolds, their scores rose 5.2 percentage points" (Rickford Testimony, 4).

# POLICY IMPLICATIONS

As a result of the very sound, well-informed, and expertly researched documentation provided by both linguists and educators (Rickford, Labov, Taylor, Williams and Casserly), in conjunction with the testimony of educators from Oakland (including Superintendent Carolyn Getridge), Senator Specter directed the members of the subcommittee to maintain funding for the Standard English Proficiency program. He also supported a line item in the 1997 appropriations budget providing one million dollars for research on the relation between the home language of African-American students and their success in learning to read and write in Standard English. The research will be jointly conducted in Oakland (under the direction of Etta Hollins) and in Philadelphia (under the direction of William Labov).

The Ebonics debate held under the aegis of the Appropriations Subcommittee was clearly one instance in which the concerted efforts of expert witnesses (teachers and researchers), as well as substantive empirical data on the underachievement of African-American students provided by school district personnel from the OUSD, served to sway the opinions of policymakers toward implementing a proactive educational policy that would hopefully redress the academic failure of such students in the public school system by recognizing the link between the primary language of African-American children and school success.

While there are clearly hopeful signs on the horizon regarding the use of the home language of African-American children as a means of raising self-esteem and academic achievement, other policy implications remain unclear or unaddressed. There are still no federal or state guidelines to assist school district administrators and teachers as to the possible pedagogical models that can be used with Ebonics speakers. As in Oakland, California, the onus is on the local education agencies to create or adopt innovative teaching strategies (e.g., Standard English Proficiency) to redress the reading and writing difficulties of African-American children functioning in Standard American English classrooms. A dire need still exists to reverse the overrepresentation of African-American children in remedial programs as well as to close the widening achievement gap between these children and their white counterparts. Culturally sensitive testing instruments need to be developed that will incorporate to the fullest possible extent the unique linguistic abilities of African-American children. Urban curricula need to be adapted to cater to the needs of the children they serve by incorporating Afrocentric epistemologies into curricula content. In terms of teacher preparation, special language sensitivity training sessions need to be conducted for beginning as well as veteran teachers in the school system so that African-American children are not stigmatized for using their primary language and are not routed into remedial programs based on a supposed "language deficiency." Finally, the absence of federal or state funding for programs that address the linguistic needs of African-American bidialectal children needs to be taken up with state and federal policymakers as an issue of equity and social justice.

# PART TWO

# BECOMING AWARE

# OF CHILDREN'S

# DAILY REALITIES

# CHAPTER SEVEN

# GOLDEN EAGLE

# GOES TO

# KINDERGARTEN

CATHY GUTIERREZ-GOMEZ, UNIVERSITY OF NEW MEXICO

Early in February 1992, our family embarked on a journey that would for-ever impact our association with the public school system. A neighbor asked us what we were going to do about our son's hair. "Mesquite has got a strict hair policy; are you sure they're going to let him go to school here?" she asked.

"We've had our daughter in the same school for three years and no one has ever said anything to us about it. I don't think there will be a problem," I said.

"I don't know, you might want to check it out," she advised.

A few days later, a second person asked the same question and voiced the same concern. Itsa-Lichii had worn his hair long since birth, like his Apache father, and now that he was about to start kindergarten it was about to become an issue.

On March 4, 1992, my husband Gregory and I wrote a letter to the superintendent of the Mesquite Independent School District (MISD) at the superintendent's urging. In the letter, we asked for a waiver of the MISD's hair policy which states that a boy's hair may not be longer than over the shirt collar. We waited for months for a response. On July 20, 1992, we wrote again and asked that a response be given as soon as possible since we only had a month before school was to start.

The long-awaited letter came in August 1992. In the letter, the superintendent stated:

> While I sympathize with the importance you attach to your heritage as an American Indian, I cannot authorize an exception to the policy on hair length for boys in this situation. These grooming guides have been in existence in Mesquite Schools for decades and continue to be valued by the Board, the community, and the instructional staff. We believe that these grooming expectations are reasonable and an important part of our goal to educate the whole person ... you may address your concerns to the Board of Education if you would like to appeal my decision.

I read the letter over and over and still arrived at the same conclusion: This had to be a bad dream! It was, in fact, an unbelievable reality. On the evening before the board meeting, we talked with the children to explain what was going on and prepare them for the next day. We assured them that everything would work out just fine. This was just a big misunderstanding, and we just needed to clear things up. We thought that this could be resolved through sincere and open communication. This was 1992, not the 1960s, and we had lots of information to share with the board about the changing demographics and growing need to incorporate multicultural education and diversity awareness at all levels of schooling.

We prepared for the board meeting by gathering information and statistics relating to changing demographics in the school district and surrounding area. In addition, we compiled information from a diversity of sources addressing the need for multicultural education and cultural diversity awareness in schools (Anti-Defamation League of B'nai B'rith, 1986; Jones and Derman-Sparks, 1992; Phillips, 1988; Ramsey and Derman-Sparks, 1992).

August 10, 1992, the day of the MISD School Board meeting, is a day I will never forget. When it came time for the board to address our appeal, we were called to the front. The board members sat behind a long set of tables. We stood before the board as my husband introduced the family members, one by one. First he introduced himself, then me, then each of the children. After introducing Dahazhi and Itsa-Lichii to the board, we asked a friend, Sandy, to take them into the hall area because we didn't feel it was appropriate for them to be in this meeting.

Gregory gave the board a brief history of our family, our backgrounds, and our beliefs. He described his Lipan and Mescalero Apache ways and customs, including the sacred traditional beliefs and practices of wearing long hair. "In our ways, wearing our hair long is another manifestation to honor our heritage and our ancestors. It means that we are tied to our sacred (religious) way of life seven days a week, twenty-four hours a day. As you have seen, all four of us have long hair. It is in keeping with our centuries old ways and protected by the United States Constitution, as relates to religious freedom and freedom of expression."

The meeting went on for about an hour. We answered question after question regarding our way of life. One board member wanted to know why we couldn't just conform and show our children that "within some systems one must conform?" He continued to explain how this would make it easier for everyone to be treated equally and fairly. "If we break the rule for your son, we'll have to deal with a bunch of others wanting the same preferential treatment," suggested the superintendent. "Haven't you ever worn your hair short, Mr. Gomez?" asked another board member. Gregory responded, "I have, I chose to join the United States Marines knowing that they would shave my head. As a proud American I made the decision to join and do my duty for my country. I wasn't forced into the Marines, wasn't forced to conform. I went to Vietnam and put myself at risk to fight for the ideals of this country; that includes the freedom to practice our religion and enjoy life and the pursuit of happiness."

I can't recall a more humiliating experience than this one. It became harder and harder to hide my anger at the total disregard for human dignity displayed during this school board meeting. Gregory made an admirable appeal for the right to freedom of religion and expressing cultural identity. Some American Indians still only cut their hair when mourning the death of a loved one. He presented more facts pertaining to the cultural diversity of the American populace and the growing trend to embrace cultural differences. "We strongly believe," I added, "that our children's future success as productive American citizens greatly depends on their ability to respect and get along with people of diverse cultures." This is a perspective we consider to be a fact, and we continue to promote it today.

As the meeting came to a close, it was agreed that Itsa-Lichii would attend kindergarten while the board reviewed our appeal. There appeared to be a glimmer of hope. We went home and attempted to explain the evening's events to our children. They were both happy that Itsa-Lichii was going to be allowed to go to school.

# ITSA-LICHII'S KINDERGARTEN

Itsa-Lichii started kindergarten on August 17, 1992. He was so excited that he had a hard time getting to sleep the night before. His sister was equally excited and told him that she had butterflies in her stomach. "Butterflies? What color are they?" he inquired with a serious look as Dahazhi and I burst out in laughter. We walked his sister to her third grade class first. She gave him a tight hug and assured him he would do all right. "Brother, if anybody messes with you, just let me know who and I'll smack 'em!" she said as she waved her clenched fist. He had a million questions as we headed to his class-room. His main concern was that his teacher would be upset with him because he didn't know how to read. I assured him that everything would be fine and that he was going to school to learn how to read. I reminded him of the many things he could read, like his name, his sister's name, and some let-ters and numbers. He looked at me with his big eyes shining and smiled.

"That's my teacher, Mom?" he asked.

"Yes, son, that's your teacher," I said.

Mrs. Adrian smiled and welcomed Itsa-Lichii. "Hi, I'm Mrs. Adrian, I'm going to be your teacher," she said. Then she showed us where he could sit and told us to look around if we wanted while we waited for the rest of the children to come in. He was all smiles as he tried out the desk and looked around the room. He watched his teacher very intently as she greeted more children and their parents. When it was time to go, he hugged my neck and gave me a big kiss on the cheek, "Bye, mom, see you later." He had no prob-lem with my leaving.

Itsa-Lichii's brief kindergarten experience at McWhorter Elementary was a good experience. He loved going to school and looked forward to it every day. Though our conversations with Mrs. Adrian were brief, she was cordial and we believed she did a good job of teaching Itsa-Lichii and his classmates. Itsa-Lichii thought she was wonderful. We wondered what she thought about having Itsa-Lichii in her classroom. She never shared her views with us or talked to us about our situation. Other teachers and staff in the school had expressed their support and sorrow for what we were having to deal with. A teacher talked with me at length after school one day. She asked me to come into her classroom while the children played outside with classmates. She wanted me to know that she supported and believed in our position. According to her, most of the teachers were on our side. Unfortu-nately, they couldn't risk showing support openly. She told me she was sorry about this, but that "going against the system" would mean losing their jobs and she couldn't afford to be without a job.

On Friday, September 25, 1992, the principal met us as we arrived at the school. This was very strange because he usually ignored us, so I knew immediately that he had some news. He waited while I took Itsa-Lichii into his classroom. From the stern look on his face, I could tell the news he was about to deliver was not what we wanted to hear, but as he started speaking I could not believe his words. "I need to talk to you," he said. "Unless you cut your son's hair, he will not be allowed to come back to school on Monday."

I couldn't believe my ears. "What did you say?" I asked. He repeated the same words, very matter-of-factly. "You can't mean that! That just can't be!" I pleaded. He stated that he was just the messenger; that it was the board's decision and he was just delivering the message.

"You know this is wrong!" I implored.

"I'm just following orders, I don't make the decisions!" he shot back.

"This is discrimination, it's racist!" I said emphatically.

At that very moment I noticed that my daughter, Dahazhi, was standing there listening to everything. She cried, "I hate it! I hate it! It's not fair!" This didn't seem to faze the principal, who simply walked away.

I held on to my daughter as we both cried and walked toward her classroom. Her teacher, Mrs. Bradshaw, saw us and came to the doorway. She hugged Dahazhi as I explained what had just taken place. She said she had expected that was what would happen and expressed how sorry she was about it. I asked Dahazhi if she wanted to go home with me. Before she could answer, Mrs. Bradshaw assured Dahazhi that if she stayed, they, Mrs. Bradshaw and Dahazhi's classmates, would help her through this ordeal. Dahazhi hugged me and said she would stay at school and go home with us at noon when we were scheduled to pick up Itsa-Lichii.

I found out later that Mrs. Bradshaw and the children had engaged in an emotional discussion about what had happened. The class of third graders wanted to know why their classmate was so distraught. Once Mrs. Bradshaw explained what she could, they wanted to know—Why? Why did the school not want Itsa-Lichii there? What was wrong with his having long hair? What was he going to do if he didn't go to school? Did that mean that Dahazhi was going to have to leave too? We decided, as a family, that Dahazhi was already going through enough and that she should stay and finish third grade at McWhorter.

# HOW OTHER CHILDREN WERE AFFECTED

Months later, I took the children for a checkup with the doctor they had been seeing for four years. They had both been experiencing stomach pains, nausea, and headaches. While we were there, I saw a parent, Claire, who had had a child in the same kindergarten class with Itsa-Lichii. She asked if we had been back to the school or talked to any of the parents from Itsa-Lichii's old kindergarten class. I told her we had not talked to or seen any of them since the last day Itsa-Lichii was at the school. Claire went on to tell me about how this whole incident had impacted the rest of the children. She said her own daughter, Chelsea, had cried because her "friend" was not going to be in her class anymore. Chelsea had asked her mother if Itsa-Lichii had done something wrong. Claire said she had explained to Chelsea that she didn't think Itsa-Lichii had done anything wrong at all, that he and his family were American Indian and that the school had a problem with Itsa-Lichii wearing long hair. Chelsea wanted to know why the school thought that was a "bad thing." Claire also shared with me that some of the other children had also cried that Friday after their parents explained why the news cameras and reporters were at their school. The most touching story she told me was about Jenny. According to Claire, Jenny had become quite emotional when her mother informed her that Itsa-Lichii, whom she referred to as her "boyfriend," would no longer be coming to her class. Again, Jenny's mother did the best she could to explain the circumstances. Still, Jenny could not understand and insisted on knowing why he couldn't come back, "He sits next to me, he liked me," she said. Jenny, a special needs child, was confined to a wheelchair for most of the day, and for group time she would either stay in the wheelchair or had to be picked up and placed on the floor. For the most part, Itsa-Lichii and Jenny had sat next to each other until his last day at the school.

# HOMESCHOOLING

For the next few months, October through February, we provided Itsa-Lichii with homeschooling. Rachel, our friend and an in-home caretaker, was tremendously helpful with this. With Gregory working full-time and me in graduate school full-time, it was difficult at first to adjust to the responsibility that comes with homeschooling. With all of us working together, we were able come up with a workable schedule that allowed us to give Itsa-Lichii a well-rounded educational experience. We were not sure how long we would be homeschooling, but we were determined to do the best job possible while we considered our options. I provided most of the educational experiences directly and instructed Rachel regarding additional activities she was to provide for Itsa-Lichii during the times I was off at graduate school.

Most of Itsa-Lichii's socialization time with other children happened once his sister and all her friends got together after school. They included him in everything, probably because his sister, Dahazhi, made certain they did this. He was the youngest in the group, which were mostly third-graders. Eventually, the group became very age-mixed with other siblings and neighbors of varying ages from different ethnicities and families.

Many times our morning involved a walk to a nearby park. Itsa-Lichii especially liked when other children were there. One day we saw a lady with three children, two girls and a boy (I figured the boy was about three and one-half years and the girls between three and one-half and four years old). Itsa-Lichii approached them very slowly the first time we saw them at the playground. He stood and watched as they went up and down the slide several times. When a little girl let him go next on the slide, he beamed a big smile at me and joined the trio for several rounds on the slide. Then they took off, ran all over the playground, tumbled, got on the swings, and went back to the slide. We saw them a couple more times the following week.

It was so difficult to take Itsa-Lichii to pick up his sister day after day and watch as he would look toward his "old" kindergarten classroom. His face spoke a thousand words. He would stare and walk around to try to sneak a peek into the classroom. We thought that maybe he shouldn't go, but he insisted; he looked forward to this part of the day. It was always the same as far as trying to answer his questions—Why can't I go there anymore? Why don't they want me there?

The bell would ring and he would run to Dahazhi's classroom. She would run out and they would hug tight. She always had something for him, a leftover cookie, a drawing, a pencil with a funny eraser in the shape of a foot. She would make a big fuss over him and ask him about his day. As he recounted some of his activities—which that day included time on the computer, painting with sponges, a trip to the park, then a walk to the grocery store for an ice cream—she looked at him with her hands on her hips and asked if she could stay home the following day.

"I want to go to school like other kids, Mom, please ..." he pleaded. It made my heart ache to hear his plea and feel totally helpless. I wondered, does the superintendent or the board members at MISD have any idea what they're doing to this family? Have they even considered that they are dealing with human lives? We never received any type of formal notice that Itsa-Lichii was expelled.

# SEARCHING FOR THE RIGHT SCHOOL

We had already planned to file a lawsuit, and it became apparent to us that other options had to be considered as far as Itsa-Lichii's formal schooling was concerned. On February 18, 1993, we submitted a formal "Student Application for Transfer," requesting permission to put Itsa-Lichii into a school within the Dallas Independent School District (DISD). While this request was being considered, we visited several DISD elementary schools as close to home as possible and tried to figure out our schedules and the distance and driving time.

We wanted "just the right school," though our criteria for what that meant to us was evolving as we visited many schools. We knew of only one other district adjacent to Mesquite, which had a strict hair policy. We heard from people in several other school districts who invited us to consider their districts or their particular school where they knew that we would not have to deal with a "hair issue." DISD seemed to be our best option for three reasons: (1) They didn't have a problem with Itsa-Lichii's hair, (2) they had an American Indian Education program (AIE), and (3) a teacher from Douglas Elementary School had called Mrs. Lamey, the AIE program director, and indicated that she wanted us to consider putting Itsa-Lichii in her class.

Gregory and I went to visit Douglas Elementary School, and we were very impressed the moment we walked in. Its appearance was multicultural—the walls and the hall displayed an array of posters, pictures, and wording that sent the message "diversity is valued here." The principal was Mrs. Delaney, a dynamic African-American woman who greeted us warmly. She was aware of our situation and wanted to help. She suggested that we visit three kindergarten classes.

We visited all three classes. All the teachers were white, two female and one male. The male teacher had a very plain classroom and a structured schedule, though he seemed to relate well to the children and they were very well-behaved and involved in their worksheets. The first female teacher did not greet us with much enthusiasm and seemed to be overwhelmed with the children and all the activity going on. She was attempting to get the children to sit and be quiet—we did not stay long. The second female teacher jumped out of her seat when we went in her classroom. She expressed her desire to have Itsa-Lichii in her classroom. She said she knew a lot about, and was very interested in, Native American culture. We saw the children in her classroom busily drawing or looking at books and watched as they interacted with their teacher. She was distracted with us, I thought, or would have been more responsive as children approached with questions. I asked questions about her beliefs and practices for teaching young children at this level. Her responses sounded good to me, she talked about how she really enjoyed teaching and believed in allowing children to be active in their own learning.

We went to Mrs. Delaney with our decision. She let us know that she would have preferred Mr. Smith, that she had some reservations about Ms. Thomas, but she would respect our wishes and place our son in her class. Mrs. Delaney also informed us that one of the local news stations wanted to go into the classroom to continue reporting on Itsa-Lichii's story. Gregory and I did not like the idea, as Itsa-Lichii was feeling very uncomfortable with all the media attention. Mrs. Delaney agreed that we should keep the media out of our son's classroom, at least for now.

# ITSA-LICHII'S PERCEPTIONS AT A NEW SCHOOL

Itsa-Lichii's transfer was approved on February 24, 1993, and we took him to Douglas Elementary. As we walked around the hallway, Itsa-Lichii peeked into one classroom and asked, "Is this it? Is this my classroom?" No, we explained, his new classroom was down the hall. "Those kids look like me. Why can't I go here?" he asked as he continued to walk into the classroom. Gregory and I followed him and attempted to steer him in the right direction. A Hispanic teacher greeted us and invited us in. We briefly explained what we were doing. She said we could visit as long as we liked and we thanked her. This was a bilingual classroom, and all of the children were Spanish speakers. Itsa-Lichii was right, they did look like him.

It was painful to hear Itsa-Lichii's questions and comments; he wanted so badly to "belong" to a classroom. He was putting together all that he was experiencing and trying to make sense of it all. When we continued to make our way toward his new classroom, he looked into another class. This one was mixed, mostly African-American and Hispanic with a couple of white children. His next comment broke my heart, "Do you think they'd want me in their classroom?" Gregory and I looked at each other in anguish. Anger swelled up in me, and I noticed my husband clench his fists as his jaw tightened. He picked up his son and smiled at him. "Son, there are a lot of classrooms with children and teachers that want you there. This is a good school, you'll like it, let's go meet your new teacher."

Itsa-Lichii entered his new kindergarten classroom and blended into the routine almost immediately. Ms. Thomas greeted us and made us feel welcome. We sat and observed while the children were getting settled. It was going so well—Itsa-Lichii was sitting at his desk and looking very content. He gave us a hug and we said goodbye. Ms. Thomas reassured us that he would be fine and said we could come back early if we wanted to observe some more. Seeing Itsa-Lichii so happy gave us a good feeling.

Finally he was in school, like he wanted to be, with other children. Everything seemed to be working out all right—our children were in classrooms that wanted them there.

# A TEACHER'S REACTION

What happened next was unbelievable and remains a mystery to us still. The following week, Mrs. Delaney called us at home to let us know that there was a problem with Itsa-Lichii's teacher. Ms. Thomas told her principal that she could no longer have Itsa-Lichii in her classroom. She said the media was being too persistent and that she did not want any part of it. According to her, having the media showing up at the school and trying to get into the classroom was too stressful. As soon as we could, we called Mrs. Larney, the AIE program director, to share this latest event. She had just received a call from Ms. Thomas, who had made her very angry with a totally different story from the one she relayed to the principal. Apparently, having Itsa-Lichii in her class was creating problems between her and some of her friends who were teachers at Mesquite ISD. She had not realized how sensitive this issue was before and did not want anything more to do with us. She told Mrs. Larney that she hoped we would lose the case. Mrs. Larney was so upset that she replied with anger, "You're showing your true colors now."

We were back at the school the following Monday meeting with the principal. She was very apologetic and reminded us that she had shared some concern about placing Itsa-Lichii in Ms. Thomas's class to begin with. There had been problems with this teacher before, but Mrs. Delaney had not wanted to appear to be biased against her. Our options were to place Itsa-Lichii with Mr. Smith, who had already agreed to take him, or look for another school. Explaining this change to Itsa-Lichii was simple once we decided to make up a story about how they really wanted him in Mr. Smith's class and we thought he should try it out. I honestly do not know how we got through this day. However, I remember vividly that I saw Ms. Thomas in the hallway and she greeted me, "Hi, Mrs. Gomez, how are you?" as if nothing had ever happened. Without responding, I stared at her in disbelief and walked in the opposite direction as quickly as I could.

After speaking with Mr. Smith briefly, we agreed that I would stay for part of the day to make sure Itsa-Lichii was going to be all right. He also agreed that I could come in at any time to check on him. I was determined to be in there as much as possible. This had to work out—we didn't even want to think of the possible outcomes if it didn't. Itsa-Lichii was now in his third kindergarten classroom and we still had three more months of school left. There were way too many worksheets and too much structure and no real learning center or child-centered types of learning. It was obvious to me that this was not the ideal kindergarten classroom, but it wasn't the worst either. Mr. Smith did a fair job, especially for someone who expressed that he hated teaching and was only there to work himself up the career ladder. Why he thought he had to share this with me, I will never know.

# DEALING WITH STRESS AND RACISM

Itsa-Lichii finished out the three months of school. Both my husband and I were there often, in the classroom, for PTA and school programs. It was a stressful time because we were running back and forth between Itsa-Lichii's school and Dahazhi's school. Gregory had his job, I had graduate school, and we had a household to maintain. In addition, we continued to meet with lawyers to prepare our case. We had not realized how stressful this whole ordeal was on the children until we took them in to see their doctor because of ongoing complaints of headaches, stomachaches, and bed-wetting. The doctor determined that the multiple symptoms were due to the stress they were experiencing.

The ramifications of this racist incident were more apparent to us when we pursued an opportunity to put the children in a private school in Dallas. As is the norm in private schools, the children were put through a series of tests. Because of these test results, Dahazhi was reluctantly placed at the third-grade level and we were advised that Itsa-Lichii would need to go to "primer," their equivalent for kindergarten. Later, it became more apparent that many of the children enrolled at this private school were placed one grade level lower than they would have been in public school.

Private school provided the children with many benefits and experiences during the next two years. Both children were very happy about going to school. For the most part, the teachers were wonderful, especially Itsa-Lichii's primer teacher.

While at the private school, it was Dahazhi that showed more signs of social and emotional stress. She questioned her self-worth and her appearance, thought the other children didn't like her, and was struggling academically. As a result of several meetings with teachers and school administrators, we decided to allow the school counselor to run a battery of tests on Dahazhi. Dahazhi's test results were quite good, and she scored in the highest percentile for reading. There was no indication of any learning disability or learning problem. The school counselor, however, started a series of counseling sessions with both children and with Gregory and me.

It was very difficult for the counselor to get Dahazhi to talk, but she was able to give information that helped us understand what was troubling her. Firstly, Dahazhi's self-esteem seemed to be suffering because she was continuously worried about how the other children reacted to her. Secondly, she was occasionally still having a recurring nightmare where the Mesquite school principal is shouting at us and telling us to leave their school. Thirdly, Dahazhi was feeling a tremendous responsibility for her brother. She felt that she had to make sure he was okay at school all the time. She worried about other children picking on him or hurting him physically.

Dahazhi was very emotional regarding her feelings that sometimes other children didn't like her because she was different. She was very aware of how people sometimes react to others because of their physical appearance. Most of Dahazhi's classmates were white, and she wondered if sometimes they excluded her because she wasn't. She was sure that was the reason for not getting invited to some of her classmates' birthday parties. She very eloquently expressed her desire to be in a school where "everyone would be treated the same, where all the kids would play together and have fun and not have to worry about someone not liking them because of their skin color."

# ITSA-LICHII'S CONTINUED STRUGGLE

Itsa-Lichii has come a long way. At the present time, he is twelve years old. He finished fifth grade as an honor roll student and will be going on to middle school. He is very tall and athletically gifted, according to his fifth grade teacher and his physical education teacher. There are, however, still some things that he has to work through. Probably the most significant ordeal he has had to struggle with, and still has to work through, is developing trust and feeling safe around middle-aged white men. His fifth grade teacher was helpful since he was a middle-aged white man who unknowingly was very instrumental in pushing Itsa-Lichii forth, both academically and socially. He challenged him academically by accepting and praising his contributions in class. He helped him form new friendships by involving him in informal sports activities (i.e., basketball and soccer games at lunchtime). Itsa-Lichii proceeded with caution when he first entered fifth grade and met his new teacher. He needed time to get to know his teacher and feel comfortable and safe around him. This way of approaching white men who were new to him came to be standard procedure.

Like his sister, he too had a recurring nightmare about the Mesquite incident, but his nightmare was obscure and hard for him to describe. In his nightmare he saw a "faceless man" walking down the school corridor toward him, and he would wake up just as the man reached for him. He told us he had other bad dreams, but he didn't remember them after he woke up except for one dream where the "KKK were just standing there" looking at him. He was adamant that he could still see them after he had woken up.

The second most apparent consequence of the Mesquite incident was that Itsa-Lichii's perception of himself was distorted. For a while he was very negative about his appearance and his abilities. He often asked me if I thought he was "ugly" or "funny looking." He also asked me if I thought that girls would ever like him. This was baffling to me because occasionally people commented on how handsome he was, but he didn't seem to acknowledge this or he dismissed it as politeness. I asked if maybe he felt this way because people sometimes mistakenly thought he was a girl. "Nah, that doesn't bother me like it did when I was a little kid," he responded (he was now about nine years old). He had learned not to get upset if someone thought he was a girl; instead, he would politely inform them that he was "a Native American Indian boy."

# INTO THE FUTURE

It is now May 1999. My husband and I understand, all too well, that we will never see the end of our ordeal with the Mesquite ISD incident. Today we still continue to suffer the ramifications in a number of different ways. As we approach the new millennium, I wonder, will things be better for our children in the future in relationship to racism, equity, and justice? Yes, there have been some positive changes, but it was so slow and has taken such a heavy toll on our children and on us as parents. In the long run, however, we became even stronger as a family and stronger as advocates for diversity, equity, and justice.

Itsa-Lichii's fifth grade teacher told us during our last parent/teacher conference that if Itsa-Lichii kept going the way he was, he had no doubt that he would be very successful. "He does great in school and he is a gifted athlete; he'll probably have his pick of colleges," he said. We returned the compliment and expressed our appreciation for his dedicated efforts as a teacher. He is a fantastic teacher, very committed and very fair. He goes far above and beyond the call of duty. Our son has a great deal of admiration and respect for him. It's teachers like this one that make all the difference in the world and make school a place where all children can be successful and reach their highest potential.

# CHAPTER EIGHT

# ARE SCHOOLS PREPARED TO SUPPORT EXCELLENCE FOR NONMAINSTREAM CHILDREN?

## LATINO/A VOICES AS A RESPONSE

MIRYAM ESPINOSA-DULANTO, THE PENNSYLVANIA STATE UNIVERSITY

US society is neither a perfectly blended melting pot nor a multicultural democracy. It is a heterogeneous, diversified, and stratified society in which race, ethnicity, language, gender, and socioeconomic status are intrinsic to issues of power and control. The case I want to build here, with the help of multiple Latino stories and the use of fiction, is how social agency is expressed in Latinos' encounters with the mainstream society; specifically, their dealing with the challenge of being "the other" in a largely white educational system. Numerous variables, overlapping layers, soft meetings, and cacophonic voices enter into the river of representations of these encounters. My intent is to share both sublime and insignificant moments of participants' lives using an *evocative* writing (Kondo 1990) and a *fictionalized self* (Slattery 1998), while experimenting with narrative forms (Behar 1996; Richardson 1997; Williams 1991) that recognize both the participants' voice and my own voice as a researcher/participant in a research project (Geertz 1995; Fisher 1986; Winterson 1995). My objective is multifold: I want to disturb the already accepted definition of who Latinos are, as well as address teachers' expectations about the abilities of their Latino students.

For many Latinos, succeeding in school and acquiring a formal education is the secure path to a better life. Every Latino/a I have interviewed, observed, and worked with has told me this. They also said that the school's environment is a small representation of the larger society. Thus, learning to deal with school helps to prepare Latinos for future social encounters. However, school and mainstream society are unknown environments for many of the people with whom I have worked. That is why I focus my research on the process of recognizing and learning how to deal with the mainstream's rules. Latino participants' stories have provided me with a variety of reactions, processes, and developments. The stories range from someone who takes the challenge to learn the new environment and succeed in it to someone who fails, gets discouraged, and quits, becoming angry at the whole world. These are the extremes. The middle points are countless, such as one who takes the challenge and manages to survive, another who plays with the idea of Westernization but manages to maintain her/his groupness, still another one who does not know what to do and goes "with the wind," to others who just decide to erase all that could identify them as Latinos and become whoever the mainstream offers to them, and the ones who have decided to recuperate their "ancestral cultural heritage."

Each of the people participating in my research project—including me—has become both a tributarian as well as an indispensable component of the large reservoir of social information. I chose the grammatically incorrect term "tributarian" instead of tributary as my recognition of the active role, the agency of the participants in this project. They are not only "flowing waters," they are creators of its own course.

The "data" is an ethnography of my ten years working in Lakeland (a fictional name for the midsize midwestern city in which I conducted my living research) from which I have learned and based my view about Latinos and Latino ethnicity in the United States. It has helped me to create a narrative genre for sharing the gathered information. The narratives are intertwined and interrelated but not necessarily organized following a pattern. They serve my objective to disturb already accepted ethnic labels and social predispositions as well as to reflect on the complexities of social agency.

My voice has become part of the research stories as well as part of the information reservoir. L. Richardson's work (1997) has shown me that one's research becomes part of the identity development of the researcher. In this specific case it is important that my academic persona recognize that my research has profited from and been part of the process of becoming who I am. At the same time, as an individual, I value the importance played by my research in this process and, in its temporary product, the person I have become.

# AN ETHNOGRAPHY IN LAKELAND

From the start, my research has been harmoniously related to and grown together with my personal quest for social identity/ies. My first academic experience as a research assistant was in a longitudinal research study, "Increasing the School Achievement of Low-Income Minority Children Through Home-School-University Collaboration (HSU)," funded by the Spencer Foundation and the Wisconsin Center for Education Research at the University of Wisconsin-Madison. The research's goal was "to study the effect of different home-school involvement and collaboration strategies on low-income and minority culture children's achievement and educational success within integrated multicultural settings" (Bloch and Tabachnick 1988). The overall idea was to learn through field-experiences why parental involvement in schools decreased as their income decreased and when their ethnic and racial background was other than white. In addition to acquiring this knowledge, we were to propose different strategies to improve parental involvement with an overarching goal of encouraging minority children's achievement. Lakeland, the midwestern city in which the project was located, had a large white middle-class population. The targeted low-income minority children were from three ethnic and racial backgrounds: black, Hispanic, and Hmong. Lakeland's population distribution by race and/or ethnicity follows in Table 8.1.

## Table 8.1: Distribution of Population by Race/Ethnicity in Lakeland County—1990

| Race/Ethnicity | |
|---|---|
| White | 244,682 |
| Black | 10,414 |
| Asian or Pacific Islander | 8,582 |
| Hispanic | 5,204 |
| American Indian, Eskimo, or Aleut | 1,326 |
| Other race | 2,081 |
| Total | 272,289 |

Information given by the Applied Population Laboratory at the University of Wisconsin-Madison.

During two academic years, I regularly observed selected Latino children at school and at home using an ethnographic approach based on the works of C. Delgado-Gaitan; C. Delgado-Gaitan and H. Trueba (1991), D. Foley (1990), M. Suarez-Orozco (1992), G. Spindler (1982), and O. Vasquez (1990). As a participant-observer, trying as much as possible not to interfere with the routine of the classes, I followed these children into their regular classroom, into special activities—physical education, music, art—and recess periods.

After many attempts to identify Latino families for the HSU project, eight families—the Ballards, the Contreras, the Cortézes, the Fernándezes, the Mesías, the Moráns, the Núñezes, and the Salazars—opened their homes to me. (The family names used here are fictional to protect the families' privacy.) All of the families but the Ballards had a Latino surname, and everybody but Pedro—the Ballards' child—was formally considered Hispanic in the school system. Through those exchanges I learned that school assumptions on parental involvement were inaccurate and were a reflection of mainstream expectations for minorities in school.

For example, the Cortéz family did not attend any school activities and were unreachable. As a consequence, they were assumed to be indifferent to their son's schooling. Nevertheless, Jorge Cortéz was one of the children the project aimed to work with, and my mission was to establish contact with his family. The single act of meeting the Cortéz family took me several months. I began by sending letters by mail. I tried sending notes with Jorge; finally, I personally left notes at their home. Nothing seemed to work; I almost gave up. However, looking at Jorge's work at school made me ask for help from the home-school liaison. She was extremely resourceful, managed to contact the family, and got me the first interview with Carola, Jorge's mother. Carola was the one who explained to me that their decision not to contact either the school or the project was due to their time restrictions.

> Carola and Jorge—the Cortéz parents—work in *la agricultura*. Their shift begins at 5:00 p.m. and finishes at 7:00 a.m. (14-hour shift) seven days a week. No holidays. They are very tired when they get home and need to sleep to recover their strength for the next shift, which will start that afternoon. Also, Carola reminds me that she is pregnant and that made her easily tired (Espinosa-Dulanto, HSU fieldnotes).

The Cortézes were very interested in Jorge's schooling, but looking at their work schedules, no one could expect them to volunteer or participate in school activities. Their schedules were not the only constraint for the Cortézes. As seasonal workers, they were not in control of the length of their stay in Lakeland. It depended on the harvest cycle, the canning production, and management planning and decisions. The only certainty was that they would leave "at the end of the season." The information provided by Carola demonstrated that school assumptions about minority families' involvement were not only incorrect but also point to the school's responsibility to provide adequate spaces for nonmainstream families' involvement.

There were many visits to the *Lanes* (a fictional name for the housing project in which the Latino families resided), which brought adventures, and sometimes complications. At the beginning of the project, when I was an outsider, an uninvited visitor that tried to connect with Latino families, there were moments in which I was scared and frustrated. A critical part of the research project was to learn about the children's home culture and recommend different strategies to improve the school environment to be more "culturally compatible" for both minority and non-minority children, with the ultimate goal of increasing children's achievement in school. Nevertheless, the bigger challenge for me was to break the barriers of the unknown and become part of the group I was studying. Following is a short piece that reflects on these issues. I use *fictionalized reality* to share some of the fears and domestic complications a Latina/Mestiza/researcher/teacher/woman/ wife might face trying to connect with a group who is partially outside of her known realm.

# WORKING A WAY INTO THE LANES ...

José:     Are you crazy? Going to the Lanes this late!? I'm serious ... really
          ... you have to be crazy ... you know what's going on there at
          night?

He keeps yelling ... José gets agitated, adding flapping arms, getting louder
and louder ... he gets closer to my face ... his right finger pointing at me,

José:     Drugs Miryam ... drugs ... you think ... they are children ... yeah
          they look like children ... fuck ... they are drug-dealers ... drug-
          dealers ... but no! ... you don't believe me ... you wanna help ...
          help who ... *te van a cortar* (they are gonna hurt you) ... you just
          don't get it! ... tell me again, why do you need to go?

Gosh! better leave, he won't stop and I don't need to be reminded of all
that ... I can't believe it! José is telling me those things, he lives with me, he
knows my work, he listens—I'm doubting it now—to my stories and he is
Latino himself ... how come he repeats all that shit? He sounds like a broken record of everything some people believe... you know? That poor people are delinquents ... lazy and so on ... It might be true for some but
definitely not for everyone ... and absolutely not for the children I'm gonna
visit tonight ... I know ... the Lanes are kind of dangerous but such is life
... like we never had been in weird situations ...

Miryam:   *Mi amor*, I need to meet Carmencita's parents. They're never
          home but today I got a note from her mother. She's expecting me
          around 7:00 ...

Nothing. José doesn't buy my soft tone and charges again, this time he
reminds me how cold it is outside ... he knows how much I hate this
weather ... and I begin to feel it in my bones ... NO! ... it's only November
... if I wait until next week it will be worse ... is gonna be colder ...

Miryam:   *Mi cielo* ... I promise you, I won't be out for long ... just a short
          visit ... why don't you come? ... they'll love meeting you ...

His face gets all grouchy, José doesn't want me to leave, he doesn't want to
go either, and he realizes that I'm on my way ... not too happy or too convinced ... I know it's cold ... and dark ... 7:00 p.m. looks like midnight but
... *ni modo*... what else can I do?
     Putting together all my strength, I walked to the bus stop. It took me
almost an hour to arrive at the Lanes. Gosh! feels weird ... It's kinda sad to
work with the people in the Lanes. Sometimes, I feel guilty for their luck ...

like a *monjita* ... then it's José ... he's not babbling ... I know ... the Lanes aren't safe ... drugs are easy to find around the apartments ... how many times did I get nauseated with the smoke in some of the buildings ...

It's so dark ... what should I do? ... run like everyone else and forget about the little ones? ... I don't think so ... they are poor but they are struggling to get out ... and who am I to evaluate these people's lives? ... I have no idea what's going on inside the apartments ... better move quickly, it's already 7:05 ...

I wanna scream! I wanna cry! Once again, nobody is at Carmencita's apartment! How many more times do I have yet to come to get to talk to someone in this family?! My frustration is mixed with fear. I don't like to be standing up in front of a closed door nor to be waiting at the bus stop ... where can I go? ... I thought that using the bus would give me mobility and security, but I just realized ... I'm stuck here ... really, I'm stuck!! Only me, who else could have had the brilliant idea of coming by bus—without checking the schedule ...

Gosh!! I'm liking less and less the movements in the near windows. I'm seeing people behind the curtains in the neighbor's apartment ... I'm standing there, waiting forever, looking/feeling vulnerable, alone with an unrequested company ... The neighbors are watching me and I have no idea how to act... I'm confused and afraid ... The whole deal is absurd ... I'm waiting for people I've not met, that I don't know by name nor have seen their faces ... This isn't easy... this thing, this ethnography, this observation, this home visit... this thing it's very difficult ... I've got to insert my presence into these people's lives, but I'm terrified, frozen by fear and cold ... sitting/standing/walking in circles on their front steps ... Why are they never home? ... I don't blame them ... who wants a weirdo to come to their home? ... to do what? ... yeah ... I'm asking to let me observe them ... in the privacy of their homes ... to take notes on how bad they are raising their children ...

It might be the cold ... I'm delusional ... poor people ... some are so ashamed of their ignorance, their poverty, their lack of everything ... whatta job I found ... Okay, okay, better knock on the door once more, nothing ... slip a note under ... Okay ... It was an eternity but my watch isn't moving ... just passed 20 long minutes in this horrible, horrible, horrible cold ... but there are 40 more—even longer—minutes to go ... waiting for my chosen vehicle, the city bus.

# WHAT IS MY ROLE? "PLEASE TELL ME AGAIN, WHAT IS IT THAT YOU WANT TO LEARN FROM US? ..."

As soon as I began the home visits and observations, I realized that no one in the families really understood what the project involved. The general idea—I learned later—was that I would perform as a reading or language tutor for their children. In their minds, I was a representative of one of the school's projects for targeted minority families "in need." To understand why this happened, it's important to remember that these Latino families were not used to dealing with mainstream institutions such as Oakhill Elementary. The parents were very young (with their oldest child entering elementary school), poor, fairly new to the area, with few years of schooling, were temporary/seasonal workers with extensive work hours, language barriers, and immigration problems. For more information on the families, please see Table 8.2.

It did not really matter that the families had granted me the permission to observe the children, nor that I had scheduled several visits every week. To have their cooperation, I needed to earn the families' trust and support. The first scheduled visits were closer to a performance than an observation. The following is an account of one:

> Julio's sisters and brother were kept out of the dining room area; they were sent to watch cartoons ... "no, Discovery channel," corrected their mother. They left the room giggling and pushing each other, just far enough to be out of their mother's sight, close enough to pick up on what was going on with Julio and *la maestra*. Julio's mother was shouting for silence all the time, even when everyone was quiet. She seemed nervous and tried to show off ... Poor little Julio ... he looked like the perfect picture of a boy ... his clothes were clean and crisply ironed, his hair wet and well groomed, sitting at the dinner table, looking at a book that he was not able to read, but repeating loudly what—supposedly—he was reading. Julio was a playful and happy boy, always playing and running around. It was the first time I saw him all groomed and looking studious. The book he was "reading" was an English-only picture book. Julio read it using the following pattern, almost as chanting:
>
> "*sombrero*, hat ... *chamarra*, coat ... *guantes*, gloves ..."

Table 8.2 HSU Latino Families

| | Place of Origin | Language Mainly Spoken | Schooling | Employment Status |
|---|---|---|---|---|
| **Ballards** | | | | |
| father | Wisconsin | English | Some college | Bus driver |
| mother | Texas | English/Spanish | Some college | Social worker |
| **Contreras** | | | | |
| father | Honduras | Spanish | Some high school | Construction worker |
| mother | Honduras | Spanish | Some high school | Cleaning lady |
| **Cortézes** | | | | |
| father | Texas | Spanish/English | High school | Seasonal cannery worker |
| mother | Texas | Spanish/English | High school | Seasonal cannery worker |
| **Fernándezes** | | | | |
| father | Honduras | Native language/Spanish | Some schooling | ? |
| mother | México | English/Spanish | High school | Home caretaker/State economic aid |
| **Mesías** | | | | |
| father | Texas | Spanish | Some high school | Seasonal cannery worker |
| mother | México | Spanish | Some schooling | Home caretaker/State economic aid |
| **Moráns** | | | | |
| father | New Mexico | Mixed English/Spanish | Some high school | Home caretaker/State economic aid |
| mother | Wisconsin | Mixed English/Spanish | Some high school | Home caretaker/State economic aid |
| **Núñezes** | | | | |
| father | Nicaragua | Spanish/English | High school | Temporary office worker |
| mother | Nicaragua | Spanish | Some schooling | Home caretaker/State economic aid |

He pointed to a picture and then, "read the word" first in Spanish, then in English. Julio's mom was very proud to show me how much reading he had learned in school that week (Espinosa-Dulanto, HSU fieldnotes).

After these performance type of visits, I had to revise my approach. The idea was to learn about the home culture, the families' lives, and how the children were using their afterschool time. My first revised strategy was to explain again the project goals and why we had asked for their involvement. I remember myself, in every family living room, giving short lectures about the goals of the project, inviting them to ask me questions and hoping for some discussion, but what I usually got were blank faces making efforts not to yawn at me. Adding to my difficulties was the fact that I was considered a special visitor to be entertained, and an outsider who was there to judge their ways of raising their children.

The families were both precise but also mistaken in their assumptions. I was an outsider, but that was not all. I was also committed to become a cultural bridge between home and school, and I needed to find how to communicate with the families. I changed the ways of explaining the goals of the research project. Instead of lecturing I tried examples. We talked about what was going on with youngsters, women, and other Latino children around the city. We exchanged our experiences in school, community, church, and within the Latino community in Lakeland. Earning the families' trust and support was neither a simple nor speedy process. I spent almost a year, with the main goal of making the families comfortable with my presence in their homes, in their playgrounds, and what is more important, around their children.

In order to observe their children, I allowed the parents and a caretaker grandmother to observe me, to interview me. It was necessary to give as much information as I was asking from them. Instead of an ethnographic model, I followed a traditional Andean norm of creating ties among interacting people. I could not be a stranger observing their children; I had to become a familiar and trustworthy person before I would be able to do my (field) work. Their response was slow but worth waiting for. They took their time but gave me enough space to observe their children at home, after school hours, and during holidays and summer. The performances to impress me gradually subsided.

It was very touching to see the change in my relationship with the Latino families in the Lanes. My Latino background together with my newcomer status, were central to the acceptance process. I became someone with a similar background to all of them and, like them, I was working my way up from nothing, having strength and endurance as my most precious skills. My gender made connections as well as limitations. I spent much more time with the children and women. My "long distance" motherhood also was a connection. Like many of the Latino people I met in Lakeland, I had to leave my child back in my country, waiting for the "right" time to bring her. Almost everyone had a similar story, leaving a close relative at home. I received the families' empathy because they saw in me a reflection of what they were going or had gone through. Furthermore, my position as a research assistant linked to the university and my ability to function in English created the generalized assumption that I had made it into the mainstream, a great achievement. A switch happened; I became a successful Latina, worthy of being emulated.

In short, the ethnography went both ways. In Dorinne Kondo's (1990) words, I "displaced the binary," in this case the researcher vs. researched, and got myself involved in the ethnography and study. I was able to see the participants not only as "my objects of study" but as entities and individualities creating a different world than mine, a world that from a distance could have passed as similar but was extremely different when seen up close. Displacing the binary meant bonding with the group. I was not able to understand "Hispanic culture" until I became a part of the world I was observing. I learned and rewrote what it meant to be a Latina in Lakeland.

Despite our overall empathy, sometimes we—the families and I—had to deal with situations that were very difficult because of our different backgrounds. As a general rule, we all recognized and respected our differences; what's more, we all preached on the need for doing it. Paradoxically, the same people were intensively ethnocentric and used broad generalizations regarding Latino traditions and culture. In these cases, each individual assured me beyond a doubt that his or her assumptions and generalizations were "the Latino" qualities or defects according to the case under discussion. In these instances, I tried to listen since I was always in the minority—a Peruvian, new to the area, and not an *Ama de casa*. One of these differences was food. For the women, it was a big deal to demonstrate they knew how to cook "real food." This meant Mexican food for the Mexicans, Nicaraguan food for the Nicaraguans, and Honduran food for the Hondurans. Of course, I was weird, Peruvians did not eat *tortillas*! In one moment, I was the observer, the researcher, and I was consulted as well as looked at as a role model. At the next, I was a woman unable to cook *mole* or prepare *tortillas*. This fluidity in the field helped me to learn much more about the families' home traditions and customs. At the same time, the issues of power were in equilibrium, enabling us to establish harmonious relationships.

For the observer at home, it was necessary to be multilingual. English and national Spanish/es were a condition of this research, adding to the difficult job of understanding people from different backgrounds. What made it worthwhile was the realization of the incommensurable wealth that national Spanish/es represent for Latinos, especially when they are in cultural interaction and transition in the United States. This development is part of the Latino cultural repertoire for asserting their/our Latinness, carving a domain in which Latinos can re-create their own ways.

# UNDERSTANDING THE SCHOOL AND HOME CULTURES: LEARNING TO RECOGNIZE OUR OWN ASSUMPTIONS

The assumption that through formal education Latinos may obtain a better life by moving up the social scale leads people into schools, only to find that these institutions are part of the oppressive system from which they want to escape. Nevertheless, schooling, with all its shortcomings, has become a necessary element of everyday life. As educational practitioners, we all hold responsibility for children's schooling. Michael Apple (1999) strongly urges us to make a difference:

> until we take seriously the extent to which education is caught up in the real world of shifting and unequal power relations, we will be living in a world divorced from reality. The theories, policies, and practices involved in education are *not* technical. They are inherently ethical and political ... whether we like it or not differential power intrudes into the heart of curriculum and teaching and they ultimately involve ... intensely personal choices.

Teachers and school officials are not free of preconceptions and social images. The widespread images of what a Latino/a is have been socially forged in an effort to cope with the fear of the unknown and as an effort to understand it—the "Other"—in this case, a growing minority in school grounds. Mirroring these assumptions, Latino children are perceived as different.

Teachers' construction of children is affected by their personal experiences (Ladson-Billings 1990), their knowledge or lack of it about children's personal stories (Heath 1983; Lareau 1989; Delgado-Gaitan 1990; Delgado-Gaitan and Trueba 1991), and ideological positions on social issues such as race, gender, language, and economic status (Apple 1990; Tabachnick and Zeichner 1991; Popkewitz 1993). As part of an educational system, teachers and school officials are also affected by the school-level system of belief concerning issues of assessment and achievement, particularly regarding developmental "level" or "readiness," and normative reference groups (Graue 1992; Shepherd and Smith 1989).

Lois Weis (1983) opens up the dichotomy, oppressor and oppressed, and presents schools as pivotal places to develop social agencies and cultural productions. In Weis's view, schools are hegemonic devices, but not exclusively. They are also places in which people's social agencies and cultural forms blossom and powerfully emerge as expressions of the processes by which children create and re-create their identities:

> [Schools are a] reflection of an economic base [in which] lived cultural forms arise in part from that base and may act in contradictory ways to sustain it. The relations between culture ... and the economy are exceedingly complex and no simple base/superstructure model will serve to illuminate them (252).

In a more general sense, I propose that we should not assume that cultural forms are determined as an automatic reflex of, but not limited to, one's class, gender, language, place of origin, race, ethnicity, religion, schooling, and traditions regardless of their importance for understanding students' attitudes and behaviors. For example, Latinos are in the daily business of creating their/our own ways in their/our own register. The struggle is permanent and democratic, a dynamic, changing, and interactive process in which people define, from the bottom up, their own culture. People's agency—using counterhegemonic devices—is the counterpoint to the social norm; it is the active creation of culture, sometimes harmonious and other times in a conflicting stance vis-à-vis the mainstream.

The following segments are illustrations of how Latino children were identified and placed in specific programs, sometimes only because of their/our ethnic profile. I focus only on the assumptions that were prevalent during the time I was working on the HSU ethnography. These were that: (1) All Latinos speak Spanish, (2) Latino parents do not get involved in school activities, and (3) Latino children are lazy, often late, and not interested in schoolwork.

## Latinos, the Spanish-Speaking People in the United States

*The official language [English] is bound with the state, both in its genesis and its social uses ... Obligatory on official occasions and official places [English] becomes the theoretical norm against which all linguistic practices are objectively measured. Ignorance is no excuse; this linguistic law has its body of jurists—the grammarians—and its agents of regulation and imposition—the teachers—who are empowered universally to subject the linguistic performance of speaking subjects to examination and to the legal sanction of academic qualification ...*

BOURDIEU (1991)

Pierre Bourdieu (1991, 1977) named the hegemonic role an official language has in marginalizing nonofficial languages and more importantly on controlling the act of teaching. In the Latino case, to acquire English—the official language in the United States—demands more than having the linguistic knowledge. It demands formally establishing that one master the English language regardless of Latino traditions and/or the social assumptions brought with the Latino label.

The assumption that all Latinos speak Spanish was largely embraced in Oakhill Elementary. All Latino children observed were entering kindergarten and all were placed in the English as a Second Language (ESL) program. This placement was done regardless of the fact that three of the seven had English as their mother tongue and did not know Spanish. However, the ESL placement was not restricted to the entering children. The following excerpt is from an older student who eagerly tried to do his ESL homework:

> "I was walking down the hallway when one child addressed me, 'Señorita [with a funny English accent], you know Spanish, right? ... You know how to write 'the door is brown'? ... I need to write it [in Spanish] for my [ESL] homework ... " (Espinosa-Dulanto, HSU personal journals).

Bourdieu is helpful in understanding that for Latinos in the United States, English is not only a tool for communication but also an object of "symbolic domination [a code] in the sense of a system of norms regulating linguistic practices ... and social uses" (Bourdieu 1991, 45–52). The unspoken rules and dreams of US culture are embedded in every aspect of life and language. For the new immigrants, for the first-generation children and/or for the "Spanglish" speakers, English—as the *officielle* language—has become a "form of prestige and reknown ... perhaps the most valuable form of accumulation ... readily convertible back into economic capital ... " (Bourdieu 1977, 179).

By the time I interviewed the ESL coordinator at Oakhill Elementary regarding the Latino children's placement, the ESL staff was informed that not all the children were there because of their lack of English. Nevertheless, the Latino children were consistently taken from their regular classes to attend the ESL program. The answer I received was that Latino children were receiving extra help with their reading and writing. In any event, I must stress that the ESL coordinator and the classroom teachers were indeed enthusiastic about helping Latino children but only within the school institutional framework. This posits problems because the mechanisms implemented for assisting these children are, in the end, critical for defining their identity as "at risk" or with "deficiencies," closing the circle of their predicaments and identifying them as of lesser status than their mainstream counterparts.

In the group observed, Latino children's behavior could be largely explained in terms of their struggles to make sense of the language used. In Oakhill Elementary, Latino children were not formally denied speaking Spanish, but they were classified with a language deficiency and placed in special programs (i.e., ESL) despite their level of English proficiency. The idea was to help the Latino children to acquire English and the culture of the school. However, attending the ESL classes and activities disengaged these children from their classmates and positioned them behind in "regular" course work. It is not so difficult to imagine the frustration of those children and why they chose to speak only in English as soon as they were able to do so.

## Lack of Parental Involvement at School Does Not Mean Lack of Parental Attention at Home

At Oakhill Elementary Latino parents were not actively participating nor were their children performing as expected. These two facts led the school to launch the *Grant Program* that supported the idea that children should be considered as partners in their families. In the program, parents and children performed tasks together. As a way to increase parental participation, Oakhill Elementary scheduled paid parent visits to their children's classrooms. This economic support was used to cover the parents' babysitting and transportation expenses. Latina mothers participated in the program, came to the workshops, made cookies with their children, read to them, and went together to the zoo.

I believe that ideas such as the Grant Program are products of good intentions and show interest in reaching the group that is not performing or participating as desired. There were several problems, though. The implementation was done without considering the ways in which Latino parents define and engage their own children. For example, the recommendation for nightly reading, which was originated with the goal of encouraging parental closeness as well as reading models, became extremely controversial when the adults at home had limited English abilities, limited schooling, or an oral storytelling tradition. In the case of gender roles, baking cookies with one's son was fun when it happened at school. It was another story at home, trying to explain to the same child—a couple of days later—why he was being laughed at, called names, and prohibited from baking cookies for his cousins. Finally, the zoo visit was a wonderful time for the ones who could make it. Money and babysitting were provided, but for such families as the Cortézes or the Contreras that was not enough because of the length of time involved in their work shifts; time was a resource not available to them.

Time was a priceless commodity for the Latino families. I learned this by trying to fit into their lives while doing the ethnography for the HSU project. As explained earlier, just to meet with the Cortéz family took me ten months. I persisted only because I "fell" for their child. Jorge had a spark. He was tall and massive for his age but gentle and kind. He always participated and volunteered to do anything; for example, he erased the blackboard, distributed the snacks, and helped his classmates with their reading. Moreover, Jorge developed impressive progress in mastering English and had high self-confidence. In short, Jorge was a picture of a successful Latino kid, and he was such a blessing to observe that I wanted, so badly, to meet his parents.

The first time I had the opportunity for a conversation with Ms. Carola Cortéz, I realized that my assumptions and expectations were absolutely dissociated from their daily life. She did not answer my calls nor was involved in any of the Oakhill Elementary programs, but she was extremely involved with her children's upbringing. There were several reasons for her choice of not being involved. She was working long hours, recently had had another baby, and her family's living arrangements were unstable. The Cortéz family life depended on the parents' work. They had to rearrange their lives accordingly, something that needs to be taken into account regarding school expectations for parents' involvement. Families like the Cortézes can't predict their immediate future and choose not to make a commitment for fear of failing the promises.

Overall, the Grant Program was condescending to minority families; they were invited and paid to come to the school to be taught how to be "better parents." However, it missed parental input and the exchanging of their own perspectives regarding their children's upbringing. And there was no adequate space for nonmainstream parents, such as the migrant workers, to participate. The idea of short workshops, at the beginning and the end of the vegetable-picking season, could be a positive response for migrant children's schooling.

## Being Late Does Not Mean Being Lazy

In a different vein, the assumption that Latinos "are always late" is also prevalent in mainstream culture, and it came up several times during the observations at Oakhill Elementary. It was a fact that some Latino children came to school late both at the beginning of the day and after lunch. It was also a fact that children across race, ethnicity, gender, and class were sometimes late. What is difficult to understand is the assumption that in the Latino case this was assumed as a tradition or as some kind of genetic trait which also implied laziness or disdain for schoolwork.

When talking with Latino parents about their children coming late to school, they all agreed that sometimes the children had a hard time waking up and got to school late, but usually, in the parents' recollection, their children were on time. An example of one of these conversations follows. I was at the Cortézes. Carola was breast-feeding little Octavio while Jorge was playing with Oscar (four) and Xochitl (one and a half). Jorge's schedule was like this:

> The school bus picks him up at 8:00 a.m. ... so he needs to wake up with enough time to catch it ... but ... [Carola smiles] sometimes, Jorge watches too much TV ... and next morning ... ahhhh ... next morning, I have to push him out of the bed ... [Carola talks softly] Yeah, a few times he's missed the bus ... then ... you get a crying boy ... He cries until I walk him to the school ... like last week ... [Carola turns to see Jorge, who is all frowning]

> Mom it was ... *mi hermanita* ...

> Carola answers back with a nod and tells me that last week he overslept because he helped her with Xochitl with her bottle and stuff ...

> You know … two little ones, at night they cry at the same time … [Carola remarks] Jorge likes school so much, he doesn't want to miss a day (Espinosa-Dulanto, HSU fieldnotes).

Thus, Jorge, as any other child, loves to watch TV but sometimes overdoes it. When he does, waking up on time to catch the bus is difficult, although very few times has he actually missed the school bus. Nor are those few times he has missed the bus always a consequence of watching TV. Jorge, like other children in that community, helps at home, and sometimes it is a big responsibility for such a little boy, causing him to be tired in the morning and perhaps late. When this conversation took place, Jorge was only a kindergartner.

Listening and spending time with Latino parents was helpful to see things in a different light, and I've always wished that other teachers could have the same opportunity to learn. Sadly, that was not the case of a kindergarten teacher from Oakhill Elementary. She told her class that a Latino child was late because that is something that "runs in his family." She based her assumption on her past experience with the boy's cousin. She never asked why he was late, but it did not stop her from assuming it to be a family or cultural trait and from sharing her ideas with the whole classroom.

A Latino friend who is a middle school teacher in the same area of the city made the following comment regarding the Latino lateness:

> I don't understand why they get so caught up with the Latino children coming back late, after lunch. Everyone in the school knows that they go home to have lunch … they are across the street. So, sometimes they are a few minutes late—so what? How much can you do in a few minutes? What about the children who get permission to travel for vacation for a week or longer during the school year? Are they lazy? Why do Latino children get the "always late," "lazy" labels and the other children do not? Why? … This really bothers me … (R. Saénz, personal communication, January 1998).

## Summary

There is no one behavior that would represent and reflect Latino ethnicity and agency. As reflected by almost everything I encountered in my research, the diversity was staggering and led me to believe that Latino ethnicity is formed precisely from that heterogeneity and complexity, despite ethnocentric assumptions by mainstream society, segments, or individuals within Latin culture. Moreover, ethnic and cultural standards are enriched when Latinos work out their differences and learn each other's ways. As a consequence, every day new cultural forms are created. No longer Mexican, nor Nicaraguan, nor Honduran, but a new creation is born from the adaptation to the available cultural traits, as tasteful *platillos* with new *secretos,* neighbors share with each other mainly as a way to re-create the Latin American heritage in the United States. This heritage is reinvented and redefined each time Latinos selectively decide what part of their traditions they will keep, what they will borrow from others, and what they will forget when dealing with the mainstream society.

Paraphrasing Ladson-Billings (1994), I conclude that Latino children need *better* schools in which "culturally relevant teaching practices would be an integral part ..." (137), meaning that, as teachers of diverse children, we need to create inclusive classrooms in which all children feel welcome and recognized. For that to happen, the inclusive classrooms have to respect and honor not only the teachers' dreams for education but also those of the community served.

# THE POWER OF FICTION— THE MESSAGE GETS THROUGH

Communicating our dreams might be one of these challenges because it requires listening and understanding over preconceptions and assumptions. Fiction and other narrative genres could be of great help in establishing the bridge of communication. What follows is a poem in which I share my teacher's dream as my own individual way of building this bridge of understanding.

## A Teacher's Dream

It was my teacher's dream
    to have a spacious
        bright
    full of fun things classroom
in which
    twenty-five smiling faces
    with twenty-five pairs of all-attentive eyes
    with twenty-five pairs of all-listening ears
were ready to follow my instruction

ready to fill themselves
   with knowledge
the knowledge
   I wanted to share
   I wanted to teach

Another is my day
   when only fourteen of thirty-one
     showed up for class
when almost all fourteen
   where jammin' their heads
   following music I couldn't hear
when almost all fourteen
   with dark shades
   were watching some movie I couldn't see
when almost all fourteen
   were tired
   lying their morning on a desk
when almost all fourteen
   have all-many dreams to become
   I have no idea what
when almost all fourteen
   come regularly to class
   and again I have no idea why

That's my dream
that's my day
   and my challenge is to connect
this my day
with my teaching
   that is my dream.

# CHAPTER NINE

# A LIFE SPAN /

# TODA UNA VIDA

## THE PAIN AND THE STRUGGLE THAT WILL STRIKE/

### EL DOLOR Y LA LUCHA QUE EMBISTE

IRENE PABON, THE PENNSYLVANIA STATE UNIVERSITY

The time has come, colonizer/colonized: pain, suffering of being, vulnerability, and submission. A soul between a rock and a hard place (*Entre la espada y la pared*). The new old reality of being what I have been and the struggle to change a past that I can't change. The time has come to end the suffering and the pain of being both the colonizer and the colonized, of being oppressed and submissive. These were my thoughts as I was reading.

While I was reading the article "The Colonizer/Colonized Chicana Ethnographer: Identity, Marginalization, and Co-option in the Field" (Villenas 1996), I had chills as if I'd had a sudden rush of adrenaline which I could not stop. My heartbeat accelerated and blood rushed to my head in a way I had never felt before. At that moment, the words "colonizer/colonized," which the author of the article had used, kept coming to my mind repeatedly, creating a new awareness along with this strong emotional response in myself. I saw myself, through the reading of the article, as a soul trying to help my fellow Puerto Ricans, but at the same time as part of the dominant mainstream culture that colonizes, oppresses, and marginalizes my life. I was actively participating in my colonization acting as a colonizer. In her article, Sofia Villenas explains the researcher's role in colonization, which would shed a little light on this point:

Researchers have illuminated the ways in which the researched are colonized and exploited. They have participated as colonizers of the researched by objectifying people's lives and not asking what the researched think about how their lives are being interpreted and described in text. They also act as colonizer when they claim authenticity of interpretation and description under the guise of authority (Villenas 1996).

Although I had heard the words colonizer/colonized before, it never occurred to me that I could be actively participating in the perpetuation of my own colonization and marginalization. So I began to think more deeply about my personal experience as a Puerto Rican, whose homeland had been colonized first by Spain and in the last one hundred years by the United States.

I think I had become a colonizer since I had failed to question my own identity and had implicitly assumed the mainstream position, seeing the lives of other Puerto Ricans as problems. However, my internalized colonization has been a veil over my eyes that I have just started to remove after many years, through this new realization about colonization.

When I went to work for a community of Puerto Ricans in the States in 1985 as a bilingual teacher, I went with the idea of helping these "poor people" get out of the ghetto (*arrabal*). Unconsciously perhaps, I blamed them for their pitiful situation, accepting the way they were depicted by mainstream teachers, administrators, and the media. At that time, I did not realize that the social issues associated with Puerto Ricans were associated with oppression, which resulted from colonization. Because I had suffered oppression most of my life, been used to it, and thus been unable to detect the oppressive forces that had shaped my life, I had become an oppressor myself. With this realization, I felt angry with myself at having had a foot in both worlds, in the dominant privileged institutions and in a marginalized community. So I began to look more deeply into my own experiences and to define those things that have made my life what it is.

# CHILDHOOD RETROSPECTION

I was my father's little princess. What made me special was that I was the youngest of six siblings and that I was a girl. I was a vivacious little girl, who at a young age was able to express herself freely and creatively, with my father's approval. I would sing and dance freely to show others my talents and creativity. As a small child I was motivated to be outgoing and expressive in different ways.

But later, through the socialization process, I was stripped of my inner self, experiencing the turmoil of contradictory feelings, inadequacy, and confusion.

The messages I received were contradictory. What was valued one moment was devalued in another. Being active, expressive, and outgoing was in distinct contrast to my prescribed role as a female in Puerto Rican society, where I was expected to be private, discreet, quiet, simple, willing to be subjugated, and dominated to fit into our social order. I learned this lesson the hard way because I still remember the worst reprimand I had as a preadolescent. First, let me describe the circumstances that prevailed in my culture at that time.

## SHAPED BY CULTURE

In our patriarchal society, Puerto Rican men are privileged. They are allowed to do things women are not. Women are expected to be loyal, submissive, quiet, supportive of men, passive, and homebound.

As a little girl, I was able to mingle with a predominantly male group with my father, but as a young lady I was not allowed to enjoy the company of the opposite sex. When I was no longer a little girl and had become a young woman, I had to learn to behave differently. As a young lady it was not socially acceptable to be outgoing. I had to stay in the house because that was the place for the woman, since going out into the street to mix with members of the opposite sex was seen as improper for a nice girl. Things were different for my beloved brothers. They were allowed to leave the house and do what pleased them most, which was a legitimate cultural practice. I could not even go out and play with my next-door neighbor because five of her eight siblings were males. To survive as a female in Puerto Rico was to not question male authority. I wanted to have fun, of course, but I did not want to upset my father with my behavior (I was between a rock and a hard place). His approval meant a great deal to me. It reassured me of my worth. But I also wanted to have fun and did not know why I felt so guilty about it.

## SUBMISSION

While dealing with the frustration of my prohibitions as a Puerto Rican young woman, it once occurred to me that I could meet my father's expectations of being quiet and submissive while being myself and having fun at the same time. One day I decided I would take a chance and go next door to play with the neighbor girl. What could go wrong? I thought. I figured that as soon as I heard my father calling me, I would run back to my house and avoid any reprimand with no further consequences. So I ventured next door.

My girlfriend and I were talking and deciding how to entertain ourselves when one of my girlfriend's oldest sisters suggested doing a variety show in which I would be an exotic dancer. Everything was set, but we needed an audience for the show and wondered who it could be. My girlfriend's oldest sister solved our problem by offering to bring her brothers to the show, but they were very critical, so everything had to be perfect to convince them to participate in our game. We decided that to have the perfect show, the older girls would improvise costumes to fit me. We also made a tent with a bed sheet and had the boys drum on the floor to make the rhythm for me to dance to. Everybody cheered and the show began, the boys playing with incredible rhythm. Then suddenly one of the kids said to me, "I hear someone calling you." Suddenly, everybody became motionless and silent. I heard a familiar voice calling my name. It was my father. My heart stopped, my face turned pale as if I were going to faint. I did not think or hesitate for a minute. I just ran back to my house in a frenzy. I got home as fast as I could, not realizing I was still dressed for the show. When my father saw me in my costume, his green eyes looked greener and full of anger. I was punished so harshly that even now it is hard for me to describe it. I carried the physical scar for many years.

After this incident, I was wrapped in great confusion and did not know how to behave. I struggled between my desire for my father's approval and my need for self-expression. How could I reconcile the two because, as a little girl, my father's approval meant love? After that I learned to hide my true self and became quiet and submissive, fulfilling my traditional role at home, although my submissive behavior made me hate the house and what it represented. A Puerto Rican woman knows what being oppressed means by the mere fact that she is female. Oppression and inequality were integral to my socialization, so it seemed normal to accept them. I never verbalized my frustrations and disappointments. I was required to fulfill my designated role in society and never questioned authority.

Our internalized oppression, our colonizer/colonized status, is sometimes like smoke in our eyes, as I have discovered through my own experience. But it is time to clear our vision by ending our silence and resisting the inequality, the oppression, and the marginalization that we are confronting. It is time to disperse the smoke of stereotypes that disguise, obscure, and mask the inequality, oppression, and marginalization of Puerto Ricans in a prejudiced and racist society.

Rediscovering my own oppression, which related to what I was reading about in regard to colonization, enabled me to realize that I needed to recognize how I had internalized my oppression and had thus been unaware of it. Similarly, I have been part of a colonized society that accepted oppression to the extent that I was unaware that I too could be a colonizer. I had participated both in my own colonization/oppression and colonized/oppressed other Puerto Ricans because my attitudes were influenced by the mainstream culture.

# OPPRESSION AND INEQUALITY

My internalized colonization gave more power to the superiority of the oppressor and diminished my self-esteem. As part of the Puerto Rican community, I have been blaming myself and blaming the victims of inequality and oppression, not the real forces that produce them. Oppression and inequality create negative social patterns that block access to economic opportunity and create welfare recipients, unemployed people, illiterate individuals, inhumane living conditions, and the ghetto, where crime and other social ills develop. Linguistic and cultural barriers are not the cause of these social problems. Rather, all of the negative social traits conceived by a racist society have been used to define what it is to be a Puerto Rican in the United States.

My aversion to violence and crime in all of its manifestations has blurred my vision as well. I have felt angry with people in the *arrabal* who cannot raise themselves above its ghetto culture and have blamed them for their misfortune. I have condemned the subculture which it has developed, the deviation of the language, and the disintegration of what I considered our cultural values within the strong family institution in Puerto Rican life. I have blamed the subculture in the ghetto for my own feelings of powerlessness, inadequacy, and inferiority. To resist accepting these stereotypes, I have had to critically analyze why this was the case. Who really made me feel this way? Who devalued my language and my culture? What was causing my pain?

Shame and pain blurred my vision as I legitimated the stereotypes created by the dominant culture that depicted my fellow Puerto Ricans—as a result of their not mastering the English language—speaking with an accent or lacking in education. I had not understood the dynamics of oppression. The images constructed about my community as persons who fail in school are lazy and violent are the opposite of my experience. In view of these stereotypes, I had to critically analyze the facts and consider the misrepresentations of Puerto Ricans in the United States. Who created these images? What is the purpose behind them? Who gains from them?

These stereotypes are perpetuated to a great extent by the failure of the dominant culture to meet the needs of Puerto Ricans migrating from the island. Language is especially a major issue for US politicians now, and bilingual education, which was instituted in schools to advance language learning for immigrants, is under attack. Bilingual children are constantly marginalized and oppressed for their language and culture, creating in them a sense of inadequacy and inferiority in the very place where they should be cherished: school.

These images constructed about my community are abominable, offensive, odious, reprehensible, insulting, repugnant, and wrong. I know and remember many Puerto Ricans who do not fit these stereotypes. As I reflected on these false perceptions of Puerto Ricans, images of my life story unfolded before my eyes, reminding me of the strong fiber that Puerto Ricans are made of.

We do not choose to be poor. There is no choice! And we don't like it either. Inequality, discrimination, and prejudice have reduced many Puerto Ricans to poverty or a lower economic status. Puerto Ricans are honorable citizens who have paid their dues fighting and dying for the North American nation of which we are citizens. We have also contributed with our talent to the arts. People like Julia de Burgos, José de Diego, José Ferrer, Pablo Casals, Rafael Hernandez, Francisco Oller, René Marques, and my own mother Antonia Fernandez, to mention a few, are among the many who have made significant contributions to our culture and society. These are individuals whose talents have contributed to the betterment of the Puerto Rican soul, through a poem, a speech, a song, a performance, a painting, a work of literature, or simply by raising a family and productive citizens. These are examples of hard-working people who are not lazy, who are sensible, intelligent individuals who exhibit great creativity and have certainly not been school failures.

Despite economic hardship after my father's death, my mother managed to raise a family of six children, attend evening school after work, and send me to college. This is not the stereotypical picture of a lazy Puerto Rican but an example of a hard-working and caring individual. This is an example of being brave, surmounting the odds, and fiercely fighting for survival.

We Puerto Ricans must fight the racism and discrimination that haunt us in mainstream society in the United States. It is a matter of survival, not a matter of violence ingrained in us. It is not an evil gene that defines us. As we are persecuted because of discrimination, oppression, and inequality, we must strike back with a compelling force and rise united, deploring injustice and inequality. One of our famous poets, José de Diego, describes the phenomenon of survival of the persecuted, with dignity, in his poem "*En la brecha*" ("To the Persecuted"):

| *En la brecha* | To the Persecuted |
| --- | --- |
| Jose De Diego | (Translation by Roberto Santiago) |
| *Ah! desgraciado si el dolor te abate,* | If suffering comes unabated, |
| *si el cansancio tus miembros entumece!* | If weariness weighs down your spirit, |
| *Haz como el arbol seco: reverdece* | Do as the once barren tree: flourish |
| *y como el germen enterrado: late.* | And like the planted seed: rise. |
| *Resurge, alienta, grita, anda, combate,* | Resurge, breathe, shout, walk, fight, |
| *vibra, ondula, retruena, resplandece...* | Vibrate, glide, thunder, shine forth... |
| *Haz como el rio con la lluvia: ʿcrece!* | Do as the river rich with new rainwater: grow. |
| | Or like the sea approaching a rocky shore: strike. |
| *De la tormenta al iracundo empuje,* | Know how to face the angry thrust of storms, |
| *no has te balar, como el cordero triste,* | Not braying, like a frightened lamb, |
| *sino rugir, como la fiera ruge.* | But roaring, like a defiant beast. |
| *Levantate! revuelvete! resiste!* | Rise! Revolt! Resist! |
| *Haz como el toro acorralado: ʿmuge!* | Do as the bull in the face of adversity: |
| *O como el toro que no muge: ʿembiste!* | Charge with confident power. |

We will resist and refuse the stereotypes created to depict Puerto Ricans by a racist society, with their prejudice, and reverse the misconceptions that become blinders that cause the exploitation and maginalization of our people.

Puerto Ricans have been exploited for hundreds of years. Oppression and inequality suffered by Puerto Ricans on the island and on the mainland has created a sense of inferiority so that the oppressor gains more power. For centuries strangers have been knocking at the door of the Puerto Rican nation, always in search of something, to get something, or to take something forcefully and openly from us (Colon 1995). Ironically, our exploitation and oppression are supported in some instances by our own socialization patterns manifested by the oppression of women in our own patriarchal society.

Puerto Ricans, like many immigrants, come to this "promised land" in search of a better life, hoping to share the American dream. But a large number of Puerto Ricans have been forced to remain in the slums. Discrimination and prejudice have created oppressive conditions that make our struggle to make a living to raise our families with dignity almost impossible, and we are blamed for this. Puerto Rican culture is being attacked, and a fear campaign beneath the guise of nationalism is being used by English-only advocates in the States to promote assimilation and devalue minority languages (Soto 1998). The sharing of the American dream will not be accomplished at the sacrifice of the traits that make us what we are as Puerto Ricans. We are strong people who have been struggling to survive as a *pueblo*. Social patterns associated with oppression emerge as violence, drug addiction, and high dropout rates among students. These results of oppression are used to depict and stereotype Puerto Ricans. Our family values are not understood in the new cultural system, and we are labeled dysfunctional by the new rules set for us by the dominant culture.

As a teacher, I have a foot in both worlds, in the dominant privilege institutions and in the marginalized community. However, teachers must change their pedagogy so that students learn how to make sense of the world by critically analyzing and exploring the hidden forces that have shaped their lives, to be able to discover their true self and change the pervasive condition of colonization. This should start in the early stage of schooling by posing strategies that will help students gain a consciousness of oppression early in life and effectively change the trend of colonization to liberate them from this oppressive condition.

As a Puerto Rican woman, and an educator, I intend to raise my voice and theorize from the position of my pain. I have been oppressed, subjugated, dominated, and discriminated against as a woman, as a mother, as a teacher, and as a Puerto Rican, both on the island and on the mainland. I have been denied my rights and have willingly accepted this fact through my own socialization. Oppression and discrimination I know firsthand.

Schools must break or deconstruct stereotypes to fight oppression and discrimination. As Puerto Ricans, we have to learn about our history, make our contributions visible to the world, and learn who we are through our culture and literature. We must know our writers, poets, scientists, and all those who mold our identity, and raise our self-esteem in order to develop pride in who we are. Teachers who emphasize equality by breaking down the barriers between themselves and their students can create an atmosphere that promotes the active participation of students in the learning process and offer strong visual images of themselves as role models who promote equity and openness.

Now is the time to learn to love ourselves and our community with a healthy love which will give us the strength we need to succeed. We have been damaged merely by virtue of being Puerto Ricans. We have been oppressed too long already, but we are still alive. What the poet José de Diego advises us to do we have done. We have refused to give up our culture and linguistic heritage after the last one hundred years of colonization. We will keep fighting oppression in our search for equality.

Fortunate are those Puerto Ricans who have survived oppression and struggled to maintain their language and cultural identity, which grew from three different roots and rich, cultural traditions: Taina, Spaniard, and African. We are still Puerto Ricans and proud of it! We must teach our children at home and at school to rise above oppression and discrimination to claim and carry on their cultural heritage.

# CHAPTER TEN

# MY STORY AND
# THE MELANESIAN
# KNOWLEDGE

LYNUS YAMUNA, THE UNIVERSITY OF GOROKA, PAPUA NEW GUINEA

The news of my birth spread like the awakening crow of the rooster, and soon crowds of women came to the bush maternal labor ward, which was built some two hundred yards away from the main village. Our beliefs and customs clearly defined the roles of women and what they should do during such times. Giving birth to a newborn baby was a sacred act that allowed only the presence of women. Our beliefs even prohibited males from eating food cooked by a new mother. Men were not allowed during early child-birth; therefore, only women from the village came to visit my mother and me.

One significant event of these early visits by the women of the village was "the naming of the newborn child." A newborn child without a name is often thought of as having come from a clan that no longer exists or whose status in the villages was of low regard. My grandmother from my father's lineage was one of the very first to come to name me. She came with a pre-determined mental list of the names she was going to place on me. She, being the mother of my father, was expected to name me first. She named me "Bagasim," the name of a great man from her clan. My father's step-mother came next and gave me the name "Garev," another great warrior also from my father's clan. My mother's relatives and clan members also came and placed their blessings on me by also giving me names that represented the prominent men in our clan. These name-giving episodes were each accompanied with gifts and food for the new mother and the child. By the end of all the initial visits to my mother, my list of names was well into the double digits. After a month or so in the labor ward, my mother and I were allowed to return to our home. More name-giving occurred as the male members of both my father's and mother's clans began to pay their visits. Giving names to a newborn child in my Murik society in the East Sepik province of Papua New Guinea signifies a very important beginning for me as an individual. It determined that I was a valued individual of the two clans I was born into.

As a child growing up in that society, I was called upon by my many names. Whenever I came in contact with my relatives, they always called me by their particular clan names. And when I was able to talk and understand, the elders from both my dad's and mum's clans told me about the significance and the status of the dead ancestors after whom I was named. For example, the name "Bagasim" was given to remind me that my grandmother came from a distant land to marry and resettled in my grandfather's village. My grandfather was a great warrior who traveled, fought, and made peace with villages afar. In one such adventure, he won the love of my grandmother and brought her to the place I now call home. The name my grandmother calls me links me to her ancestral lands and people. It is a heritage she wishes for me to keep and know. It is very much part of who I am. The name "Garev," on the other hand, is very much linked to power. I was expected to emulate the power of a great warrior ancestor. By constantly calling me by that name it reminded me to be brave and strong in times of trouble, that I have my great ancestor's blood running through my veins. This name made me an important member of my tribe or clan.

My clan, therefore, had an important responsibility of grooming me to be like the dead great ancestors whose names I now bear. All my elder male relatives, especially my mother's brothers, had the sole responsibility of passing on the cultural beliefs, norms, values, and patterns of behavior to me. Being the firstborn child of my father, as soon as I started eating solid food, my paternal grandmother took on the responsibility of being my guardian. I spent a lot of my childhood with her listening to her tell me lots and lots of legends. If my mum's relatives wanted to take me anywhere, they had to first obtain permission from my paternal grandmother. I come from a clearly patriarchal society and therefore my father's clan was the dominant authority in my upbringing. Nevertheless, my mum's clan still took an active role in shaping who I was and who I am today. They, too, told their stories and made sure that I was very well accounted for during my early childhood. In fact, my maternal uncles were revered as my role models for manhood. All my initiation ceremonies for manhood came directly under their responsibility.

Between the ages of three to five, my father started taking me to the *haus boi* (the men's spirit house). There I witnessed the greatest acts of oratory. The great men of all the village clans would march up and down the house floor and recite the historical battles our great ancestors fought and won. I was always amazed and felt proud to see my grandfathers take the floor and stake out their claims as well. The men's house was indeed the house of power. There the levels of power were clearly determined into three power categories: the elders, the middle-class, and the lower-class. Where you took your seat on the floor of the men's house was clearly determined by the rites and rituals an individual has previously undertaken and passed. The elders of the men's house were the chief examiners of such practices, and they also determined where you took your seat. Whenever men gathered for important occasions in the men's house, there was always food. Women cooked and brought the very best food to the men's house. This food was again distributed and consumed according to the power hierarchy in the men's house. The most powerful and important men (the elders) always consumed the very best food, the next best went to the middle-class, and the least powerful ate what was left over. As a young child, I quite often sneaked to where my grandfathers were seated in order to taste the kind of food they were consuming at such times. Another significant characteristic of the men's house was the obvious fact that it was "the spirit house." This fact was signified by the storage of some of the most ancient carvings and artifacts that are centuries old. A sacred flat form was built and attached to the roof immediately above the elders' section of the men's house. It was where all the sacred spiritual figures were kept secluded from the naked eyes. The presence of these spiritual figures made the men's house a place of honor and respect. All young boys were brought to the men's house to observe and learn these qualities of honor and respect for the elders. Severe discipline was also executed in the men's house. Young boys who broke the expected patterns of behavior were often brought into the men's house and flogged. To cry and scream in the men's house was a sign of a very weak person, and the young boys were taught to swallow hard their pains and face up to the beatings like a "real man." A young boy who hardly came to the men's house was generally labeled as still living "under his mother's grass skirt." Every young boy knew that to be labeled as such was shameful and derogatory, and thus every attempt was made to live up to expectations. By continually going to the men's house, I soon realized that not only was it a house of spirits, it was also my entire classroom in the village. The various *garamuts* (huge wooden drums) had their specific functions. The many messages that the specialized drummers beat out of them carried over many miles. Even individual clan leaders had their personal drum messages. For example, if such individuals were out of the village they could easily be called back immediately by sending out their personal drum messages. All the people in the village were quite familiar with two particular drum messages: firstly, the message to announce the death of a person; and secondly, the message of public curse for someone who was caught stealing. This particular drum message I will call the "ridicule of the bastard." Everyone in the entire village knew this drum message quite well and tried their best to avoid being cursed by its message. The former was obviously more frightening, especially if it is heard in the odd hours of any given day.

The men's house wasn't my only classroom. Outside of it my dad also continued his own responsibilities of passing on what I needed to learn and know. There were many learning activities my dad and I went through. I will now spend some time to focus on one that seems to stand out. This particular event is about the time I first learned to swim. I was about five years old when my dad put me in a canoe and we paddled to a shallow lake. We found a place where I could stand in the water with my head clearly above the water level. My dad turned the canoe upside down and then asked me to dive from one side of the canoe to the other. I was scared to dive on my own initially, so my dad took hold of my hand and we dived together for several times. After that I was able to do it on my own. My dad explained that this initial step of submerging in and out of the water was done to remove my fear of the water. In order to learn to swim, the beginning swimmer must first adapt to the natural learning environment. In addition to diving in the lake, my dad also took me to the beach many times to face the waves crashing on the beach. At times he would carry me into the sea and we would swim through the waves together. At other times he would let me play on my own and let the small waves roll over to where I was. All these encounters of the lake and the sea led toward my interest in swimming, and soon I quickly learned to swim.

My education in the village also came with a cost. My dad was both loving and firm, and he ruled his household with a firm hand. On one occasion he sent me to the store to buy him some tobacco, but on the way I accidentally lost his money for the tobacco. When I reported the matter to him, he got very angry and chased me with a spear. In fact, he actually speared me on my left thigh. Later on, as he got more involved in his missionary work, he became more loving and humble.

The many education experiences I received from my parents, grandparents, relatives, and the elders of the men's house are clearly the foundations that helped to determine who I am today. I continue to show a lot of respect for the village elders and all our beliefs and value systems. Even though my Western form of education puts me well above all my kinsmen, my place in the men's house still remains with the lower-class men. According to village customs, I must be initiated before I can really have any power to even address my kinsmen in the men's house. Right now, my Western education gives me no power in the men's house whatsoever. The issue of initiation is not mine to decide. It is the responsibility of my maternal uncles. In fact, after completing my graduate studies at Penn State, I will be seriously considering taking a leave from my job and returning to the village to prepare for my initiation. By then, the village elders will most likely view my successes in the West as relevant qualifications toward my village initiation. I view this village initiation as the missing link between my Western education and the indigenous education. In order for me to effectively use my education to help my kinsmen, I must first achieve the relevant means to really connect me to their day-to-day experiences and livelihood.

Personally, I am quite proud of the significant link I have maintained between the Western and the village lifestyles. From time to time I take leave from my work and return to my village. My kinsmen always look forward during such times to welcoming me home. Since I am married to a wife who comes from a far-off province, my visits to my village are quite limited. Since my marriage I have visited my wife's village more times than my own village. And as a father of four sons, I know deep down I have not prepared my own sons to live in my village. I hardly take them there as we generally spend most of our holidays in their mother's village. My four sons are more comfortable living in their mother's village than mine. Whenever an opportunity comes for me to take them to my village, I will have to quickly give them some sort of a survival lesson on how to withstand the public gaze from the village community. One great advantage they currently have is my dad, who does most of the teaching. But the problem now is that my father is aging and soon won't be around to pass on our village ways to his grandchildren. When God finally calls dad away to his eternal rest one day, so much of our traditions, values, and norms will die with him as most of our Melanesian knowledge exists in oral form.

Many parents in Papua New Guinea hardly take their children to their home villages during school term breaks or even during Christmas vacations. As a result, many urban children in Papua New Guinea grow up only in towns and cities. For such children a village way of life is meaningless and often boring. No wonder our towns and cities are now filled with unemployed youth. No Western school experience can teach our children to return to their villages. This is simply because the schools in the country strictly follow a prescribed formal school system from our colonial era.

What then can our schools do? What roles should school institutions in Papua New Guinea play? Can Western and indigenous forms of education be integrated into one system? The answers to such questions are hard to come by, and in order for us to locate some sort of response, we have to critically view the kind of educational system operating in Papua New Guinea. The country's education system must make a serious effort toward bridging the gap between the "Western knowledge" learned from our current schools and the "Melanesian knowledge" that is available in our village communities throughout Papua New Guinea. The current educational reforms taking place in the country must aim toward addressing the issues of integration between the Western and indigenous knowledge.

# CHAPTER ELEVEN

# PARENTS
# AS GUARDIANS
# OF THE MOTHER
# TONGUE

REBECCA BLUM-MARTÍNEZ, THE UNIVERSITY OF NEW MEXICO

It is parent-teacher conference week at the Alamo Elementary School in a major city of the Southwest with a very large, Latino population of mostly recently-arrived Mexicanos.[1] The fifth-grade teacher's parting words to her students is a reminder of the appointments she has made with their parents. Setting up these appointments is no easy task. The teacher must share the one phone in the teachers' lounge with forty other staff members who are also making arrangements to meet with the parents of their students. And these are made during the half-hour recess and lunch breaks, or in the evening after their workday is supposedly over. At the end of the week, she complains that many parents failed to show up. In the case of one child, an older brother—a known gang member—was sent as a substitute for the parents. "The trouble is these parents simply don't care," she tells me in a familiar refrain (Benjamin 1996).

Over the last twenty years, the focus on parental involvement in the schools has gained a great deal of attention, particularly in the case of language minority students (U.S. Department of Education 1992; Moll et al.

1992; Trueba 1989; Valdés 1996). Parental involvement has been identified as a positive factor in student achievement (U.S. Department of Education 1987; Olsen 1988; Soto 1988). Similarly, as test scores of language-minority students continue to lag behind those of their English-fluent counterparts, language-minority parents are often blamed for their children's lack of progress (Valdés 1996).

At one level, the "blame game" around language-minority students' academic failure is easy to understand. Politicians and the media would have the public believe that a disproportionate amount of money is being spent on special programs for the education of language-minority students (Meyer 1988; Crawford 1989). When there is no dramatic rise in test scores despite these programs, school systems are blamed, particularly the teachers who work with them. The teachers, in turn, frustrated often by their own lack of knowledge about language-minority children, blame the children's parents.

Those who have worked in this area know that these educational issues are quite complex, and far exceed the parents' sphere of influence. There are cultural discontinuities between the children's culture and that of the school (Valdés 1996; Heath 1986). There are sociopolitical and economic realties that often conspire to maintain social inequalities found outside the schools' walls within them (Ogbu 1986). And there are sociolinguistic issues that are also involved (Labov 1982; Zentella 1988; Cummins 1995; Benjamin 1997). But it is easy to blame the parents given their absences at parent-teacher conferences and at school gatherings.

In this article I argue that most language-minority parents are quite involved in their children's lives, and their children's schooling, but that school personnel fail to see this. In some cases teachers and administrators are simply unaware of what is happening in the homes of their students. In other instances, parents define involvement differently than do teachers. More fundamentally, however, there is a basic difference in goals. While educators see academic achievement as the primary means to a better life, the vision that the parents have for their children's future is not limited to successful schooling. I describe two very different groups of parents and the vision they hold for their children. The strategies they have employed, and the changes they have made to ensure this vision are frequently unrecognized by the school. Language-minority parents care about their children's schooling, but they are also concerned with their children's continued membership in their families and in their culture. They also worry about their children's ability to succeed in the world of work (Valdés 1996). A fundamental skill needed for these contexts is fluency in the native language—something the schools will not, or cannot, provide.

I present two scenarios of parental involvement in guarding the mother tongue, one of immigrant Mexicanos in an urban setting and the other of American Indians in rural areas. In both places there is a great deal of concern for the maintenance of the native language. In each setting, however, the strategies that have been adopted reflect cultural, historical, and structural differences of the locales in which they live.

# EL ROBLE: A MEXICANO COMMUNITY

El Roble[2] is a large urban neighborhood in a major city of the southwestern United States. The presence of Mexicano immigrants has been noted since the turn of the century (Portes and Bach 1985). In the last twenty years, the number of Mexicanos has increased dramatically (U. S. Census 1992). As in other "daughter" Mexicano communities in the United States, El Roble has close ties to a specific "sending" region in Mexico, where most of the immigrants have originated (Portes and Bach 1985). Similarly, the migration of Mexicanos to El Roble is characterized by what is called "revolving door" migration. During the course of a worker's lifetime, there may be an average of four to five trips to the daughter community in the United States for a period of roughly one to two years. In the interval, the men go home to Mexico to do seasonal work. Over time, these men may migrate more permanently to the United States, with their wives, or they may form families while in the United States. Mexicano immigrants usually follow brothers, sisters, or other relatives who have settled more permanently. Nevertheless, returns to Mexico are frequent and often lengthy (they can stay up to four months at a time). Many of them plan to return to Mexico for a permanent stay once they have enough money saved to buy land or a small business. In the interim, their children—whether they have been born in Mexico or the United States, or whether their mothers are American or Mexican—are sent to Mexico during vacations.

In El Roble, many of the fathers of Mexicano families are employed either by permanent settlers from the sending communities or by Chicanos who speak Spanish. Although the fathers are usually more exposed to English than the mothers, many of them work with other Spanish speakers. If the mothers work, it is usually alongside their relatives who have been here a little longer; in restaurants, hotels, and factories. Their immediate working world speaks Spanish. If they stay at home, Spanish is the medium of communication—in the stores, the Laundromats, churches, and so on. The exception is the school, where Spanish is used only as a means of rapid transition to English, and where their children are encouraged to use English exclusively.

Luz, Adela, and Caridad all live in El Roble. Luz is thirty-two, married, with two daughters, Elisa and Nora, and a homemaker. Adela, also married, is about the same age, with three children: Lorena, Mayra, and Cristina. Adela is receiving disability compensation after suffering an accident at a meatpacking plant where she was employed. Caridad is in her mid-fifties. She is married and has had nine children. They range in age from eight to thirty-two. Caridad stays at home, but takes in blanket piecework in order to supplement the family income.

Each of these women wants their children to succeed in school, to know English well, and to achieve more in their lives than they themselves have. With this in mind, they have adopted specific strategies to help their children succeed in school. All three women are very vocal about the opportunities their daughters have for a better life in the United States because of the perceived advantages women have for education and equality. But this awareness or the desire for their children to succeed in the English-speaking world does not diminish their desire for their children to continue speaking Spanish. For this reason they have adopted certain measures to ensure that.

When Luz and her family first arrived in El Roble, Nora and Elisa were placed in a day care center so that Luz could work. Elisa was placed in a class with Spanish-speaking teachers. Three-year-old Nora was not so lucky. After several months, Luz and Elisa realized that Nora was losing her ability to speak and understand Spanish. Luz's reaction was definitive. She asked to be placed on the night shift at her work, and during the day she began reteaching her daughter Spanish. She said about this experience, *"Entonces dije nó, éso no está bien. Ella no me entiende. Ni yo me puedo comunicar con ella, ni ella conmigo porque no hablábamos lo mismo. Entonces le dije, ¡ Nó! vamos a empezar a enseñarte lo que debes saber. Decirle, enseñarle, ésto se llama así. Lo repetía. Y así poco a poco hasta que volvió a agarrar su lengua de ella."* ("I said no, this is not right. She doesn't understand me. I can't communicate with her and she can't (communicate) with me, because we didn't speak the same. So I said, 'No, we are going to start teaching you what you should know ... to tell her, show her, this is called this.' And that was the way, little by little, until she began to grasp her own language again") (Benjamin 1994).

After this experience, and once her husband was making a more comfortable salary, Luz decided to stay at home and increased her efforts on behalf of Nora and her sister. She devised a prize system for good grades for her daughters and nieces, volunteered at Nora's school, and became an active

PTO parent. In terms of Spanish-language maintenance, she had her daughters read to her one half-hour in Spanish every afternoon. She took them to the Spanish language library once a week. She found them Spanish-language pen pals and was always vigilant of their grammar and word usage in Spanish.

Adela and Caridad have each made certain adjustments in their lives as well so that their children can succeed in school. Adela, who has more schooling than Caridad, checks her children's homework every evening to make sure it's complete, even though she doesn't understand enough English to know what it says. She buys her daughters English-language books and encourages them to write in English on weekends or during vacations. Adela has taught her daughters how to read and write in Spanish. For several months when Lorena was first learning to read in English, Adela sat with her in the evenings and taught her to read and write in Spanish. She has since done the same with her younger daughter. In addition, besides purchasing Spanish-language books, she purposely puts Lorena in situations where she must read or write in Spanish. For example, she makes Lorena read any correspondence from Mexico aloud to her with the pretext that she is not feeling well enough to read it herself on account of her disability. When Lorena's grandfather comes from Mexico, Lorena becomes his companion, translating for him and being his scribe when he writes letters home. It could be argued that translations are not the best way to maintain a language (Wong Fillmore 1982). Nevertheless, these are strategies that Adela and her husband have consciously adopted to help their daughters maintain Spanish. Finally, when they go to Mexico, they do not assist their daughters in any way in any communication or transactions that take place, telling them they must be able to say anything they need to on their own.

Caridad has purposely never worked outside the home so that she can dedicate herself completely to the housework and thereby free her children to do their schoolwork and succeed. She does not ask her children to help her with the housework until their homework is done. Caridad volunteers in the Chapter One room and the clothing bank at her children's elementary school. She believes that the best way to raise her children is through example and the giving of advice. Therefore, in comparison to Luz and Adela, her strategies appear less proactive. Giving advice may be more important to Caridad because of her age or more rural background. She often recalls the good advice she received from her parents and how it has guided her to this day. Therefore, this is the strategy she often employs with her children. In terms of the maintenance of Spanish, she says, *"Yo me creo, que uno de madre o de padre tiene que inculcarles, día trás día y momento trás momento que no pierdan su idioma. Que así como aprendieron el inglés, que es muy bonito, entonces que sigan también con su español. Por que para mí, se me hace que con esos dos idiomas en cualquier parte pueden trabajar, con cualquier persona pueden hablar."* ("I think that as a mother or father, one has to instill in one's children, day after day, moment by moment that they not lose their language. In the same way that they learned English, which is very pretty, they have to keep up their Spanish. Because for me, I think that with those two languages they can work anywhere and talk to anyone.")

Caridad, Adela, and Luz never lose sight of their responsibility to prepare their children for the world of work. They recognize, given the characteristics of Mexicano migration, that working may mean either a return to Mexico, or at the very least the necessity of communicating with future migrants. These are very realistic and hard-nosed reasons for wanting their children to continue using the language. But there are other reasons for this desire that are just as compelling. One of them is that the children must be able to speak the language so that they can maintain relationships with their relatives, grandparents, aunts, uncles and cousins living in the United States and in Mexico. The family continues to be very important. Luz talked about this as she described the case of one family where the older son had lost his ability to speak Spanish: *"El que viene de México no habla español, nada. Estos niños se los trajeron chiquitos aquí. Ellos aprendieron inglés muy bien ... La señora no habla inglés. El muchacho nacido aquí él es el que habla español entonces la mamá le tiene que preguntar a su hijo qué dice el otro hijo para poder entender. (Es) negativo en el sentido de que él viene de una cultura hispana y tiene que aprender su lengua. Buena o mala, tiene que aprender su lengua para poder comunicar. Si él tiene familiares en México ¿cómo se va a comunicar ? ... en México no hay mucha gente que hable inglés ... Tiene que saber comunicarse con las personas —simplemente con su mamá."* ("The one who comes from Mexico doesn't speak Spanish, nothing. These kids were brought her very young. They learned English really well; their mother doesn't speak English. The one that was born here is the one who speaks Spanish, so the mother has to ask her son what the other one is saying so she can understand. [This] is negative in the sense that he comes from a Hispanic culture and he must learn his language. Good or bad he has to learn his language to be able to communicate. If he has relatives in Mexico, how will he communicate with them? In Mexico, not many people speak English. He has to know how to communicate with people, more simply with his mother.")

But even as Luz discusses the importance of maintaining a relationship with family, there are allusions to another, more intangible reason for maintaining Spanish: its role in personal and ethnic identity. For Luz, the fact that the boy she is referring to comes from a Hispanic culture means that he must know his language. *"Buena o mala tiene que aprender su lengua."* (Good or bad he must learn his language.) In conversations with Caridad about the importance of Spanish-language maintenance, she says very similar things: *"A mí en lo personal me da tristeza, ... porque si saben el español entonces a mí sí me da tristeza que lo pierdan. Yo he visto en muchos casos que se avergüenzan del español y no lo deben de hacer. Nada menos que mi hijo, él habla el español pero sus amigos, todo, es de puro inglés. Entonces a mí en lo personal, a mí me da tristeza porque él es mexicano y él sabe español. Pero no debe de negar su origen, no debe de negar su idioma, no debe de negar sus costumbres. Entonces yo les inculco, No se avergüencen de su origen y que no se avergüencen. Porque es muy bonito decir, 'Yo soy mexicana.' Que no nieguen su origen, y que no olviden su idioma, ni sus costumbres."* ("Personally, it makes me very sad ... because if they know Spanish and lose it, it is very sad. I have seen a lot of cases where they are ashamed of Spanish and they shouldn't be. Just in the case of my son, he speaks Spanish, but his friends, everything is all English. So personally, it makes me sad, because he's Mexican and he knows Spanish. But he shouldn't deny his origins, he shouldn't deny his language, he shouldn't deny his customs. So I try to instill in them, don't be ashamed of your origins. Don't be ashamed. Because it's beautiful to say, I am Mexican. Don't deny who you are. Don't forget your language, nor your customs.")

Adela, Luz, and Caridad all believe that the ability to speak Spanish is necessary for their children. However, because of their relative newness to the area and because of the particular configurations of these communities, they have no ties or connections structurally to any of the institutions in the community—the schools, churches, or other social organizations—to effect broader changes for a large number of children. They work at helping their own children, but in a very real sense they work alone.

# PUEBLO COMMUNITIES OF THE SOUTHWEST: AN INDIGENOUS SCENARIO

In the American Indian Pueblo societies of New Mexico, the people have lived continuously in the same area for many centuries (Sando 1992). The ties to the land are both historic and religious. Autonomous governments which reflect native forms of government are in place, still adhered to, and deeply respected by tribal members (Sando 1992; Benjamin et al. 1996).

Social and religious organizations are very much intact which tie people to each other through various forms of kinship and shared responsibility (Sando 1992; Suina 1990). In addition, these are generally small communities of several thousand people living in a rural area but within one to three hours from a city. The Pueblo people in New Mexico speak five distinct languages. Among most of these tribes there is a deep concern for the preservation of language and culture. This concern has been heightened by the erosion of the native languages in persons younger than thirty. Presently, there are efforts under way in several of these communities to preserve and revitalize the language. Below, I describe the strategies and initiatives that have been undertaken in two different Pueblo communities.

Joseph lives with his wife and three daughters in one of the more traditional Pueblos. He was raised in a Keres-speaking home and did not learn English until he went to school. He participated in most of the religious and cultural activities of the village throughout his childhood. After a few years in the army, Joseph and his wife came home to raise a family. When Joseph's first daughter was in the local Head Start program, he was heartened to see that her teachers were using the native language with her and the other children and were teaching them some of the dances and other cultural activities. He became an active volunteer in his daughter's school. During this same time, Joseph's wife, who had been raised outside the village, was becoming involved in the religious and social societies of the community. She therefore had to learn the language. In order to avoid a similar situation with their children, he and his wife made a conscious decision that Joseph should start using the native language exclusively with their children. In addition, they moved their younger daughters from an English-speaking day care center to a native-language-speaking day care environment. However, when their first daughter moved from the Head Start program to the BIA elementary school in the village, they discovered that there was no use of Keres in the school and that, in fact, its use was discouraged by the principal and the non-Indian teachers who worked there. Joseph then became involved in the local PTO organization to see how he could influence these practices. After several years, he ran successfully for the local school board. Over the course of several years, Joseph was able to convince the other school board members, all of whom were from his community, to begin planning for a native-language program.

Joseph recalls that it was his daughter's attendance at Head Start and his wife's growing involvement in the social and religious life of the community that brought to mind his own upbringing:

"Then that's where I realized as I sat back and thought about when I was just a kid and dancing ... when everything was over, they used to give us lectures all the time, those older folks. They used to sit and tell us, 'You kids, keep up your language, let your hair grow ... that's who we are ... this is us. If you don't keep it up, if you don't keep up the language, if you don't keep up the hair, you're going to lose it. And you're gonna lose who you are, what we are, because it's not written. There's no way we can turn back and read up, turn a page and find out this is how you do it. If you don't maintain what we have now, we'll just start losing it, and then we'll lose it all.' That's what was preached when I was a kid. And that's what I realized as I sat there."

The wisdom of the elders and Joseph's personal situation of being the only parent in the house to speak the language are what spurred him to action, to ask that the language be reinforced at school.

In Joseph's community, as in the situations of Luz, Adela, and Caridad, there are both practical and other reasons for maintaining the language. In order to participate in most activities in the tribe, people must be able to speak the native language fluently. In addition, in order to know their history, people must be able to understand songs, narratives, and certain practices that are all based on the language. This is especially crucial in an oral society as the elders pointed out to Joseph and the other young people. Without a sense of history, of culture, and most importantly, religious practice, there can be no maintenance of what is, for them, a Pueblo way of life.

As in the case of the Mexicanas, what appears crucial is the role of language in ethnic and personal identity (Smolicz 1989). Joseph speaks again:

They used to tell us, "You parents, you Mom and Dad. You, you're the ones that are responsible to teach your kids the language and basically what is involved in the household, what's expected of you. We as a group, we as a group, we are responsible for keeping things like the dances going and that's where the kids learn. You fathers are responsible for taking your sons over to where there's a dance going on so they can see and learn, so they can be a part of it, put it in their heads, this is what's supposed to happen. So everything is connected. We try to live how we preach. It has to be a community affair because if we lose our language we lose who we are. What makes us different is our language. What makes us (Pueblo) is us speaking our language."

A few miles down the road, there is another Pueblo community of about the same size as Joseph's village. Although it is less traditional, there is a deep concern for the loss of the native language among the younger members of the tribe. The Tribal Council has formed an Education Task Force that is charged with looking after the educational well-being of the tribe. In this community, there is a strong cohort of college-educated people, many of whom sit on this Task Force, and all of whom are parents. Over the years, they have tried repeatedly to dialogue with the public school district which serves them to become more culturally and linguistically sensitive to their needs and expressed goals. But this has been difficult.

For example, at one of the Task Force's meetings with a public school representative, the school district employee bemoaned the lack of participation by parents in school affairs. When she was reminded that the Task Force members, who were the official representatives for the tribe at the school, had been present at most school functions, she dismissed it because not all members had children of elementary school age. It appeared that what the school staff desired was the presence of individual parents. The tribe, on the other hand, believed they were being proactive by appointing a group to speak on behalf of all of the parents.

Similarly, the Task Force began implementing a native-language revitalization program within the community for the children who no longer spoke their heritage language. The link between language and the continuation of their culture was of utmost importance. "Language is the essence of our existence, our spiritual being." Over and over again, the Task Force members talked about the need to involve the children in the central aspects of their community life, and about the tensions between their traditional way of life and that of mainstream society. "We need to turn our children around. It's difficult for them to understand the inner, spiritual rewards of our life versus the material rewards of the greater society."

Establishing the language revitalization program was a complex and labor-intensive job. Meetings were held once a week and often lasted for five to six hours. Fluent native-language-speaking adults underwent intensive training in order to become language teachers. Community meetings were held with all age groups to get their input. All of this work was sponsored and funded by the Tribal Council, for the benefit of the children of the community (Benjamin et al., 1996). And yet, many of the teachers in the public school continued to claim that the parents did not care.

Likewise, in the communities where Luz, Adela, and Caridad lived, one could hear teachers and staff complaining about the parents. For them, it was not important that Luz and Caridad walked their children to school and back every day. They did not see the sacrifices that those women made by changing work schedules, forgoing an additional income, teaching them to read and write in Spanish, and teaching through example and advice.

Because their behavior did not conform to the expectations of the schools, they were labeled as uncaring parents (Valdés 1996).

While these scenarios describe a very small sample of language-minority parents, they point to the implicit responsibility parents feel to prepare their children for the future. Valdés's descriptions of Mexicano families reveal a preoccupation with preparing the children for the world of work (1996). Similarly, Moll et al. describe the many ways in which Latino families share their knowledge of the world (1990). Language-minority parents know that their children's future includes both worlds, the one they have come from and the one represented by the school (Valdés 1996; Moll et al. 1996).

For this reason, they realize that the schools have only been able to do half the job. The schools have concentrated on teaching English, on the development of academic skills and information that children will need to succeed in mainstream society. But who will prepare the children for a successful life in their communities, where different skills are needed and other values are held (Wong Fillmore 1991)? And who will help these children form healthy identities (Benjamin 1997)?

The pressures to perform well academically seem to have overridden all other concerns in the schools. Administrators and teachers are especially sensitive to these pressures, and appear to have developed a blindness to those other aspects of a student's life that do not directly involve the school. When my son was preparing for his bar mitzvah, his English teacher complained that he was not completing all of his homework. When I explained all of the studying my son had to do in preparation for his bar mitzvah, his teacher commented that it was too bad that this event got in the way of the children's education, and wondered if it wouldn't be better not to have a bar mitvah, or at the least to postpone it until the summer! Seemingly, anything that does not place successful schooling as the first priority is suspect.

Ultimately, it is the children who must decide what direction to take in their lives. The contrast between their parents' vision and that of the school puts many language-minority children in a bind (Benjamin 1997). Some lose the mother tongue in an effort to become part of the mainstream (Wong Fillmore 1991). Others, like some of the children in the Pueblo communities I have described, avidly seek to learn and retain it. Some find other ways of resisting the system (Fordham and Ogbu 1986; Weinberg 1994; Matute-Bianchi 1989).

After knowing Nora, one of Luz's daughters, for more than a year, I asked her about the apparent gap that existed between the school's objectives and those of her mother. At that time Nora was only nine years old. Already, however, she was aware that her mother and the teachers in her school disagreed on a fundamental issue. She answered, "I say, believe in my mother. Because, mothers are, they know every time what could happen to you or what could not. Right now here at this school, they don't know if I could go back to Mexico or not. They don't know. I don't want to forget Spanish, because that's the language I was born with. They can't just take it or forget it … It's important to keep it."

## NOTES

1   The term "Mexicano" is being used here to refer to those people either born in Mexico, or those born into families from Mexico.
2   El Roble, here, actually represents two different communities in the southwestern United States. There are sufficient similarities between them, in terms of the Mexicano population, to permit me to combine them into one community for the purposes of this article (Benjamin 1996).

# PART THREE

# PROMISING

# PRACTICES

# CHAPTER TWELVE

# ON THE

# THRESHOLD

# OF BILITERACY

## A FIRST-GRADER'S PERSONAL JOURNEY

MARÍA DE LA LUZ REYES, UNIVERSITY OF COLORADO-BOULDER

LISA COSTANZO, UNIVERSITY OF COLORADO-BOULDER

## INTRODUCTION

A common and perhaps narrow interpretation of Cummins's (1981, 1996) minimum threshold hypothesis and linguistic interdependent theories forms the crux of the theoretical framework for bilingual education. It posits that to avoid negative cognitive effects, children must be solidly grounded in their primary language *before* embarking on a second language. The logical implication is that teaching a second language before a child has acquired the first would *not* be advisable. An extension of this implication is that it would be equally reckless to introduce *literacy* in *two* languages. The findings from the report on *Improving Schools for Language Minority Students* (August and Hakuta 1997) support the notion that "reading instruction in a language not yet mastered orally ... is too great a cognitive challenge for most learners" (59).

Among the majority of bilingual educators, the prevailing view is that the simultaneous introduction of two graphophonic systems would seriously jeopardize a child's development of literacy. In many school districts across the country, debates still rage over whether Spanish-speaking students should learn to read and write in their native language or be immersed in English. But what about children who embark on a *biliteracy* journey on their own initiative? What do they gain, or lose? Are the warnings warranted, or are they simply conclusions based on labels for bicultural children that may not always be useful or appropriate? Moll and Dworin (1996), who have written about biliteracy among elementary school children, suggest that the terms such as *native language* and *second language learners* are not useful constructs in bilingual contexts where literacy in two languages is taking place simultaneously.

In this chapter we present an ethnographic case study of a first-grader on the threshold of biliteracy. We use the term "biliteracy" to mean some degree of mastery of the fundamentals of speaking, reading, and writing (e.g., sound-symbol connections, conventions of print, accessing and conveying meaning through oral or print mode, etc.) in two linguistic systems. Central to this is constructing meaning by making relevant cultural and linguistic connections between print and the learner's own lived experiences. In addition, it includes the learner's view of literacy as a means of accessing others' perceptions of the world and what they have written (Wallace 1989).

# BACKGROUND ON THE CASE STUDY

This case study is part of María de la Luz Reyes' longitudinal study of the development of bilingualism and biliteracy in the primary grades. The theoretical framework for the research is based on a Freire's (1985) and Vygotsky's (1978) critical sociocultural view of language and literacy; that is, that language and literacy are more than speaking, reading, and writing. Moreover, their development is affected by the world in which meaning is constructed, particularly by the larger social context of learning in the home, school, and classroom. We also consider the learner's own view of self as a learner, as well as her effort and motivation, to be important influences. Like O'Loughlin (1992), we believe that "each student possesses multiple frames of reference with which to construct knowledge by virtue of their ethnic background, race, class, gender, language usage, religious, cultural, and political identities" (5).

Data were collected from weekly classroom observations over a period of eighteen months, from the second semester of her kindergarten year through the end of first grade.[1] Besides analyzing field notes and videotapes, writing samples in both languages were collected and scored holistically using a developmental rubric. These were analyzed for content, form, and bidirectional transfer of literacy skills. We used Cortés's (1986) Contextual Interaction Model as a framework for analyzing the influences of the larger sociocultural context, the home, the school, and the classroom on the student's emerging biliteracy. By adapting Cortés's model to reflect the sociocultural contexts specific to the focal student, the model elucidates the factors that directly or indirectly influenced her biliteracy.

# LUCIA[2]

Six-year-old Lucia is the second daughter of native Spanish speakers. Her father was born in Guatemala but raised in the United States, and her mother is from Perú. Lucia describes herself as being from "Perú-Guatemala." Like her mother, she has long, shiny, straight hair framing her round, smiling face. Also, like her parents, Lucia is a native Spanish speaker with bilingual proficiency. Lucia loves to read. Clearly, this delight began at home, listening to her parents, grandparents, and older sister read. Later, it was in school, in environments that nurtured biliteracy, that she began to blossom in reading and writing on her own.

## Home Influence

Academic achievement, bilingualism, and biliteracy are very important to Lucia's family. Since she was a baby, both parents have read to her daily—her mother in Spanish and her father in English and Spanish. Because her parents are bilingual, bicultural, and biliterate, they have created a home with opportunities for her to develop her own bilingualism and biliteracy. When they lived in the South, her parents knew no Spanish speakers. Afraid that their daughters would lose their Spanish language, Lucia's parents began paying them for speaking Spanish as part of their allowance. Lucia's mother explained to us how this payment system worked: "*Nosotros vamos contando qué días nos hablaron español y cuál hablaron inglés.*" ("We count which days they speak to us in Spanish and which days in English.") "*Obediencia paga dies centavos, hablar español dies centavos ... y ... rocoger su cama cinco centavos.*" ("Obedience pays ten cents, speaking Spanish ten cents, and making their bed five cents.") Although their older daughter had begun school in a monolingual English program, and most of their books were in English, both she and Lucia continued speaking and understanding Spanish. To this day Lucia's parents still pay their daughters ten cents a day for speaking Spanish. Maintaining their Spanish language is viewed as simply another family expectation—just like other household responsibilities.

Lucia's allowance is not her only incentive to speak Spanish. Her maternal grandparents, monolingual Spanish speakers, live with them. Lucia herself says it is important for her to speak Spanish because they speak "only a little English." She identifies with being bilingual and views it as a natural process, stating that she expects her new baby brother will speak "both" [Spanish and English] like the rest of the family.

## School Setting

Lucia attends Williams Elementary School, located just outside a large urban center in Colorado. At the time of the study, the school boasted an enrollment of about 600 students, 45 percent of whom were of Mexican origin, and 61 percent of whom received free or reduced lunch. The bilingual program within this K-5 school is transitional, with one designated bilingual classroom per grade, totaling about 125 students.

In general, the bilingual program model includes an alternate-day approach: Spanish one day, English another. Rather than emphasize the transition from Spanish to English, teachers expect children to be able to follow instruction in both languages according to the target language of the day. Although all the bilingual classes adhere to this structure, its exact implementation varies from class to class. For example, Lucia's kindergarten teacher followed this alternation religiously, but the first grade teacher did not; she used English nearly 80 percent of any given day.

# CLASSROOM INSTRUCTION

## Kindergarten

Kindergarten consisted of two full days on Tuesdays and Thursdays and every other Friday. Mrs. Bravo, Lucia's teacher, carefully structured children's language and literacy experiences. On Tuesdays, instruction was in Spanish, Thursdays in English, and Fridays varied, sometimes half-day Spanish/half-day English, or the language varied by subject. Regardless of the language of the day, children's formal reading instruction was conducted in the child's dominant language.

Lucia was placed in English reading instruction. Despite the fact that at the time Mrs. Bravo was completing a master's degree in whole language literacy, her reading instruction was heavily phonics-based. As a native Spanish speaker, she told us she instructed "based on the knowledge [she] had of how [she] learned Spanish, [she] started with the syllables, vowels first, and then syllables, and then words with syllables" (Interview April 9, 1997). She lamented that there were not enough literature books in Spanish. She relied on making photocopies but was concerned that it "[was] not the same as having a REAL book." The English speakers, including Lucia, started reading before the Spanish speakers. Mrs. Bravo believed this was because there were so many more books available to children in English.

## First Grade

Lucia's first grade teacher, Mrs. Norman, provided reading in students' native language. Initially, Lucia was placed in the English literacy group. Soon, however, she expressed that she "felt sad" she was not writing or reading in Spanish. Her mother, a bilingual paraprofessional in the same school, also expressed concern over this. To accommodate Lucia's needs, Mrs. Norman gave Lucia the option to read and write in either language, encouraging her to do so in English on English days and Spanish on Spanish days. Although Mrs. Norman was neither a native nor a fluent Spanish speaker, she valued and supported her students' bilingualism.

In general, both Lucia's kindergarten and first grade teachers created a safe learning environment where students could experiment with both languages. This encouragement and freedom to choose their language of instruction nurtured students' voice, enabling them, to some extent, to participate in the direction of their own learning. In both classrooms, children were immersed in social interactions with their peers where they could learn from others. Although it is not clear whether this "space" for social interaction was intentional or not, it provided children the opportunity to help each other with both languages and to experiment with reading and writing in Spanish or English as they so desired. This structure promoted bilingualism and biliteracy as "normal" and even fun. In fact, on some occasions the children seemed to promote each other's biliteracy more than the teachers did. Both teachers recognized Lucia's own initiative and curiosity about language and literacy. Their "additive" approach to bilingualism allowed Lucia to speak, read, and write in both languages, underscoring the belief that both languages are legitimate, of equal value for learning purposes, and constitute the intellectual culture of the classroom. As Moll and Dworin (1996) have found, "in these learning contexts, biliteracy clearly represents a particularly powerful means for thinking, strategic tools for gaining access to important social and cultural resources" (214).

# LUCIA'S BILITERACY DEVELOPMENT

As a kindergartner, Lucia was one of only two students speaking and reading two languages. As early as March of her kindergarten year, Lucia's writing demonstrated writing conventions far ahead of her grade level, such as sentences and correct spelling. Figure 12.1 shows her kindergarten writing.

## Figure 12.1: Lucia's Kindergarten Writing Sample

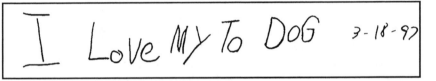

By the first semester of first grade, Lucia was reading in both Spanish and English at a mid–second grade level. Her writing had progressed to express complex ideas, cause and effect, the use of pronouns as well as invented and conventional spelling. Figure 12.2 is a sample of Lucia's English writing. In this example, Lucia expressed three complete thoughts in simple sentences using the conjunction "and" as a cohesive device to link the narrative.

Note that the English story begins with a capital letter, but has no period at the end. All the words are spelled correctly, including words that contain vowel digraphs (*ea* in "bread," and *ie* in "died"), which are normally confusing for first graders. Lucia's handwriting is clear; the letters are well formed, each sitting on the appropriate base line. The letters, *l, d, f, h, I, b, d,* and *t* extend to the top line as they should, and the *g* and *y* hang below the base line. Even more impressive is Lucia's ability to use the pronoun "it" to substitute for the subject, goldfish, rather than repeating the subject, as is common for most 6-year-olds. The use of the antecedent signals an under-

## Figure 12.2: Lucia's First Grade English Writing

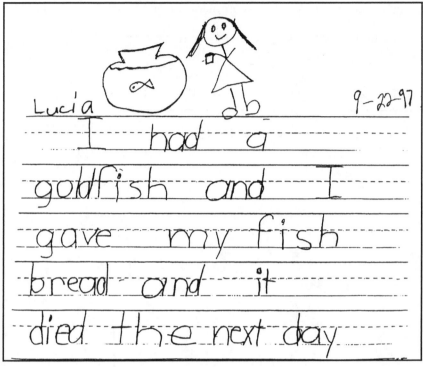

Lucia    9-22-97

I had a
goldfish and I
gave my fish
bread and it
died the next day

standing of complex structures. Her illustration enhances the story, focusing precisely on the main action: feeding the fish.

In contrast, in her Spanish story, Lucia does not use a capital letter for her beginning sentence, but she does end with a period. (See Figure 12.3.)

This example suggests that Lucia is aware of the need to capitalize the beginning word in a sentence and use a period at the end of the sentence, but she may not have a firm grasp of this rule, or may be more focused on using the alternate language code. She fails to put accent marks over "*mamá*" and "*compró*," but she was not, after all, receiving any formal reading or writing instruction in Spanish! Lucia misspells "*fui*" [I went] and "*tienda*" [store], but her use of the phoneme /ye/ for /ie/ yields the same sound. This is a good strategy, but an incorrect choice. In contrast to the simple sentences used in her English narrative, this piece of writing consists of a complex-compound sentence—a structure not commonly used by children in first grade. The following is an analysis of the sentence structure (in English):

I went to the store (independent clause)

where they sell dogs (adverbial/dependent clause)

and my mother bought me two dogs (independent clause)

## Figure 12.3: Lucia's First Grade Spanish Writing

Although the Spanish narrative contains more errors in form than the English writing, the Spanish writing illustrates a more sophisticated use of language and grammar, suggesting that Lucia's knowledge of language structure is stronger in Spanish. Graves (1983) and others report that students often ignore form when they are focusing on complex constructions of writing, or on how to express their message. This does not mean that children do not know how to use a particular grammatical element, for example, but that they are not attending to it *at the time*. Given Lucia's work in both languages, we are fairly certain that if she were asked to reread her work, paying attention to capital letters and spelling, she would correct some of these errors. Note that Lucia *does* use the appropriate sociocultural conventions of written language in her use of dates: " 9-22-97" in English and "*jueves el 13 de noviembre* 1997" in Spanish. In all aspects, Lucia shows considerable bilingual proficiency and demonstrates developing control of the writing system (the graphophonic, syntactic, and semantic aspects) of not one, but *two* languages *at the same time*.

In another writing sample, Lucia assumed a third person voice to write about herself in a note to her teacher. As Figure 12.4 demonstrates, this required highly advanced abstract thinking, uncommon to most first graders. First, Lucia had to decide what she wanted to tell the teacher, then assume her mother's perspective to write about her daughter (herself). She is completely accurate in her use of voice, including signing the letter "Marisol," her mother's name.

## Figure 12.4: Lucia's Note to the Teacher

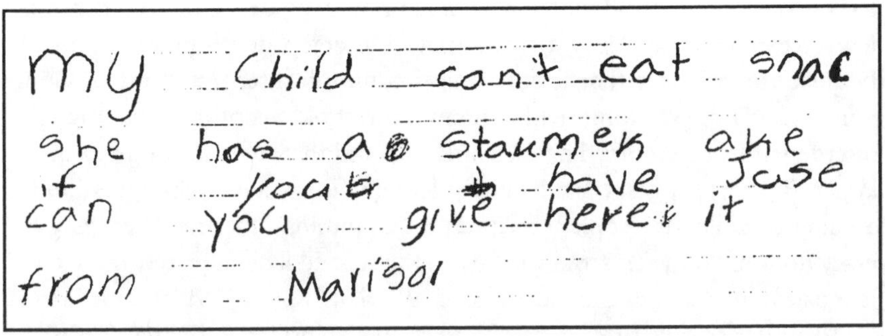
my Child can't eat snac
she has a Staumek ake
if you have Jase
can you give here it
from Marisol

# LUCIA'S READING CAPABILITY

In December of first grade, we asked students to select a book to read for us on video. As might have been expected, most students chose one at an emergent reading level, with simple pictures described with one or two words, or with repetitive text. We expected that Lucia would select a book in English because her reading instruction, and the majority of her writing, were in English. She surprised us by selecting one in English (*The Mystery of the Missing Peanut*) *and* one in Spanish, *Tikki Tikki Tembo* (Mosel 1994). Although a popular story in the primary grades, *Tikki Tikki Tembo* is a very difficult book requiring a high level of reading fluency. In Spanish, the text is even more difficult. It is a story situated in China, about two Chinese brothers. The first two sentences are: "*Hace muchos, muchísimos años, todos los padres y las madres de China tenían por costumbre poner nombres largos y complicados a sus honorables hijos primogénitos. Pero a los hijos menores casi no les daban ningún nombre*" (1). ("Once upon a time, a long, long time ago, it was the custom of all the fathers and mothers in China to give their first and honored sons great long names. But second sons were given hardly any name at all.") In spite of this difficult vocabulary, Lucia read confidently and clearly; she read familiar words quickly, slowed to decode new words, and even self-corrected.

# DISCUSSION

Lucia's biliteracy journey illustrates that given opportunity and choice (in a socioculturally supportive learning environment), children have the potential to become bilingual and biliterate *even* in primary grades. Until recently, very few researchers have investigated early biliteracy development, possibly because there is fear that it contradicts common interpretations of Cummins's (1981, 1996) long-held minimum threshold hypothesis and linguistic interdependence theory. The case of Lucia (and that of other students in the larger data set) suggests that language learning is not a linear progression for a bilingual child, as people may interpret Cummins's theories. Learning literacy not only transfers from the first to the second language, but the second language can also advance learning in the first. Reyes (1999) and Barrera (1998) refer to this process as "bidirectional transfer." Bilinguals' learning appears to be circular rather than linear. This seems to be the case with Lucia;

her literacy instruction in English facilitated her Spanish literacy and vice versa.

The analysis of Lucia's biliteracy development using Cortés's (1986) Contextual Interaction Model reveals that schools and classrooms that support bilingualism can mitigate the overriding negative view of bilingual education in society. Cortés's model examines the interaction of different sociocultural contexts that influence a student's academic performance. It rejects single-cause explanations to perceived outcomes. In explaining a child's academic performance in biliteracy, for example, it takes into account the multiple encapsulating layers of contexts in which biliteracy is situated.

The largest sociocultural context influencing Lucia's development of biliteracy is the US society, where English is viewed as preeminent and all other languages as subordinate. Mass media perpetuates negative views of bilingual education and of immigrant groups while promoting white middle-class culture. In contrast to this are the sociocultural contexts of family and specific educational and instructional factors of her school and classroom that may facilitate biliteracy and foster Lucia's own academic qualities. For example, Lucia's home strongly supports her bilingual and academic development. Not all the parents of Lucia's peers are biliterate, nor are they as focused on academics as Lucia's parents. In spite of these differences, these students, too, are emerging as bilingual and biliterate (Reyes 2001). We cannot assume, then, that coming from a biliterate family environment is *the* essential element in the development of biliteracy. In the case of Lucia and her peers, we believe that a significant, positive influence on the development of children's biliteracy has been their teachers, who have structured culturally relevant, receptive bilingual learning environments. For children like Lucia, the emergence of biliteracy in these supportive environments has occurred naturally and spontaneously.

Lucia's case also lends further support to the belief that "bilingual children exhibit greater sensitivity to linguistic meanings and may be more flexible in their thinking than are monolingual children" (Cummins 1996, 104). This may be because Lucia, like other bilinguals, has two words for the same idea. She also has two ways of expressing the same thought, accessing knowledge, relating to experiences, and playing with language. Additionally, she possesses two cultural sources from which to draw knowledge. In mastering two linguistic systems, a bilingual child like Lucia has had to decipher much more language than a monolingual child. Conceivably, she has had more practice in analyzing and constructing meaning. Because of this, Lucia and others like her can access knowledge from two linguistic sources, or they can use one language to bridge the other. It is clear that Lucia is an intelligent child whose bilingualism and biliteracy have enhanced her cognitive capabilities.

While the majority of research on bilingual education places primary importance on children's English development, this study reveals that for many children, "English proficiency" is only half of their potential. Lucia and children like her *thrive* in bilingual, biliterate environments. Lucia, like many of her Latino peers, arrives at school possessing the "seeds of biliteracy." She and her peers express curiosity in language, play with two languages constantly, and encourage each other to experiment with the use of two languages in a variety of forms. To encourage and value only these children's English language would stifle their expression and limit their experiences. With diversity in the United States on the rise, especially among Latinos, tomorrow's leaders need multiple channels of communication, multiple perspectives for relating to others. Children like Lucia have the potential and motivation to become fully developed bilingual, biliterate, and bicultural individuals. To fail to nurture their bilingualism, to purposefully discourage what is truly natural to them, is an unconscionable waste of human resources and goes counter to what we know will be best for them as adults.

Lucia and her peers provide evidence that developing their native language and native literacy does not detract from English literacy. On the contrary, bilingualism and biliteracy enrich their total experience in both Spanish and English. Had bilingual education not been available to Lucia, she most certainly would be working on grade level in English only, and by traditional standards, she would be considered successful. However, because she participates in bilingual education, in an environment nurturing and encouraging biliteracy, she does not have to give up anything. She can be successful in *both* English and Spanish. Given the benefits of bilingualism and the *natural* potential Lucia and children like her have to become biliterate, why should we settle for "less" when they can be so much more?

# NOTES

1   The authors are indebted to Eloise Andrade Laliberty, who contributed to the collection and analysis of data during the eighteen months of this case study. Without her support and dedication to the project, this collection would not have been completed.

2   Throughout the chapter we use the student's actual first name to match the presentation of her written data. All other names of persons or places are pseudonyms.

# CHAPTER THIRTEEN

# HERE

# THEY COME

## CREATING RICH LANGUAGE-LEARNING ENVIRONMENTS
## FOR CHINESE-SPEAKING KINDERGARTEN STUDENTS

JOFEN WU HAN, WESTERN MICHIGAN UNIVERSITY
GISELA ERNST-SLAVIT, WASHINGTON STATE UNIVERSITY

*"That's America!" Kirsten said happily. She stood*
*at the ship's railing with her friend Marta and pointed*
*to the green strip of land beyond the waves.*
*Overhead, the tall sails creaked in the wind.*
*Marta shaded her eyes and pressed against the*
*railing as though that would make the Eagle sail faster.*
*"I can't wait to walk on land again," she said, and shivered.*
MEET KIRSTEN: AN AMERICAN GIRL
(SHAW 1986, 1)

As shown in the above excerpt, the excitement of coming to America shared by two European girls in 1854 is still vivid for children who are now coming from the Eastern Hemisphere of the globe. Perhaps every child has thought that at the end of the halfway-around-the-world journey lies the reward of having a new home in a new land, with a life full of opportunities ahead. Probably not many children who come with their parents to the United States have ever imagined that their trip may mean starting school surrounded by a strange language and a new culture. This challenge is particularly true in College Hill, where families from all over the globe come to study.

During the 1994–1995 school year, six children whose native language was Mandarin Chinese started kindergarten in College Hill, a small college town located in the Pacific Northwest. Four children came from China and two from Taiwan; they were all joining their parents who were studying at a land-grant state university, which has long been the hub of College Hill.

Like many other districts throughout the United States, College Hill was not ready for the steady growth of language-minority students that has taken place in the last ten years. Most mainstream teachers are unprepared to teach ESL children along with native English-speakers, and administrators are not aware of the language and cultural needs of immigrant children. In the last three years, the number of ESL students in the district has averaged sixty to seventy students speaking twenty different languages attending kindergarten through high school; yet the only certified ESL teacher in the district does not hold a full-time position. One additional point needs to be made regarding native language instruction. Even though current research has demonstrated that the most effective programs for language-minority students are those which include cognitively academic instruction through students' first language (Thomas and Collier 1997), it appears certain that a district like College Hill will not be implementing a program that includes native language instruction for ESL students in the near future.

In the last years, a growing body of research has focused on understanding how language-minority students acquire English in school. One line of research considers how various classroom activities constitute an optimal environment for ESL students. In essence, studies in this area suggest that major factors determining whether a classroom is supportive toward second language acquisition include the quality and quantity of the language used by the teacher (Ernst 1994a; Guthrie and Guthrie 1987; Wong Fillmore 1982); the nature of the literacy practices in the classroom, such as using literature to encourage children to talk about and write about stories (Allen 1986; Ernst and Richard 1994; Han and Ernst-Slavit 1999; Lindfors 1989); and an understanding of students' cultural and linguistic backgrounds (Allen 1986; Fu 1995; Igoa 1995; Scarcella 1990). Although numerous studies have focused on the effectiveness of pedagogy, including teaching approaches and appropriate materials, very few studies have documented the initial behaviors and sense-making experiences of ESL children in an all-English environment. By documenting the newly arrived children's initial experiences to new school contexts, the present case study aims to shed light on the transition processes experienced by children as they learn English in all-English settings.

More specifically, this chapter describes the actions and interactions of six newly arrived children in both their mainstream kindergarten classroom and their pullout ESL program. The report focuses on the language behaviors of six Chinese-speaking children as they participate in four different language-learning contexts: (1) teacher-directed whole-class activities, (2) adult-assisted small-group activities, (3) free-choice activities at the "choice centers," and (4) the ESL classes. Results of the analysis document how a balance of these four diverse environments for language learning prepared these six Chinese-speaking children to transition to the first grade. It will be argued that language programs for immigrant students—whether bilingual or ESL—need to include the following four aspects: an ESL component to support the acquisition of English; a variety of opportunities to use the native language; a diversity of language-learning contexts; and an array of classroom environments where meaningful communication takes place. Data for a larger study, gathered during a two-year ethnographic study, included systematic classroom observations; students' works; classroom materials; in-depth interviews with teachers, parents, and students; review of school documents; and the regular classroom teacher's newsletters.

## THE COMMUNITY

The state university in College Hill, a Northwest rural town, has the greatest influence on the community. Because the university attracts many students from all over the world, it can be viewed as a small college town with an international community composed mainly of graduate students and their families. Like many other college towns in the United States, "community members share a rhythm of life set by the university calendar, and a common thread runs through the diverse lives of each family—the pressure of student life and the promise of a better life after obtaining a higher degree" (Willet 1995, 480).

## THE SCHOOL

Mountainview Elementary School is one of three elementary schools in the College Hill School District. Most of the students at Mountainview Elementary School come from the faculty, staff, and international students of the local university. Around twenty-five different countries are represented among the K–5 student body of approximately three hundred students on any given year. During the 1994–95 school year, forty-two children were learning ESL.

Mountainview Elementary School publications reveal that the reality of a diverse student body is recognized and valued at the administration level. According to the mission statement of the school, the faculty and staff "value the cultural/racial diversity" and "are committed to celebrating cultural diversity." In its efforts to address the reality of cultural diversity, the school has chosen the song "This Land Is Your Land" to represent its belief that cultural diversity enriches the individual and society.

# THE KINDERGARTEN CLASSROOM

Ms. Miller's kindergarten classroom occupied the last room at the end of a long hallway. Wall decorations, including big letters, numbers, signs of all sorts, and Sesame Street characters, indicated that the classroom was intended to be a print-rich environment. In addition, many of the signs and posters included terms and phrases in several languages—including those languages spoken at home by the students. A poster of the song "This Land Is Your Land" hangs on one wall.

A visitor to Ms. Miller's room might notice immediately that it is arranged for a variety of independent and small activities (see Figure 13.1). Ms. Miller planned her choice centers to "maximize learning, enable children to learn through play, and build all the self-study skills," according to the teacher's own words. Children could choose to work on computers, figure out puzzles, listen to tapes (audio center), build with Legos and blocks, play pretend (in the kitchen and doll center), and make puppets from brown lunch bags (make-and-take center). Five other choices (woodworking, music, paint, water/wheat, and Play-Doh centers) were set up in another room next to the classroom. When the time block for choice centers was in process, students were also allowed to play with building blocks or ride toy carts and bicycles in the hallway outside the classroom.

# THE STUDENTS

During the 1994 school year, Ms. Miller's kindergarten class included fourteen children who spoke English as their first language and ten children who came from homes where languages other than English were spoken. As

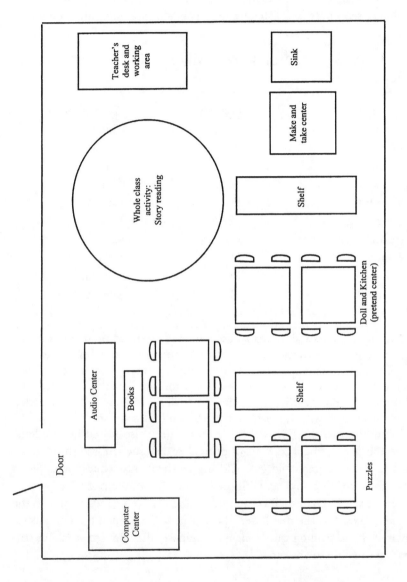

Figure 13.1: Classroom Floor Plan

illustrated in Table 13.1, there were six children whose first language was Mandarin Chinese. Ms. Madison, the ESL teacher, tested the ten ESL children early in September. The assessment focused on six areas: following commands, pointing to pictures, naming objects, repeating what the teacher says, completing sentences, and listening to a short story on tape and retelling.

## Table 13.1: ESL Children in Ms. Miller's Kindergarten Classroom

| Name | Gender | Home Country |
|------|--------|--------------|
| Pei-wen | F | China |
| Jin-yi | F | China |
| Wei-li | F | China |
| Guan-lin | M | China |
| Shao-min | F | Taiwan |
| Ning-ning | M | Taiwan |
| Insook | F | Korea |
| Abuda | M | Malaysia |
| Zelta | M | Malaysia |
| Raghu | M | Afghanistan |

During the assessment, Shao-min, who had attended preschool for one semester, was able to respond to most of the questions in all six areas. The other Chinese students, who arrived in the last three months, could not understand basic commands such as "Give me the pencil." Based on the assessment, the ESL teacher determined that all six Chinese children needed additional support with English via the ESL pullout program.

In addition to the ESL screening, Ms. Miller also tested her students early in the year. Using a concept-of-print checklist, she assessed students for print awareness. All ten children could answer the first two questions: "Show me the front of the book" and "Show me the back of the book." However, very few of the ESL children could understand the commands "Point to the title" and "Point to the first letter of the page." Even when the first author translated the remaining questions into Chinese, the Chinese-speaking students were unable to answer.

# THE DAILY SCHEDULE

There were two kindergarten classes, one in the morning and one in the afternoon. The ten ESL students were part of the afternoon kindergarten class, which started at 12:15 p.m. and ended at 2:55 p.m. The entire class period could be divided into relatively discrete segments of time in which certain activities regularly occurred. A typical day was as follows:

12:15–12:45  Choice centers (Monday through Thursday)

12:45–1:50   Whole group

12:45–1:45   Opening (ESL children go to ESL class)

1:15–1:35    Story time

1:35–1:50    Language (breaking into small groups)

1:50–2:00    Recess

2:00–2:15    Snack

2:15–2:45    Small-group science, math, language, reading activities

2:45–2:55    Closing, reflection, and line up for bus.

Everyday, as children arrived they lined up near the middle entrance of the school building. Then at 12:15 p.m., Ms. Miller or a teaching aide led the whole group into the classroom. Before children entered the classroom, they placed their backpacks into the lockers outside the classroom and inserted their name cards into the pockets of the attendance chart hung on the door. Then they "signed" their names at the table close to the entrance of the classroom. The act of signing meant that children tried to copy the letters in their names as written by the teacher. After they finished delineating the letters of their names, they immediately chose centers and immersed themselves in various activities. Songs signaled the transition of different time blocks. For example, when it was time to clean up, Ms. Miller said, "Clean up time," and asked children to "freeze" for a second. Then teacher and children sang the "clean up" song while children became busy putting things away.

# FOUR DIVERSE LANGUAGE-LEARNING CONTEXTS FOR ESL STUDENTS

Learning activities in Ms. Miller's classroom are organized around three types of learning contexts: whole-class, single-focus activity directed by the teacher; small-group activity with adult assistance and peer interaction; and choice centers—the more loosely organized, multi-foci activities which the children initiated outside the direct supervision of the teacher. In addition, a fourth learning environment—the ESL classroom—provided another set of learning opportunities for ESL students. Each of these four language-learning environments will be described below followed by a description of the level of participation of ESL students in general and the Chinese-speaking students in particular.

## Teacher-Directed Whole-Class Activities

A good example of this type of activity is teacher-directed story reading. Ms. Miller read a variety of Big Books (i.e., large-size and large-print storybooks) to the students. When she read aloud, she pointed to every word so students could match sounds and letters. While the teacher was reading a story, students were to listen carefully. At times, students were encouraged to repeat after Ms. Miller's reading, answer in unison her questions, make predictions about the plot, or express their opinions. Actions often accompanied the reading. For instance, when reading a book about birds swooping down, the teacher asked the children to do the action and say loudly "swoop."

Snack time provided a great opportunity for poetry time—another teacher-directed language activity. After recess, children automatically went to the lockers to get their snacks; they sat down at their table and while eating their snacks, they listened with interest to Ms. Miller's selection of poems.

Whole-class instruction created a rich and safe language environment that allowed the Chinese-speaking children to intake large amounts of information about how the second language works. Almost daily, students listened to various stories, songs, poems, and clear instructions about diverse activities. Continual repetition and rephrasing by the teacher helped ESL students understand how to proceed; in addition, students were able to consult with each other using their native languages. Furthermore, whole-class activities did not require students, at the beginning stages of language learning, to answer the teacher's questions or produce language. This kind of set-ting created a safe environment for the ESL students, many of whom were going through what Krashen (1982) calls the "silent period," a stage where second language learners are internalizing many aspects of language that will eventually help them produce language.

## Adult-Assisted Small-Group Activities

Adult-assisted small-group activities were often preceded by an explanation or demonstration given by Ms. Miller. For example, on one occasion, when demonstrating how to make a booklet about the parts of a tree, Ms. Miller showed a poster of an oak tree. As she pointed to each part of the tree, she clearly enunciated each name (i.e., trunk, crown, treetop, limb, bark, root, etc.). Then she showed the students a sheet with all those names which she promptly cut and affixed to the proper location in the poster. Twenty-four pairs of alert eyes were following every move she made! Afterwards, she grouped children by fours and while she worked with one group, all other groups worked with a parent helper or the teaching assistant. Once in their small groups, generally made up of two ESL students and two English-speaking students, participants were able to interact with peers and the par-ticipating adult in a low-risk, low-anxiety atmosphere.

For ESL students, this type of activity was especially beneficial; not only did they have the opportunity to interact with English-speaking children and adults but they were also able to learn from each other and from the adult helper. While the adult-assisted small-group activities provided an ideal con-text for practicing the new language, the initial modeling done by Ms. Miller afforded ESL children the opportunity to intake bits of information neces-sary to construct meaning. Later, when students were in their small groups, the adult helper was able to continue modeling the second language while at the same time allowing students to take control of the interaction.

Research suggests that the benefits for language learning of this form of engagement are not only for the participating speaker but also for those doing the listening. By listening to other students and adults, learners can observe, and later produce, different communicative strategies used by oth-ers to keep the conversation going (Allwright 1980, Ernst 1994a).

## Choice Centers

This was one of the most lively times in the afternoon. Children were dispersed around the room, free to choose activities and cohorts. Ms. Miller sometimes used this time to assess individual children's oral language development by focusing on fluency, vocabulary, and pronunciation. Sometimes she visited different centers, talked to individuals and small groups, hugged children, and always made zestful comments about children's productions. Ms. Miller commented that her role at this time was not of an authority figure, but of someone who "facilitated learning."

Choice centers allowed students thirty minutes per day to make decisions about whether they wanted to work alone or join others, to talk or remain silent, and to stay in one place or walk around. The nature of the activities chosen affected the frequency and amount of talk during this time. For example, in the "pretend center," where a fantasy world of many new and complex roles and relationships was continuously being worked out, a great amount of conversation seemed to be needed to keep things going. However, in other activities, talk was hardly needed at all. When coloring, arranging puzzles, or making puppets, children often worked alone and spoke less frequently.

The choice centers, regarded by the six Chinese-speaking children as playtime, unintentionally created a context for them to use their native language. However, as weeks went by, choice centers began to serve as a bridge to smooth the transition from home to school. That is, choice centers allowed ESL students to decide when to try out the new language and when to fall back to the safety net provided by the mother tongue. Evidence of the influence of native language development on academic achievement in a second language derives from program evaluation studies of the 1980s and 1990s. These studies have demonstrated that the more the native language is supported in academic settings, the higher ESL students are able to achieve academically (Krashen and Biber 1988; Ramirez et al. 1991; Thomas and Collier 1997). Research on second language acquisition indicates that when students have control over the activity and the ensuing conversation, they are more likely to use a variety of communicative strategies to overcome the problem of communicating with limited second language resources (Ernst 1994a; Pica 1987).

Within the ebb and flow of naturally occurring contexts created by the setup of choice centers, interesting patterns emerged. Chinese-speaking children tended to form a subgroup wherein almost all communication was done in their native language. A favorite activity for this group, during the first three weeks of school, was the pretend center. Although traditionally this activity may be considered more a "girl activity," the two Chinese-speaking boys often joined the activity. In the pretend center the six Chinese-speaking children cooked together, cleaned the house, got sick, called the doctor, and danced as brides and grooms. The most obvious patterned behavior was that they always communicated in Chinese. It seemed that the pretend center had become the "niche" in which they chose to house themselves.

By the ninth week, however, this strong subgroup of Chinese-speaking children became less obvious. They started falling into three different groups (two in each) and gradually played with other children. In this case, code switching—shifting from one language to the other—was obvious. Shao-min and Ning-ning, a girl and a boy from the same region, often played together with Legos. At first, they talked in Chinese, with some English vocabulary mixed in. If an English-speaking child joined, Shao-min and Ning-ning often spoke English to the third child, yet when they talked to each other, they used Chinese. For the other four Chinese-speaking children, Chinese was, for the most part, the predominant language during playtime or whenever they were alone.

## The ESL Class

ESL classes began in mid-September. From Monday through Thursday, at 12:45 p.m., Ms. Madison went to the kindergarten classroom to pick up her ten ESL children. She tapped the xylophone fastened on the wall and announced, "ESL class." The ESL children immediately stopped their work, ran out of the classroom, lined up in the hallway, and followed Ms. Madison to the Language House, a former residential house located next to the school building. Children were always excited as they walked on the path leading to the Language House.

Colors, numbers, food, greetings, and directions were some of the survival topics covered early in the year. Children's participation was always boisterous and lively. For example, when Ms. Madison showed pictures of vegetables, all the children said in unison after each picture, "Peas!" "Onion!" "Lettuce!" "Spinach!" When it came to a picture of a tomato, the teacher asked, "What color is it?" "Red!" shouted the children, with confidence. Their voices were so loud that Ms. Madison had to remind them to keep the volume down. During hands-on activities, children often shouted and argued for their materials. "Give me green. I want it." "Who has the scissors?" "Where is the glue?" It was during this kind of interaction that children learned new words and phrases and ventured to ask for the materials they needed to accomplish the task at hand.

In the ESL class, there was only one big group of ten ESL kindergarten students. There, the six Chinese-speaking children would seldom use their first language to communicate. The size of the group, the nature of the instruction, the length of the class period, and, most importantly, the ESL teacher's instructional style allowed students to participate actively and successfully in all the activities. The ESL teacher's instructional talk was characterized by an exaggerated enunciation, continual repetition and rephrasing, greater overall loudness, and substantiated by more real objects and demonstrations. This type of "comprehensible input" (Krashen 1982) allowed learners to understand most of the content of the talk even though the teacher was consistently using language that is roughly one step beyond the students' present level of competence in English. In addition to listening to the teacher, students in this class had ample opportunities to engage in meaningful communication with the teacher and peers. Several of the ESL students, often quiet in their classroom, were willing to take risks in this classroom by practicing their recently acquired linguistic knowledge.

# DISCUSSION AND IMPLICATIONS

Vygotsky's educational theory indicates that the direction of intellectual development goes from social to individual. Humans use cultural tools, such as speech, literacy, mathematics, and computers, to mediate their interaction with each other and their surroundings. Children develop skills in higher mental processes through immediate social interactions. Adult guidance and collaboration with more capable peers are two major ways of social interaction, which lead eventually to the "zone of proximal development." Vygotsky (1978) defined the term as "the distance between the actual development level as determined by individual problem solving and the level of potential development as determined through problem solving under adult guidance or in collaboration with more capable peers" (86). Therefore, from a Vygotskyian perspective, a major role of schooling is to create social contexts for mastery of using cultural tools. In light of Vygotsky's learning theory, the kindergarten experience at Mountainview Elementary, as described above, provided ESL children with ample opportunities to practice their second-language skills in carefully designed rich social contexts.

Table 13.2 presents a summary of the four language-learning contexts (i.e., teacher-directed whole-class, adult-assisted small group, choice centers, and ESL class). The 2x2 matrix compares these four contexts in relation to the size of the group and the amount of personal interaction that transpires for all ESL students but especially for the Chinese-speaking children.

## Table 13.2: 2×2 Matrix of the Four Different Language-Learning Contexts as Related to Group Size, Amount of Interpersonal Interaction, and Opportunities to Produce the New Language

|  | Opportunities to Produce the New Language | |
| --- | --- | --- |
|  | Less | More |
| **Teacher-directed larger group** | | |
|  | **Teacher-directed, whole-class activities** | **ESL class** |
|  | ESL children may not understand all the stories being read but enjoy them. | There is more comprehensible input (i.e., exaggerated enunciation, overall greater loudness, and more realia). |
|  | ESL children are taking in new information (internalization) even though they do not speak much in the whole class setting. | ESL children understand the purpose of the class. |
| **Self-formed smaller group** | | Children are willing to learn. |
|  | **Choice Centers** | **Adult-assisted small group activities** |
|  | Intended effects: learning is maximized through children's self-exploration and discovery. | Teacher and adult helpers are able to interact with children on an individual basis. |
|  | Unintended effects: Chinese ESL children form a subgroup and use native language. | Children are able to learn content and language together. |
|  | Subgroups dissolve gradually. | There is more peer interaction between native and ESL children. |
|  | More English is being used by ESL children. | ESL children feel free to hypothesize about using the new language. |

The point here is not to suggest that one context generated more opportunities for language learning than the others, but to highlight the importance of having four diverse contexts which offered an array of instances for using and learning language. Furthermore, the differential demands placed by each setting on the ESL students provided opportunities to respond to those demands differently. For example, during their first month, Chinese-speaking children used Chinese almost exclusively while in the choice centers, whereas they only used English in the ESL classroom. Having the opportunity to use the language of their choice in most of their activities helped students feel at ease in spite of being surrounded by a new culture and a strange-sounding language. In fact, all Chinese-speaking children mentioned during early interviews that they liked their school. For instance, when Jin-yi's was asked, "Do you like school even though you do not understand English in the classroom?" she responded with aplomb in Chinese, "It's fine. I love it and I am learning English."

In classrooms, everyday activities are organized around different kinds of situations and events. With the increasing number of linguistically diverse families in our nation, more and more children are learning English as their second language while at the same time coping with a new way of doing school. There is no doubt that the acquisition of a new language and culture can be a shocking and difficult experience. In this regard, several studies have clearly demonstrated that the impact of these early experiences will in part determine whether the immigrant child successfully acquires the second language and becomes capable of thriving within the dominant culture (Ernst 1994b; Ernst and Richard 1994; Igoa 1995; Soto 1997). Ms. Miller's kindergarten classroom has successfully fostered an enjoyable and effective language-learning environment for both ESL children and native speakers. In her classroom meaningful communication is not just encouraged but carefully organized and nurtured.

As mentioned earlier and discussed at length elsewhere (Ernst 1994; Han and Wenger in press; Han 1996; Han and Ernst-Slavit 1999), the six Chinese-speaking children not only enjoyed a smooth transition to the first grade, but were extremely successful in first grade—even when compared with their native-English–speaking counterparts. After weathering unsettling storms and a myriad of assorted waves, the Chinese-speaking students in this study were finally able to walk on land again, as Kirsten had hoped in the opening quote of this chapter.

It is clear from this study that four important aspects are needed to support ESL students' acquisition of the second language. First, an ESL program is necessary to provide a supportive environment with rich opportunities for students to be successful while they extend their receptive and productive repertoires in the second language. Second, second-language programs—especially in the primary years—need to provide opportunities for students to use the first language for meaningful activities; this will ensure that students feel that their first language and culture are validated by the teacher and school. Third, classrooms need to offer a variety of language-learning contexts so students can hear the new language spoken by competent speakers in an assortment of situations. And third, students need classroom environments where meaningful communication is not only encouraged but carefully orchestrated, supported, and monitored by the teacher.

# CHAPTER FOURTEEN

# EARLY

# CHILDHOOD

# BILINGUAL

# CLASSROOMS

JOCELYNN SMREKAR, CLARION UNIVERSITY

The challenge for early childhood teachers is to understand the relationship of language and culture, and then to reflect critically on the philosophies that drive early childhood programs. Teachers who wish to respond sensitively to the unique culture each child brings to the classroom will "use culturally appropriate pedagogies to create liberating learning environments" (Trueba and Zou 1998, 17) while staying constantly on the alert for cultural stereotyping.

In addition to the deficit view of linguistically and culturally diverse children that school personnel often unknowingly hold, critical pedagogy must prompt early childhood educators to examine how the asymmetrical power relations of society are maintained and reproduced in schools (Anyon 1998, Freire 1985). Early childhood programs created for specific groups tend to create socioeconomic segregation and legitimize the belief that one group of children is inferior to another (Cannella 1997). Little interaction occurs between the poor children who attend subsidized programs with a curriculum designed for remediation and the affluent children who attend private programs with a curriculum designed to develop their full potential.

The current interest in finding instructional methods that will improve the academic performance of linguistically and culturally diverse children tends to obscure other important reasons for the children's performance; namely, the homes and the communities in which the children reside (Bartolomé 1998).

# CRITICAL UNDERSTANDINGS

There is a need for early childhood teachers of linguistically and culturally diverse children to critically reflect on the theories that guide their thinking and practices. It is critical for teachers to understand bilingualism, the need for consistency and cultural congruency in children's lives, the connections of culture and language, and the need to maximize the linguistic and cultural capital that children bring to school. These will be addressed next.

## Teachers' Beliefs Regarding Bilingualism

Teachers' beliefs are realized in their classroom practices; therefore, teachers' beliefs about language acquisition are relevant to children's academic achievement in bilingual classrooms (Beckett 1997). In a recent study in Texas, Beckett found that most early childhood teachers surveyed who spoke Spanish felt reluctant to use it in the classroom. In addition, teachers surveyed who could not speak Spanish felt that proficiency in two languages—bilingualism—was unnecessary for a good education. The results of this study point to the fact that improvement is needed in the preparation of pre-service teachers who will serve linguistically and culturally diverse children. Teachers oftentimes have a mistaken idea that "one size fits all" when it comes to teaching linguistically and culturally diverse children (Bartolomé 1998). They believe that teaching approaches (e.g., cooperative learning, whole language, process writing) that fit one minority population will routinely fit another. A more beneficial approach would be for teachers to modify and individualize the teaching approaches they use for each group.

## Congruency

Another element critical to the success of linguistically and culturally diverse children is cultural congruency or consistency. Cultural congruency has been defined as one-to-one correspondence between what happens at school and what happens at home—or more simply, consistency in the home-school experience (Mohatt and Erickson 1981; Hyun 1997).

According to Hyun, early childhood education needs more consistency between home and school cultures than formal education at other levels. Maintaining cultural congruency between young children's home and school is the core of early childhood critical pedagogy for DCAP [developmentally and culturally appropriate practice] (Hyun 1997, 8).

"Children learn best when there is consistency in their lives, including keeping children tied to their home language and culture" (Jang and Mangione 1994, 47). Children especially need cultural congruency when family values, beliefs, and attitudes are very different from the dominant culture. By critically inquiring whether each child is receiving a culturally congruent classroom experience, teachers move closer to the goal of all learners reaching their potential. We will return to the ideas of empowerment and cultural congruence in the "Recommendations" portion of this paper.

## The Connection of Culture and Language

An underlying issue in the education of linguistically and culturally diverse children is the connection between culture and language. The language one speaks is closely tied to culture (King, Chipman, and Cruz-Janzen 1994; National Association for the Education of Young Children 1996). On the surface, it may seem that children learning a second language are simply learning a large number of new words, grammatical rules, phonology, discourse, and pragmatics, but this is not the case. Lourdes Díaz Soto says, "Language is one of the most powerful transmitters of culture and is crucial to the survival of a community. For many families language is at the heart of their cultural knowledge and traditions" (1997, 356). Since language and culture are so closely connected, one really cannot learn a second language without also learning a second culture. Children must want to learn a new language in order to succeed (Tabors 1997), and they must also want to become part of the new culture to some degree. Conversely, if the child doesn't want to take part in the Euro-American culture, then she will reject it and the English language along with it, especially if she is being forced to learn it.

## Linguistic and Cultural Capital

All children bring knowledge and beliefs, experiences and language to the classroom. Too often these things which have been referred to as linguistic and cultural capital have been ignored in linguistically and culturally diverse children (Lima and Lima 1998; Trueba and Zou 1998). Early childhood education programs have used the middle-class way of life as a standard for everyone (Cannella 1997). Cannella writes

> This [middle-class] perspective has disqualified the knowledge(s) of those who do not espouse middle-class values and beliefs and constructed a message that these "Other" people and their children are inferior (112).

The linguistic and cultural capital of all children should be recognized (National Association for the Education of Young Children 1996). When the school does not recognize the child's cultural behavior and experiences as legitimate, or worse (the child's cultural heritage is thought of negatively), this instills a feeling of failure that accompanies the child through school (Lima and Lima 1998). The feeling of failure is counterproductive to learning and cognitive development. A much brighter picture would be for teachers and students to learn from and value the language, knowledge, and life experiences of all children, including ethnic minority, working-class, and low socioeconomic status children, rather than valuing only the language and experiences of the affluent children (Anyon 1998).

# MILESTONES IN THE TYPICAL SEQUENCE OF DEVELOPMENT

One myth that must be dispelled is that young children learn a second language so quickly and easily that it seems almost like magic. In reality, children who actually know very little language are able to appear as if they have much greater language abilities because it is appropriate for children to interact and respond with less language (e.g., single-word answers). They are not called upon to produce discourse that would provide a more accurate indicator of their language abilities.

Although many parents and educators worry that children will become confused by learning two languages, researchers now believe that this is not the case (Tabors 1997) and that bilingualism actually has cognitive and social benefits (Hakuta 1986). There have been few extensive longitudinal studies on the development of bilingual children, but what studies have been done indicate that bilingual children appear to reach the same basic milestones as monolingual children (Genesee and Nicoladis 1995). Of course, the same individual variability that characterizes language development in monolingual children exists in bilingual children.

The exposure to and experiences that children have in a language have an effect on the rate of development. "Bilingual children exhibit more rapid progress and more ability in whichever language dominates in their social environment" (Genesee and Nicoladis 1995, 23). The development and use of each language fluctuates according to how much a child is exposed to each of the languages (Tabors 1997).

Changes in the composition of children's families or moving to a different community may greatly impact children's bilingual development. The language environment may also prompt children to use what is called situation-specific language. Bilingual children may have a preference for using one language or the other in specific situations. It is not known why some children do this and others do not; however, it has been attributed to children's personality preferences or attitudes.

# FEATURES OF BILINGUAL CHILDREN'S LANGUAGE PERFORMANCE

While in the process of acquiring two languages, young bilingual children's speech appears to have many of the same features as monolingual children's speech. These characteristics are a reflection of the children's knowledge of both languages and also demonstrate the strategies the children have at their disposal to aid them in using and acquiring language.

One type of error bilingual children make is known as a transfer error. These can be one of two types: code mixing or developmental errors that all children make. Code mixing refers to bilingual children using words from one language interspersed in a conversation that is otherwise in a second language. Code mixing is now known to be a form of lexical borrowing along the same lines as overextensions or underextensions in monolingual children (Genesee and Nicoladis 1995). Overextensions are overgeneralizations. An example of overextending would be for a child to refer to all four-legged animals as "doggy." When children overextend, they are making use of the vocabulary words that they already know to communicate. As their vocabulary expands, the children will use more appropriate words. For bilingual children, overextending or code mixing means they are using words from two languages to meet their communication needs. Bilingual children also use underextensions too, or overly restricted use of some words, in much the same way that monolingual children do. Underextensions are less noticeable than overextensions, and underextensions are gradually used less as more appropriate vocabulary is learned by the children.

To summarize, bilingual children will use any and all linguistic strategies they have acquired at a given moment in time to communicate, as do their monolingual peers.

# SOCIAL COMPETENCE AND COMMUNICATIVE COMPETENCE

Social competence and communicative competence are closely linked and both are clearly needed by children who are second-language learners. The rules of social and linguistic competence seem harsh. If a child is a poor communicator, he or she will be ignored socially by peers. If he or she is ignored by peers, then he or she does not have opportunities to become a better communicator. Tabors (1997) calls this a "double bind."

When children with a home language other than English enter a classroom in which English is used, they have a big adjustment to make. They are often ignored by the English-speaking children because of their lack of English proficiency (Tabors 1997). The children who don't yet speak English are left to play alone silently, and they typically sing, hum, or talk to themselves. They wait for their peers to initiate interactions, and only rarely do they try to get one of the other children to do something for them. They do things for themselves or do without because they intuit that they have no social capital. Fortunately, the situation improves rapidly for most second-language-learning children as they gain enough English to become social members of the group. Also, as they participate more frequently in group interactions, they encounter more situations to use language. What at first was a "double bind" (Tabors 1997) now becomes a double blessing for the second-language-learning children.

# RECOMMENDATIONS: RESTRUCTURING BILINGUAL EARLY CHILDHOOD EDUCATION

How will early childhood bilingual education be transformed to meet the needs of the young children of the next century? What kinds of changes will we see in the way teachers are prepared? In the future, where will the knowledge come from that informs early childhood bilingual education? Several important changes will take place: (1) children will become empowered, (2) teachers will engage in inquiry and reflection, causing them to take a critical look at their own beliefs about language and culture, and some long-held assumptions, and (3) taking a critical look at their own beliefs, teachers will engage in critical pedagogy.

## Empowerment

We, as early childhood educators, are challenged to learn ways to empower all children, especially those who are culturally, linguistically, socially, or economically diverse, in order that they may succeed in schools in appropriate learning environments. Before they can empower children, teachers must examine their own assumptions about childhood, diversity, and education. Empowerment will be discussed first.

Research has shown that young children's awareness of and attitudes toward race and ethnicity are formed very early in their lives (Banks 1993). At four years of age, Anglo children in Banks's study began to demonstrate ethnocentric attitudes and make negative comments regarding people of other races and ethnicities. Banks's studies also revealed that as children grew older, it became more difficult to influence their racial and ethnic attitudes. That being the case, it is more productive for early childhood educators to use opportunities they encounter in their classrooms to positively influence children's attitudes toward race and ethnicity, than it is for teachers of older children.

Young children's attitudes are influenced by teachers who express the idea that children's unique cultures and native languages are treasures to be conserved, rather than obstacles to be overcome. When children's culture and language are valued, the children are empowered. The development and maintenance of children's home language is important to the children in constructing positive self-identities and in maintaining communication with parents (Soto 1999). Some educators go so far as to say that a multicultural curriculum should also be a multilingual curriculum (King, Chipman, and Cruz-Janzen 1994).

New approaches which empower linguistically and culturally diverse children are being employed by some early childhood bilingual teachers who understand the process of empowerment and its benefits. Empowerment has been shown to benefit linguistically and culturally diverse children through greater academic achievement (Trueba and Zou 1998). Reaffirmation of children's ethnic identities empowers children, thus creating learning contexts in which students are able to empower themselves (Bartolomé 1998).

## Inquiry and Reflection

Becoming a better early childhood bilingual teacher in the next century will mean making more use of inquiry and reflection. George and Louise Spindler believe that teachers ought to undergo "cultural therapy," meaning they would reflect on their own cultural biases (1998). In my research, I have interviewed white, middle-class, preservice teachers who deny that they have any culture because it is invisible to them. The first step in their cultural therapy would be to realize everyone has a culture, and the second step would be to examine how that culture has biases. Tabors (1997) also writes of the importance of teachers examining their own belief systems because they often do not know what those systems are. Teachers need to understand the way their own language works together with their culture before they can fully realize the importance the children's language has relative to their culture (Beckett 1997). Teachers can come to this understanding about the way language works and the importance of language to a child through inquiry and reflection.

Through inquiry and reflection, teachers come to the realization that each of us wear our own particular cultural lenses. As Trueba and Zou state:

> What is more difficult is to recognize the cultural lenses we carry and the biases, mis-expectations and assumptions that contextualize our interactions in daily life, especially if our daily life exposes us to deal with people very different from us (1998, 22).

Trueba and Zou go on to say that teachers, more so than others, need to become reflective and aware of their own cultural lenses in order to be more effective with children from diverse backgrounds.

# Critical Pedagogy

Becoming a reflective teacher involves self-study, journal writing, and discussion. All are valuable because they help teachers thoughtfully analyze their own attitudes. As teachers inquire and reflect, they may find it worthwhile to keep a reflective study journal in which they engage in critical pedagogy.

Engaging in critical pedagogy can help teachers gain an understanding of the dynamics of diverse languages and cultures in their own lives, in children's lives, and in society (Beckett 1997). According to Freire (1985), all educational endeavors are inherently political. If teachers do not reflect and make themselves aware of oppression, they may be unaware that they are oppressing linguistically and culturally diverse children through a hidden curriculum or in other insidious ways (Trueba and Zou 1998).

Some scholars in the field of early childhood are beginning to question long-held assumptions, especially regarding the paradigm of child development and the concurrent philosophy of developmentally appropriate practice. The knowledge base in early childhood has been dominated by psychological perspectives which have effectively silenced other voices. Developmental psychology has silenced or disqualified knowledge from sources such as teachers, caregivers, and the children themselves (Cannella 1997; Delpit 1995). Early childhood educators must be willing to be silent and listen to other voices, even if these voices challenge us and make us uncomfortable. While a Euro-American, middle-class, male perspective may be one way among many of looking at children's development, it is not the only way of viewing it (Hyun 1998; Jipson 1998; Cannella 1997).

Traditionally, child development has been a "single linear paradigm that focuses on only one way of looking at human growth and changes" (Hyun 1998, 2). Based upon developmental psychology, child development espouses the idea that individuals may do things at a certain age or not do them, but development always proceeds in the same direction, with the last stage of development being the highest level of development. Child development theory precludes different or multiple ways of knowing because it is a linear model.

Soto, for one, proposes that we move beyond the scientific and biologically derived theories of child development, toward a "critical constructivist paradigm" (Soto 1997). She advises us to examine the issues related to power and to pursue a "utopian early childhood dream of equity and social justice" (1999, 227). Early childhood curriculum is now in the process of being rewritten in such a way that it will integrate multiple ways of knowing (i.e., the knowledge bases of critical constructivism, multiculturalism, critical pedagogy, issues of power and feminist views) (Soto 1999).

For many teachers trained in the past decade, the book of guidelines of developmentally appropriate practices published by National Association for the Education of Young Children in 1987 (Bredekamp 1987) and revised in 1997 (Bredekamp and Copple 1997) is considered their "bible." How can we help early childhood teachers move beyond the limitations of developmentally appropriate practices that are based on child development theory? Teacher preparation needs to move toward critical pedagogy and reflective study. We need to instill in teachers the idea that an "individual's developmental growth and learning characteristics can be appropriately understood only within one's own cultural contexts" (Hyun 1998, 3).

## Teacher Preparation in the Twenty-First Century

Given the rapid demographic and cultural changes taking place today, National Association for the Education of Young Children (1996), Tabors (1997), and others have proposed specific recommendations for making early childhood teacher preparation more effective. Their recommendations are learning how to deliver culturally responsive instruction, understanding cultural congruence, participating in holistic field experiences, understanding the role of language and culture in planning curriculum and assessment, and understanding second-language acquisition. Each of these will be discussed in the following paragraphs.

Teachers need to free themselves from blindly adopting so-called effective or teacher-proof strategies and instead begin the reflective process. The process of inquiry and reflection allows teachers to recreate or reinvent teaching methods and materials, while taking into account the "sociocultural realities" of their students (Bartolomé 1998).

In the future, good teachers of young children will make education more culturally responsive. Teachers will realize that developmentally appropriate practice includes the development of children experienced in cultures other than the white, middle-class, Euro-American culture. Using culturally responsive instruction, teaching strategies can "recognize and build on culturally different ways of learning, behaving, and using language in the classroom" (Bartolomé 1998, 241). Teachers need to be made aware of the ways in which they may unknowingly disregard and disrespect culturally and linguistically diverse students' learning preferences. Typically, teachers tend to teach entirely from their own cultural perspective unless they've been taught to reflect on their own attitudes and cultural lenses (Tabors 1997). The savvy teacher who belongs to a different cultural group than her students can use negotiation to achieve a balance between her preferences and those of the children.

An idea that is closely related to cultural responsiveness is cultural congruence or cultural consistency (Hyun 1998; Mohatt and Erickson 1981). Cultural congruence is defined as close correspondence between what happens in school and what happens at home. Hyun states, "Successful early childhood education relies more on consistency between home and school cultures than on formal education at any other level" (1998, 8). Hyun goes on to say that cultural congruency is the core of early childhood critical pedagogy for developmentally and culturally appropriate practice.

She believes that, conversely, culturally incongruent communication is a major source of academic difficulties for the linguistically or culturally diverse children. Cultural incongruence may occur even in classrooms where teachers and children speak the same language. Cultural congruence, according to Hyun, may be achieved by teachers who: (1) allow and encourage children to express and show the importance of their own family culture and identity, (2) utilize children's personal experiences, family culture, and diverse language expressions as important sources of learning and teaching, (3) respect differences in perception and understanding, and (4) plan instruction based on children's diverse styles of decision-making and social interaction (1998, 12).

Teacher preparation in the future also can be improved by including a new type of field experience that enables preservice teachers to see children in the whole context in which they live (Beckett 1997). In addition to regular school-based field experiences, preservice teachers can benefit from holistic field experiences that allow them to study children outside of school, in the contexts of family and community, enabling them to understand children's total experiences. Holistic field experiences can help teachers better understand the competing forces in children's lives and, in turn, teachers can help children succeed without negating either the school, family, or community.

Early childhood educators of the twenty-first century need to be aware of children's cultural and linguistic differences in order to plan curriculum and make assessments (Tabors 1997). Some cultural differences have more of an effect upon children's learning than others, and that effect may be compounded by the children's ages, personalities, and life experiences (Bowman and Stott, 1994). For Hispanic children, who are the largest single group of culturally diverse children in the United States, Espinosa suggests that pertinent knowledge for early childhood educators would be understanding Hispanic child-rearing and socialization practices, communication styles, and orientation toward formal education (1995). For example, a cultural difference that teachers need to be aware of because it may be a barrier to educational success in children of Mexican-American or Hawaiian cultures is that these children prefer to work cooperatively rather than compete against each other. Being aware of this cultural difference, the classroom teacher may decide to use cooperative learning groups and to steer clear of competitive activities such as spelling bees.

Another suggestion to improve early childhood teacher preparation in the new millennium is to add the requirement that all teachers study second-language acquisition (Milne and Clarke 1993; Smrekar 1994; Soto, Smrekar, and Nekovei 1999). Commonly, bilingual teachers have this requirement but as we move into an era when more than half of the children in classrooms are from diverse cultural and linguistic backgrounds, all early childhood teachers need this as part of their knowledge base. "The study of second language acquisition in young children should be a compulsory part of initial training for all early childhood educators, as should the study of the methodology of first language maintenance in second language learners" (Milne and Clarke, 12).

Valdés (1996) proposed that teachers reflect on their teaching and, in the process, critically analyze their educational goals, instructional strategies, and curriculum with respect to the empowerment of children as future citizens in a democracy.

In summarizing, early childhood educators need to reexamine some long-held beliefs, especially the model of child development embedded in NAEYC's developmentally appropriate practice. Developmentally appropriate practice may be culturally limiting some children.

# CHAPTER FIFTEEN

# CARING LITERACY

# AND IDENTITY

# STRUGGLES

## THE TRANSFORMATION OF A CHICANO STUDENT

MARÍA E. FRÁNQUIZ, UNIVERSITY OF COLORADO-BOULDER

> *The word "identity" is useful because it is the everyday word for people's sense of who they are. However, it is a misleading singular word. The plural word "identities" is better because it captures the idea of people identifying simultaneously with a variety of social groups; for example, a person may simultaneously identify herself as a student, a feminist, black, an experienced worker, and more. One or more of these may be foregrounded at different times; they are sometimes contradictory, sometimes interrelated. A person's diverse identities constitute the richness and the dilemmas of her sense of self.*
> IVANIC (1994, 4)

Much current research in the field of literacy argues that the choices teachers make about instruction are moral ones, as these choices have consequences on student identity formation. Advocates see literacy as building a foundation for establishing relationships among texts, learners, and groups in ways that have potential for transformation. This transformation is "not merely a means for individual liberation; rather, it is a quest for equity, a moral vision that is grounded in an ethic of compassion and care" (Powell 1999, 6). From this perspective, literacy promotes a vision of freedom and justice for all. Teachers sharing such a view place equity front and center and commit themselves to learning about and engaging in the challenges of teaching students from culturally and socially dominated communities.

## WHAT IS AN ETHOS OF CARING?

Some researchers offer useful approaches for promoting an ethos of caring in the teaching of literacy. O'Donnell (1998) makes one suggestion. He argues that teachers must engage in a process of *re-cognizing* that, in spite of gains in civil rights, we continue to live and participate in a race-conscious society. For him, *re-cognition* is a process teachers can use to consciously recover early experiences with racism and other biases in their own as well as their students' lives.

In *White Teacher*, Vivian Gussin Paley describes her process of conscious recovery. She began her journey by observing the effect of color blindness in her kindergarten classroom community. Paley compared the similarities and differences between her white, Jewish background and those of her children of color. Over one academic year, and across years teaching in increasingly diverse kindergartens, she began to see the effect of race on student participation. For example, Carol Shen was a five-year-old who avoided "any activity or discussion that had to do with her own people and culture" (p. 36). During her kindergarten year, she also refused to speak Chinese with her non-English-speaking grandmother. Although Paley worked hard to make Carol comfortable about using her family background as a resource for learning, the child was not able to overcome her feeling of inhibition in the public space of the classroom. However, in a private space with her teacher, she whispered, "my grandmother doesn't speak English." Carol made explicit her identification with the status language, English, and her alienation from the heritage language that marked her background as different.

Caring theorists (Noddings 1992) understand that teachers such as Paley are concerned when the school and curriculum are not actively promoting a search for connection between teacher and student, between student and family, and among students themselves. These interpersonal connections are the ones Ivanic (1994) claims have profound consequences on how students' identities develop and whether literacy is a material resource in the process. Literacy resources for learning are subtracted when teachers, curriculum, and institutional structures do not place value on the native languages, histories, and cultures of students (Valenzuela 1999). Fostering an ethic of care, then, endows educators with the responsibility to engage themselves and everyone at school with ideas and practices that align with literacy for social justice (Edelsky 1991).

Literacy for social justice challenges the widespread belief that educational success for ethnic groups, such as Chinese speakers or Latinos, is about halting the use of native language and abandoning native traditions, an assimilation process portrayed by some scholars as "subtractive assimilation" (Gibson 1995). Instead, literacy for social justice promotes a view of ethnic culture that is characterized with continually shifting and emerging struggles among students identifying themselves in relation to others and in relation to the changing and unchanging social structures that link their lives. Educators for social justice agree with Banks (1995), who argues that students need opportunities in their classroom communities where they can struggle with complex ideas (e.g., racism, sexism, ethnic cleansing, war). In the struggle, students are encouraged to use all available linguistic and cultural resources to explore the ways in which these complex ideas influence their individual and collective lives. (See Fránquiz 2000 for an extended analysis of fifth grade students learning about and struggling with issues of (in)tolerance.)

# DATA COLLECTION

In this chapter I draw from over two years of ethnographic fieldwork in an alternative high school classroom I refer to as Access to Learning Class (ALC). The school will be referred to as Vista High and is located in the Front Range of the Rocky Mountains. ALC was conceived over a decade ago in order to address the needs of students who experience difficulty in regular high school classes. During fieldwork, the students enrolled in ALC were predominantly male and Chicano, a group that represents two-thirds of the US Latino population and who are considered to be more educationally disadvantaged than other Latinos (Valencia 1991). The ethnographic fieldwork consisted of: (a) video recordings of particular periods (i.e., social studies, English, math), (b) interviews with teachers and students, (c) personal field notes and field notes collected by Title VII graduate student assistants, and (d) participant observations in an afterschool group that many ALC students attended. I focus on one male Chicano student who chose the pseudonym Elway and his white teacher ally White Chocolate, a pseudonym chosen by the ALC students. I examine ways that teacher and student produced oral and written texts that influenced the reconstruction of an academic identity. Academic identity, or scholar ethos, refers to the definitions of scholar and scholarship that students develop which permits them to achieve academically (Welch and Hodges 1997). Learning about identity breakdowns and buildups among Latino students provides a way of identifying, examining, and, when necessary, working to change the material and symbolic forces that affect their lives.

# FOSTERING COMPASSION AND CARE IN THE ACCESS TO LEARNING CLASSROOM

On April 7, 1999, during social studies, students in the ALC read the local newspaper's front-page article titled "NATO Snubs Cease-Fire: Allies Answer Serb Proposal with Most Intensive Day Yet in Air War." Underneath the title was a picture of a ten-year-old boy, Dren, with his doctor pumping antibiotics into his bullet-shattered right arm. All nineteen students in the class read the boy's tale of survival. During the reading of the common text, students learned that his family was killed before his eyes. The *Denver Rocky Mountain News* reported that they were "accused of being supporters of the Kosovo Liberation Army, the ethnic Albanian separatists fighting the forces of Yugoslav President Slobodan Milosevic." Dren was hit by a bullet in the arm, fell, and pretended to be dead. The police set the remains of his family and their home ablaze. When they left, Dren ran for safety. Because of his injured arm, he could not pick up his baby sister. Dren could hear the cries of his sister as she burned to death.

Reading such accounts can evoke multiple sentiments, tensions, or text-to-life connections among youths that are exposed to increasing violence, whether they live in urban or suburban settings. After reading the newspaper article, the teacher in this study asked students to write a letter from Dren's point of view in Kosovo to a ten-year-old boy in Colorado. She expected students to feel compassion and care, and to possibly make intertextual connections between the text of Dren's life and the text of their own life. The Chicano students had deep respect for their teacher and her choice of reading material because as a white woman she worked hard to understand the struggles of being brown (Mexican) in this school and in this town.

Elway lived in a community where the history of Americans of Mexican descent was tainted by many discriminatory acts recorded in a collection of oral histories, *We, Too, Came to Stay*. However, racism in the community is not manifested along white and brown lines alone. Chicanos and Mexicanos are also divided. Mendoza-Denton (1999) has traced intragroup divisions and their manifestation in school gang affiliations in Northern California. She shows how the concept of gang membership is not always restricted to a small group inducted through a ritual beating. Rather, "many more students participate in the oppositional dynamics of gang identity than are actual members of the gangs. Often the official members are indistinguishable from the unofficial wanna-bes" (43). In her study these affiliations were split between *Norteñas* ("native" Chicanas) and *Sureñas* ("recently arrived" Mexicanas). In this study, the same split existed between Eastsiders ("native" Chicanos) and *Sureños* ("recently arrived" Mexicanos). The ALC students identified with Eastsiders. The same issues found by Mendoza-Denton in California plagued the identities of Eastsiders in the ALC alternative program: Who is the real Mexican? Who can use the name Mexican? Do you have to speak Spanish to be Mexican? These identity issues are at the heart of the ongoing conflicts that exist between Eastsiders and Sureños in the same school, in the same community.

Students of Mexican descent who do not claim their cultural identity are considered suspect. For this reason, recruitment into the gangs is not only ongoing but also directly competing with the organization of literacy instruction in school. In the case of Elway, an older brother disengaged from high school and became heavily involved with the movement of illegal drugs between the town's two gangs. Elway's brother was murdered in a deal gone sour, and the community had to take a long, hard look at the differences in the seemingly monolithic Latina/o group.

Elway had disciplinary problems in school during his freshman year. When his brother was murdered, his disciplinary problems escalated. The loss of his brother affected Elway's attitudes toward life and school. The loss was baggage Elway carried into all his classes. For the assignment in social studies, Elway produced a letter from the young Kosovo boy's perspective that suggested he might have taken up an opportunity to make connections with losses in both of their lives.

Dear Tommy,

This is Elway. I'm writing this letter to inform you about our living conditions and [to] tell about one of the worst experiences that happened in my life. It all started about a week ago as me and the rest of my family were hiding because the president is trying to eliminate all the ethnic Albanians. I was so scared as my mother cried because the house we lived in was burned down leaving us with no personal belongings but the clothes we have on. It was our fourth day in hiding and our president's armed forces came in. One by one the soldiers shot down the people from oldest to youngest. It was the most terrifying experience hearing my Mom scream and yell before she was brutally murdered right before my eyes. I then started crying.

As I was weeping, thinking about all the things my Mom had done throughout the years to give me comfort, I was then smacked with a closed fist and then told to shut up because my time is coming. I was the third youngest person. As I looked around I see blood and people as they lay dead on the ground. A soldier walks up to me points the gun and fires at me. I felt the bullet enter my left shoulder. My first instinct was to play dead. As I was laying there feeling the blood leave my body I am suddenly kicked in the chest by the cowardous soldier that shot me. The soldiers then left the house we were in. At this point I look around to see if anybody was still alive but there were no signs of life so I quickly got up and carefully ran for help all alone bleeding, crying and feeling lonely.

I'm told that this is part of the beginning of the hardships that I'm going to face in life. *Please*, Tommy, pray for me and also pray that my family is in heaven. Your life in Colorado must be so much easier. Please don't take all that you have for granted because you don't know what you have till it's gone.

I'm not certain that I will write another letter but if I get the chance then I will. So pray for me and wish me luck in my future. I hope this ends soon.

> Sincerely,
> Elway

In his letter, Elway used the first person in the opening "I'm writing this letter to inform you about our living conditions and to tell about one of the worst experiences that happened in my life." He was able to meet the assignment by putting himself in the place of Dren. However, he used his own name and not Dren's. He proceeded to explain living conditions in Kosovo, his worst experiences in the ongoing war, and details regarding the latter. Elway explained how the president was eliminating all ethnic Albanians, that his family's house was burned down, and that they were hiding without personal belongings. He changed one of the facts in Dren's life by stating his terror in hearing his mother scream and yell before she was murdered. In the news account, it was the younger sister and not the mother who screamed.

When Elway placed himself in the Kosovar boy's shoes, he spoke of the violence and its effect on him: "I was smacked with a closed fist … told to shut up … kicked in the chest … a soldier shot me. My first instinct was to play dead ... I got up and ran for help all alone bleeding, crying and feeling lonely." These personal details were more elaborate than the news account. Elway went on to explain, "I'm told that this is part of the beginning of the hardships that I'm going to face in life. Please, pray that my family is in heaven. Please, don't take all that you have for granted because you don't know what you have till it's gone ... pray for me and wish me luck in my future." This last statement was particularly interesting in light of the sorrow that Elway's family had endured with the loss of their older child. I wondered where the text of Dren's life blurred into the text of Elway's. Was it Dren who lay alone bleeding, crying, and feeling lonely, or was it Elway's brother? Were the prayers and luck desired for Dren, or for Elway? I wrote these notes next to the textual analysis of the letter.

# THE WIDER SCHOOL CONTEXT: SAME SCHOOL, SEPARATE LIVES

Vista High is where Elway attended school when he wrote his letter during social studies. It is located in a sprawling two-story modern brick building on the east side of town. During the 1997–98 school year, the student body numbered 1,249, and the ethnic composition reported by district personnel indicated 70 percent of the student body was white, 26 percent Latino, 3 percent Asian, 0.7 percent American Indian, and 0.3 percent African-American. In this school district, Latino students earned diplomas at a rate that was 20 percent less than their European-American peers did. In the 1997–98 academic year, high school diplomas were earned by 68.4 percent of Latino seniors. During that year, ninety-one Latino students, or 6.7 percent, dropped out of school (Bounds 1999). Although these figures do not represent the depressing statistics that often define Latino youth nationally, many folks in the district continue to "question whether it is more appropriate to focus on lack of fit between mainstream classrooms' discourse and Latino ways of displaying knowledge, or on the people, practices, and institutions that structure educational inequality and interpret differences as deviance" (Zentella 1997, 278). Given that "disciplinary technologies" served to label Latinos in this community negatively (Davidson 1996 reports similar influences in diverse urban high schools), their contribution to the shaping of identities in and among youth are central in ongoing local reform efforts.

Elway was officially enrolled in the ALC at Vista High School. As previously stated, ALC is a special "school-within-a-school" alternative program for youth in grades ten through twelve who do not experience success with the regular high school curriculum and schedule of classes. He had applied to the program after many disciplinary problems in his freshman year. In the 1998–1999 academic school year, all nineteen students enrolled in ALC were of Mexican origin and 75 percent of the students were gang affiliated. There was a higher representation of males than females in the class (thirteen Chicano males vs. six Chicana females). According to the teacher, she received referrals for "Anglo" students, but most of them did not feel comfortable in the class and chose not to become a part of it. On the other hand, the students of Mexican origin in her class reported during ethnographic interviews: "People get along here. Everybody talks to one another so, it's not like being in other classes where some people are quiet and others do all the talking ... In here it's not like that. We're all part of something ... We're a family." In this family there was no discussion of gangs except during the one-hour-per-week "group" time. The positive relationships between students and teacher in ALC and the safe space for learning are important elements to support healthy identity formations.

Students referred to the second floor of the high school that Elway attended as the "smart" place. The white students controlled this area and it was where the advanced courses were taught. The first floor was where "Taco town" was located. ALC was located on the first floor. The physical distance between the two tracks (college prep on top floor and other programs on bottom floor) has endured for generations. Ethnic identification was attached to physical location and, in turn, was attached to social status in school. The strategy of "acting white" (Fordham and Ogbu 1986) was used by some Latino students when taking classes upstairs. In these situations, some young people internalize "the belief that it is wrong to preserve linguistic or cultural identities" (Benjamin 1997, 37), while others are distrustful of classmates who display an assimilated ethnic identity.

The school is examining and addressing complicity in implicit or explicit reproduction of racist structures and unequal outcomes (Fine 1991, Sleeter 1993). Among positive attempts to address institutional racism are the ALC, Unity Class, Chicano Studies Class, Latino Mentorship Program, Latino Culture Class, and a High Intensity Language Training Program for English-language learners. Some of the faculty are also asking students to think about and make a decision to develop a bicultural orientation (Rotheram-Borus 1993) rather than choosing to be strictly identified with mainstream culture or solely identified with one's own ethnic group.

# CONNECTIONS: ELWAY'S LETTER FROM KOSOVO AND HIS FAREWELL SPEECH

In May 1999, Elway finished all credits needed for high school graduation. During the final "group" for the year, an hour set aside each week for discussing important issues in ALC, the students congratulated Elway on his accomplishment. One student said, "This is why I look up to you. I mean you do all your work like it was nothing, man. I have a hard time doing my work." The teacher, White Chocolate, was in "group" and reminded everyone of the many times when Elway did not want to do his work. She mentioned that once he set his goal on a meaningful end, Elway did what was necessary to achieve it.

The conversation shifted to what Elway planned to do next, and White Chocolate said, "I could see you teaching this class." Elway responded, "But see, I mean, every teacher doesn't get a class like this. So that's why I get scared. That's why I get scared, 'cause I get scared, what if I can't teach the students like I wanted to, you know, what if they leave my class knowing nothing? Then I'll feel like a failure and that's the last thing that I want to feel like." White Chocolate interjected, "That's a sign of a really successful person though, someone who *cares* enough to worry about those things. 'Cause I think there's a lot of people that just go through life just doing not caring." This is an excellent example of ways she diffused student fears and encouraged trying on new roles or identities. White Chocolate also made clear that a caring heart is the critical component for success.

Elway continued, "I can't see myself any other way either, you know, than being successful. But right now there is so much going on. It's just hard, you know. There's a lot of stress and stuff." Emulating the affirmative comments provided by their teacher, a male student interjected, "You've been through so much and I look up to you." A female student added, "And you always get through it!" Elway followed these comments with words very similar to what he wrote in his letter from Kosovo. He said, "And everything that I have now will probably be stuck with me the next five years, and that's going to make it hard in college and stuff." His cousin, who also attended the Access to Learning Class, reminded him, "But you've been through so much. I think you can make it through college. Easy!" With all these votes of confidence the discussion culminated with Elway reconsidering the idea originally suggested by his teacher: "I want to become a teacher for ninth grade.

The reason I want to is because ninth grade is when I really messed up bad. And I figure I can, you know, relate a little bit to what the students, you know, what their problems are. And I can get them to come to class."

In his letter from Dren's point of view, Elway wrote, "I'm told that this is part of the beginning of the hardships that I'm going to face in life." During his farewell speech, Elway said, "Everything that I have now will probably be stuck with me the next five years, and that's going to make it hard in college." Both the written and oral texts indicate that rising above pain is hard work and will require time and further struggle. Having lived in the ALC class for four years and having had opportunities to identify with other people's pain made it clear that the effect of the murder of a loved one is lasting. However, the literate actions of reading, writing, and discussing can be used as material resources for examining the context of pain as well as tools for reconstructing a positive attitude toward learning.

Elway is currently attending community college and working to pay for his expenses. At the beginning of high school he did not own a positive academic identity. He did not finish a single credit hour during his freshman year. However, in the alternative classroom where feelings were processed regularly, where a teacher took responsibility for creating a feeling of belonging to family, and where assignments from ordinary texts such as newspapers were used to evoke compassion and care, Elway's academic identity had an opportunity for reconstruction.

For literate activities in ALC, students were expected to do their work and to care about its usefulness. This meant connecting the content of schooling with the context of their lives out of school. Students were expected to move beyond mere comprehension of text to the struggle with the content and context proposed by complex ideas such as ethnic cleansing. It makes sense that in such a learning environment, Chicana/o students are not falling through the cracks. They are graduating, and considering becoming teachers for the next generation.

# NOTE

The research for this study was partially funded by the National Academy of Education Spencer Postdoctoral Fellowship Program. I wish to express my sincere gratitude to Title VII graduate research assistant, Sandra Wolf.

# CHAPTER SIXTEEN

# RIGHTS AND RESPONSIBILITIES OF EDUCATORS OF BILINGUAL/ BICULTURAL CHILDREN

JIM CUMMINS, UNIVERSITY OF TORONTO

This chapter (or essay) focuses on the right and the responsibility of educators to make a positive difference in the lives of bilingual and bicultural children. I argue that every educator has the *right* and the *responsibility* to make a positive difference in children's lives. This claim might not seem particularly contentious, but it entails major implications for how educators define their roles in the education of children. In a context of overt and covert societal racism directed against the languages and cultures of marginalized communities, educators not only have the *right* to become proactive advocates for children's linguistic rights, they have the ethical *responsibility* to do so.

I will illustrate the reality of societal racism directed against children's languages and cultures in two contexts: community and legislation. These examples are drawn from a US context, but similar historical and current examples can be found in countries around the world—for example, Canada's brutal treatment of its indigenous First Nations population in residential schools up to the 1970s (e.g., Haig-Brown 1991) or the current educational repression of Kurds and the Kurdish language in Turkey (Hassanpour, Skutnabb-Kangas, and Chyet 1996). Then, I will present case studies of three schools in the United States, Belgium, and New Zealand that have made a positive difference in the lives of bilingual and bicultural children by affirming in every facet of the school operation the value of children's languages and cultures. Finally, I will discuss a theoretical framework that attempts to articulate the relationship between power relations in the wider society and the reality of teachers' work in schools.

# COERCIVE RELATIONS OF POWER AT THE SOCIETAL LEVEL

I am using the term "coercive relations of power" to refer to the exercise of power by a dominant individual, group, or country to the detriment of a subordinated individual, group, or country. Racism, homophobia, sexism, etc., represent examples of coercive relations of power. The first illustration comes from Lourdes Díaz Soto's (1997) description of the eradication of a successful bilingual program in "Steel Town," Pennsylvania.

## Community

The bilingual education program in "Steel Town" served primarily Puerto Rican students and had operated successfully for more than twenty years. However, as the bilingual population increased in the area, so did expressions of racism in the wider community. The bilingual program became a symbol of linguistic and cultural difference that had to be eliminated. Opposition to the bilingual program was expressed by the school superintendent, school board, and majority community. The growth of racism in the wider community is vividly illustrated by Soto:

Listeners heard about the "Blue E" on the local radio station. The "Blue E" referred to a proposed city ordinance encouraging local merchants to post a "Blue E" on their doorways to signify their support for the English-only ordinance. The ordinance provided store owners with the ability to price goods based upon the English language proficiency of their prospective buyer. For example, if the store clerk detected an accent or felt that the buyer's English was not up to par, they were expected to pay an additional 10 percent to 20 percent on their purchase since this signified additional paperwork and expense for the merchant.

Supporters of this ordinance called the radio talk show, expressing views such as: "Send all the spics back to their country," "This is America ... for whites only," "Our city was better off without all this trash," "English is the language my grandparents had to learn," "One state should be set aside for these people ... but not Pennsylvania" (Soto 1997, 65).

The reemergence of this racism was no doubt stimulated by the fact that the Puerto Rican community decided to stop "swallowing hard" and remain silent in the face of discrimination as they historically had done; instead, they mobilized to demand their educational rights and became both audible and visible. In the eyes of the dominant majority, they no longer knew their place.

Despite the unprecedented mobilization of the Puerto Rican community and a positive report on the bilingual program from a districtwide committee, the bilingual program was eliminated in favor of an English immersion program. In addition, a new school was commissioned in a white middle-class district rather than in the much more overcrowded South Side where the Puerto Rican community lived; South Side students was bused out of their neighborhood because of overcrowding and the refusal of the school board to construct additional facilities; the school superintendent got generous salary increases and accolades from the board; an outspoken Puerto Rican advocate for the bilingual program lost his job in a community college; pastors and priests from various religious groups who supported the community were transferred to other locations; a complaint from the community to the Office of Civil Rights remained in limbo; and the Puerto Rican community emerged from the struggle with emotions ranging from frustration and anger to despondency and resignation.

The discourse that propelled the elimination of the bilingual program illustrates well the rhetorical veneer that often rationalizes coercive relations of power. For example, the school district superintendent justified his proposal to eliminate the bilingual program as follows:

Its main premise is early English acquisition, which would ensure success equipping students with the ability to communicate in the language of this country—English! The fact is that English immersion programs are legal and have been implemented successfully all over the United States for many years ... As superintendent, please know that my single motivation for changing the current bilingual education program is my deep and sincere belief that the earlier children master the English language, the better their chances for success (Soto 1997, 76–7).

There is no reason to suspect the superintendent of hypocrisy; he no doubt had (and probably still has) a "deep and sincere belief" that English immersion is in bilingual children's best interests. Those who hold power also usually hold "deep and sincere beliefs" that they act in the best interests of the society as a whole and that they have more insight than marginalized communities regarding what is in the best interests of these communities. Apartheid in South Africa was rationalized in these terms.

## Legislation

The bilingual education debate across the United States changed dramatically in June 1998 with the passage of a referendum on bilingual education entitled Proposition 227. California voters reversed almost twenty-five years of educational policy in that state by passing Proposition 227 by a margin of sixty-one to thirty-nine percent. Proposition 227 essentially eliminated the use of bilingual children's first language (L1) for instructional purposes except in very exceptional circumstances. The debate leading up to the June referendum crystallized all of the arguments that had been advanced for and against bilingual education in the previous quarter century. Both sides claimed "equity" as their central guiding principle. Opponents of bilingual programs argued that limited English proficient students were being denied access to both English and academic advancement as a result of being instructed for part of the day through their L1. Exposure to English was being diluted and, as a result, it was not surprising that bilingual students continued to experience difficulty in the academic aspects of English. Only maximum exposure to English (frequently termed "time on task") upon entry. to school could remediate children's linguistic difficulties in that language.

Proponents of bilingual education argued that L1 instruction in the early grades was necessary to ensure that students understood content instruction and experienced a successful start to their schooling. Reading and writing skills acquired initially through the L1 provided a foundation upon which strong English-language development could be built. Transfer of academic skills and knowledge across languages was evidenced consistently by the research literature on bilingual development. Thus, L1 proficiency could be promoted at no cost to children's academic development in English. Furthermore, the fact that teachers spoke the language of the children's parents increased the likelihood of parental involvement and support for their learning. This, together with the reinforcement of the children's sense of self as a result of the incorporation of their language and culture in the school program, contributed to long-term academic growth.

In the context of Proposition 227, bilingual advocates argued that bilingual education itself could not logically be regarded as a cause of continued high levels of academic failure among bilingual students, since only thirty percent of limited English proficient students in California were in any form of bilingual education. Less than eighteen percent were in classes taught by a certified bilingual teacher, with the other twelve percent in classes most likely taught by a monolingual English teacher and a bilingual aide (Gándara 1999). Thus, they argued that educational failure among bilingual (particularly Latino/Latina) students was more logically attributed to the absence of genuine bilingual programs than to bilingual education in some absolute sense.

Despite the fact that logically the academic difficulties of bilingual children could not be attributed to bilingual education, the media both in California and elsewhere consistently distorted the role of bilingual education (Krashen 1999). Latent anti-immigrant xenophobia was mobilized through the media and backed up with assertions that flew in the face of massive research evidence. For example, Proposition 227 claimed that one year of intensive English instruction was sufficient for bilingual children to acquire sufficient English to succeed academically in the mainstream classroom without any further support. Several large-scale studies show that at least five years is typically required for English language learning (ELL) students to catch up to native speakers in academic English (e.g., Cummins 1981; Klesmer 1994; Thomas and Collier 1997).

It is clear from both the conflict in "Steel Town" documented by Soto (1996) and the Proposition 227 debate that the discourse of the wider community can exert a dramatic impact on what happens in the classroom. Not only does it result in prohibitions on using children's L1 in the classroom, but it also affects the mind-set of educators who teach bilingual and bicultural students. School board administrators, school principals, and classroom teachers are all placed in a position where they have to make choices. They must decide what their educational beliefs are and how they are to act on them in a context where racism and xenophobia rule the day in the discourse of the wider society. For example, what choices are available to a teacher in a school where the principal has ruled that no Spanish shall be spoken in the classroom either by teachers or children, no Spanish books will be used in the classroom nor given to children to take home for reading with parents, and parents should be encouraged to speak English with their children? This scenario is based on accounts of teachers in California (as of December 1999).

My argument is that teachers have both the *right* and the *responsibility* to resist these coercive injunctions. When the classroom door closes, there are many ways in which teachers can communicate accurate and affirmative messages to their students regarding the value of their languages and cultures. They can also communicate to parents what the research says about the importance of first language (L1) development for children's overall academic progress as well as for continued communication in the home. To take these steps, however, teachers must define their role as challenging coercive relations of power.

The three programs described in the next section illustrate how bilingualism and trilingualism, and strong academic achievement, can be promoted in schools where educators have been willing to establish a "counter-discourse" (Freeman 1998) to the discourse of exclusion that prevails in the wider society.

# THE COLLABORATIVE CREATION OF POWER IN THREE SCHOOL PROGRAMS

Collaborative relations of power reflect the sense of the term "power" that refers to "being enabled" or "empowered" to achieve more. Within collaborative relations of power, "power" is not a fixed quantity, but is generated through interaction with others. The more empowered one individual or group becomes, the more is generated for others to share, as is the case when two people love each other, or when we really connect with children we are teaching. Within this context, the term *empowerment* can be defined as *the collaborative creation of power*.

In describing each of the three programs, I first provide a summary of the main features in tabular form and then draw out some of the commonalities that characterize all three programs. These programs illustrate what educators, students, and communities *can* achieve when the ideology that permeates the school challenges the constricting and devaluing ideology that subordinated groups have typically endured in the wider society.

---

### Richmond Road School

| | |
|---|---|
| **Location** | New Zealand (Auckland) |
| **Languages** | Cook Islands, English, Maori, Samoan |
| **Students** | Cook Islands L1, English L1, Maori L1, Samoan L1 |
| **L1/L2%** | Model A: 100% English<br>Model B: 50% Maori, 50% English<br>Model C: 50% Samoan, 50% English<br>Model D: 50% Cook Islands, 50% English |
| **Goals** | To affirm and incorporate the languages and cultures of the students within the school. |
| **Results** | By the end of elementary school, students' reading attainment improved dramatically compared with their performance in the first few years of schooling. Most children (26/35) in the cohort analyzed longitudinally were performing at or above grade expectations compared with only 3/35 who were at or above grade norms on entry to school. This contrasts with the pattern in large-scale studies which showed similar students in New Zealand far below grade level, with the gap increasing as students progressed through the grades (Elley 1992). |
| **Comments** | The classes were organized in vertical family groupings rather than according to chronological age. Peer tutoring and cooperative learning were central to the instructional approach. Students stayed in the same program from five to thirteen years of age, and parents were given the choice of which model to enter. Thus, children from English-speaking backgrounds also entered the bilingual (Maori) program (Cazden 1989; May 1994). |

---

### Oyster Bilingual School

| | |
|---|---|
| **Location** | USA (Washington, DC) |
| **Languages** | Spanish, English |
| **Students** | Approximately 60% Spanish L1 (primarily Salvadorean), 40% English L1 (about half African-American, half Euro-American). |
| **L1/L2%** | Approximately 50% Spanish, 50% English; students read in both languages each day. Each class was taught by two teachers, one responsi- |

ble for English-medium instruction and one for Spanish-medium instruction. This organization was achieved through larger class sizes and by assigning ancilliary or resource teacher allocations to classroom instruction.

**Goals**        The development of students who are biliterate and bicultural.

**Results**      Grade 3 Reading, Mathematics, Language, and Science scores were more than one median grade equivalent above norms (percentiles 74–81); grade six equivalent were more than 3.5 years above norms (percentiles 85–96) (1991 data). The school was ranked in the top 8% of Washington, DC schools in reading and mathematics on the SAT-9 test (1998 data).

**Comments**     Started in 1971, the school has evolved a *social identities project* (Freeman 1998) that communicates strongly to students the value of linguistic and cultural diversity. In the words of one of the teachers: "It's much more than language."

---

### The Foyer Model of Trilingual/Bicultural Education

**Location**     Belgium (Brussels)

**Languages**    Dutch, French, and one of the following: Arabic, Italian, Spanish, Turkish

**Students**     Students from the following backgrounds: Italian (2 schools), Spanish (2 schools), Turkish (1 school), and Moroccan (1 school).

**L1/L2%**       Nursery school (ages 3–5): 50% L1 (L1 grouping), 50% Dutch (integrated in multiethnic groups)
                 Primary school (ages 6–12): Year 1—60% L1 (reading, writing, mathematics); 30% Dutch-medium (L1 grouping), 10% Dutch-medium (multiethnic groups); Year 2—50% L1 (language, culture); 20% Dutch-medium (L1 grouping), 30% Dutch-medium (multiethnic groups); Year 3+—10% L1; 90% Dutch-medium plus French lessons (multiethnic groups)

**Goals**        To prepare *all* children and teachers to live together in a complex, multicultural society; to enable migrant children to acquire fluency and literacy in three languages by the end of elementary schooling; to increase migrant children's opportunities for integration in both the host country and in their countries of origin; and to increase family involvement in the school and society in general.

**Results**      Project students developed better L1 knowledge than those in monolingual Dutch schools, although their L1 knowledge was less than that of students in their countries of origin. Students also developed a level of Dutch sufficient to enable them to keep up with subsequent classes at secondary school, although there were still differences between them and Dutch-L1 Belgian students.

**Comments:** Started in 1981 by Foyer (a nonstate organization concerned with the well-being of immigrant communities in Brussels), the project assumed as axiomatic that children should be taught in part by teachers of the same origin as themselves in order to support their sense of identity (Byram and Leman 1990; Reid and Reich 1992). According to the evaluation report on Dutch proficiency, "children in the experimental group succeed in catching up on most of their arrears in proficiency in the course of primary school" (Jaspaert 1990, 47).

---

Some commonalities among the schools are immediately obvious. All three schools articulate the value for individual students and their families of developing strong L1 proficiency in both oral and written modes. In doing so, they are challenging the still pervasive devaluation and sometimes "linguicidal" orientation toward the mother tongues of subordinated groups in the wider society (Skutnabb-Kangas 2000).

The following quotations from evaluation reports and other documentation illustrate other aspects of the deep structure of collaborative empowerment and willingness to challenge the coercive relations of power that characterize these schools.

## Richmond Road School

From Cazden's (1989) report comes these quotes from teachers in Richmond Road. They illustrate the ways in which identities are negotiated between teachers and students and among teachers from different backgrounds:

We, as teachers, share our various ethnic backgrounds with each other. This helps to enrich us as a group working together. And not only that—the children also share their backgrounds with each other and with the teachers. The whole basis of the subject content matter of the school is who we are in *this* school.

I'm learning from the kids—their cultures, and not only that, their languages as well (1989, 148).

It's taken a long time, but for me—like many people before—I think of Richmond Road now as my *turangawaiwai* [a place to stand]. It's the place, and what it represents to me, in my mind and my heart. I left Fiji with a chip on my shoulder, and I had nothing to do with Fijian people for

ten years. It's only by being involved with the philosophy here: we're constantly telling people not to be sucked up in the system that says you have to
speak English and be like an English person before you can succeed. And I
realized that here *I* was, telling them to do these things, and *I* wasn't even
doing them myself. I had never spoken to *my* children in Fijian. This was a
big discovery to me. I felt good about myself before, but as a *New Zealand*
person. Whereas now, because of the experiences that I had here, I feel
totally different (1989, 149).

When I was a child, my mother never came near the school, because she
felt she didn't have a place in it. Here people come and feel they're *helping*,
and I think that's what's important—that everybody's got something they
can *do* for the school. If parents and children feel that school is a special
place for them, then the child benefits from this liaison. When you, as a
teacher, have the support of the parents who feel good about the place,
then there's nothing that can't be done for that child. That's special about
Richmond Road. And, of course, it's happening for *each* ethnic group
(1989, 158–19).

When teachers who belong to groups with differential status in the
wider society share as equals within the school, this constitutes a challenge to
the pattern of coercive macrointeractions in the society. Similarly, when
teachers *learn* from their culturally diverse students, a shift in the pattern of
power relations has occurred. When the school creates a climate of two-way
partnerships with parents from varied backgrounds and values the language
and cultural resources they can bring to school, collaborative empowerment
is taking place.

## Oyster Bilingual School

Freeman provides detailed discourse analyses that illustrate how the microinteractions between educators and students in the Oyster Bilingual School
"refuse" the discourse of subordination that characterizes the wider society
and most conventional school contexts. She points out that the discourse
practices in the school "reflect an ideological assumption that linguistic and
cultural diversity is a resource to be developed by all students, and not a
problem that minority students must overcome in order to participate and
achieve at school" (233). Specifically, educators have *choices* in the way they
organize discourse practices, and these choices entail significant consequences for both language-minority and -majority students. The school
*requires* all students to become bilingual and biliterate in Spanish and Eng-

lish, and "to expect, tolerate, and respect diverse ways of interacting" (1998, 27).

> Oyster's bilingual program has two complementary agendas that together challenge the unequal distribution of rights in mainstream U.S. schools and society. First, the dual-language program is organized so that language minority and language majority students have the opportunity to develop the ability to speak two languages and to achieve academically through two languages. Second, the social identities project is organized so that language minority students gain experience seeing themselves as having the right to participate equally in the academic discourse, and the language majority students gain experience respecting that right (1998, 231).

In other words, the school "aims to promote social change on the local level by socializing children differently from the way children are socialized in mainstream US educational discourse":

> Rather than pressuring language minority students to assimilate to the positively evaluated majority social identity (white middle-class native English-speaking) in order to participate and achieve at school, the Oyster educational discourse is organized to positively evaluate linguistic and cultural diversity... This socializing discourse makes possible the emergence of a wide range of positively evaluated social identities, and offers more choices to both language minority and language majority students than are traditionally available in mainstream US schools and society. The Oyster educators argue that students' socialization through this educational discourse is the reason that [limited English proficient], language minority, and language majority students are all participating and achieving more or less equally (1998, 27).

The Oyster Bilingual School Local School Plan for the 1999–2000 school year provides more information about the outstanding achievement levels of the students and insight into the conditions that nurture this achievement. It notes that Oyster has moved from being ranked 25th out of 119 Washington, DC elementary schools in the results of standardized tests in 1982 (top 21 percent) to being ranked 9th out of 111 elementary schools in the results of the SAT-9 reading and mathematics assessment in 1998 (top 8 percent). On the Spanish achievement test (APRENDA), 51 percent of Oyster students scored at the proficient or advanced levels in reading and 77 percent scored at the proficient or advanced levels in mathematics (Oyster Bilingual School, 1999).

The Local School Plan also notes that

the hallmark of Oyster's dual-language immersion program is that it nurtures students' valuing of themselves and their valuing of others. That cherishing of human growth comes in significant measure from the way that the dual language immersion program is delivered at Oyster. From Pre-Kindergarten, students learn in an atmosphere where language and culture are integrated... the equal valuation of two languages communicates to the children that cultures and the people who are products of those cultures are also to be equally valued (1999, 3).

## The Foyer Model

A number of themes run through the various evaluation reports of the Foyer project. One is the necessity for schools to focus directly on issues of *identity* if they are to prepare students to thrive in a complex, multilingual, and multicultural social context. In Brussels (and Belgium as a whole), French is the more prestigious language, but Dutch is the majority language. Because of the similarity of languages, Spanish and Italian children often acquire French on the street and are frequently more fluent in French than their Dutch-speaking peers. These students speak their L1 in the home and frequently visit their countries of origin during the summer. So three languages permeate many aspects of their lives and constitute significant components of their *Belgian* identity.

At one level the school simply reflects and positively valorizes this multilingual and multicultural reality. However, the apparent logic and "obviousness" of this approach masks its uniqueness and the challenge it constitutes to the educational status quo. Unlike more traditional schools that ignore and (implicitly or explicitly) devalue students' home language and culture, Foyer communicates to students (and their parents) the fact that their languages and cultures are *resources* that provide them with expanded options or *choices* with respect to both identity and future life choices (e.g., employment possibilities, place of residence, etc.).

Also clear from the Foyer case study is that trilingualism can be developed at no cost to students' achievement in the dominant language of society and school (Dutch). Although the evaluation comparisons involve small numbers, it is clear that teachers, researchers, and parents consider the program to be highly successful, with most students coming close to Dutch (L1) norms by the end of elementary school.

In short, the organizational structures of the project, together with the ways in which educators have defined their roles or identities, result in a pattern of microinteractions that expand the identity options and academic opportunities available to language-minority students. The *language as resource* orientation that permeates the ethos of the Foyer schools challenges and refutes the *language as problem/minorities as inferior* orientation that characterizes more typical educational contexts.

These three case studies illustrate that educators are not impotent to affirm the value of students' languages and cultures and to promote language enrichment together with strong academic achievement. The framework presented in the next section attempts to depict the underlying structure of this process. Reversing the legacy of school failure has much more to do with challenging coercive power structures than with technical aspects of instruction (e.g., specific ways of teaching reading).

# A FRAMEWORK FOR MAKING A POSITIVE DIFFERENCE IN CHILDREN'S LIVES

The framework (Figure 16.1) proposes that relations of power in the wider society (macrointeractions), ranging from coercive to collaborative in varying degrees, influence both the ways in which educators define their roles and the types of structures that are established in the educational system. Role definitions refer to the mind-set of expectations, assumptions, and goals that educators bring to the task of educating culturally diverse students.

Educational structures refer to the organization of schooling in a broad sense that includes policies, programs, curriculum, and assessment. While these structures will generally reflect the values and priorities of dominant groups in society, they are not by any means fixed or static. As with most other aspects of the way societies are organized and resources distributed, educational structures are contested by individuals and groups.

Educational structures, together with educator role definitions, determine the microinteractions between educators, students, and communities. These microinteractions form an interpersonal or interactional space within which the acquisition of knowledge and formation of identity are negotiated. Power is created and shared within this interpersonal space where minds and identities meet. As such, these microinteractions constitute the most immediate determinant of student academic success or failure.

Microinteractions between educators, students, and communities are never neutral; in varying degrees, they either reinforce coercive relations of power or promote collaborative relations of power. In the former case, they contribute to the alienation of culturally diverse students and communities; in the latter case, the microinteractions constitute a process of empowerment that enables educators, students, and communities to challenge the operation of coercive power structures.

## Figure 16.1: Coercive and Collaborative Relations of Power Manifested in Macro- and Micro-Interactions

COERCIVE AND COLLABORATIVE RELATIONS
OF POWER MANIFESTED IN MACROINTERACTIONS
BETWEEN SUBORDINATED COMMUNITIES
AND DOMINANT GROUP INSTITUTIONS

EDUCATOR ROLE DEFINITIONS ←→ EDUCATIONAL STRUCTURES

MICROINTERACTIONS BETWEEN
EDUCATORS AND STUDENTS
forming an
INTERPERSONAL SPACE
within which
knowledge is generated
and
identities are negotiated
EITHER
REINFORCING COERCIVE RELATIONS OF POWER
OR
PROMOTING COLLABORATIVE RELATIONS OF POWER

The macrointeractions between dominant and subordinated groups in the wider society give rise to particular forms of educational structures that are designed to reflect the priorities of the society. Since dominant groups, almost by definition, determine the priorities of the society, education has historically tended to reproduce the relations of power in the broader society.

Examples of educational structures that reflect coercive relations of power are

English submersion programs for bilingual students that actively suppress
their L1 and cultural identity

Exclusion of culturally-diverse parents from participation in their children's
schooling

Tracking or streaming practices that place subordinated group students disproportionately in lower-level tracks

Use of biased standardized tests for both achievement monitoring and special education placement

Teacher-education programs that prepare teachers for a mythical monolingual, monocultural white middle-class student population

Curriculum content that reflects the perspectives and experiences of dominant groups and excludes those of subordinated groups

These educational structures constitute a frame that sets limits on the
kinds of interactions that are likely to occur between educators and students.
They *constrict* rather than expand the interactional space.

In summary, a central principle of the present framework is that the
negotiation of identity in the interactions between educators and students is
central to the students' academic success or failure. Our interactions with
students are constantly sketching a triangular set of images:

An image of our own identities as educators

An image of the identity options we highlight for our students; consider, for
example, the contrasting messages conveyed to students in classrooms
focused on collaborative critical inquiry compared with classrooms
focused on passive internalization of information

An image of the society we hope our students will help form

In other words, an image of the society that students will graduate into
and the kind of contributions they can make to that society is embedded
implicitly in the interactions between educators and students. These interactions reflect the way educators have defined their role with respect to the
purposes of education in general, and culturally diverse students and communities in particular. Are we preparing students to accept the societal status
quo (and, in many cases, their own inferior status therein), or are we preparing them to participate actively and critically in the democratic process in
pursuit of the ideals of social justice and equity which are enshrined in the
constitutions of most democratic countries?

This perspective clearly implies that in situations where coercive relations
of power between dominant and subordinated groups predominate, the creation of interpersonal spaces where students' identities are validated will
entail a direct challenge by educators (and students) to the societal power

structure. For example, to acknowledge that culturally diverse students' religion, culture, and language are valid forms of *self*-expression, and to encourage their development, is to challenge the prevailing attitudes in the wider society and the coercive structures that reflect these attitudes.

The necessity for bilingual classrooms to become "sites of resistance" (counterhegemonic) if they are to be truly successful in promoting bilingualism and academic achievement is illustrated in a case study of one classroom documented by Shannon (1995). She points out that teachers must recognize how the power of English as the high status language in the school and society undermines children's desire to speak Spanish and identify with their home culture. They must also take active steps to challenge and resist the unequal language status in bilingual classrooms by conveying an enthusiasm for Spanish and ensuring equity in materials and attention to each language. In Shannon's account of one bilingual classroom, we see how issues of power and identity are virtually inseparable from issues of language learning and academic achievement.

In summary, empowerment derives from the process of negotiating identities in the classroom. Interactions between educators and culturally diverse students are never neutral with respect to societal power relations. In varying degrees, they either reinforce or challenge coercive relations of power in the wider society. Historically, subordinated group students have been excluded educationally in the same way their communities have been excluded in the wider society. It follows from this analysis that subordinated group students will succeed academically to the extent that the patterns of interaction in the school challenge and reverse those that have prevailed in the society at large. It is the *right* and the *responsibility* of educators both individually and collectively to contribute to this challenge and thereby make a positive difference in the lives of their students.

# BIBLIOGRAPHY

Adams, M. V. *The Multicultural Imagination: "Race," Color, and the Unconscious.* New York: Routledge, 1996.

Allen, V. G. "Developing Contexts to Support Second Language Acquisition." *Language Arts* 63, no. 1 (1986): 61–66.

Allwright, R. "Turns, Topics, and Tasks: Patterns of Participation in Language Learning and Teaching." In *Discourse Analysis in Second Language Research*, edited by D. Larsen-Freeman, 165–187. Rowley, Mass.: Newbury House, 1980.

American Patrol. "Voice of Citizens Together: American Patrol." 26 March 1999. *<http://www.americanpatrol.com>*.

American Patrol. "Voice of Citizens Together: American Patrol." 6 April 1999. *<http://www.americanpatrol.com>*.

Anderson, P. "Renewals." *New Left Review* 1 (January–February 2000): 1–24.

Anti-Defamation League of B'nai B'rith. *A World of Difference: A Prejudice Reduction Program of the Anti-Defamation League of B'nai B'rith.* New York: Anti-Defamation League of B'nai B'rith, 1986.

"The Anti-Immigration Pill." *St. Louis Post-Dispatch*, 22 June 1998: B6.

Anyon, J. "Social Class and the Hidden Curriculum of Work." In *Curriculum: An Introduction to the Field*, edited by J. R. Gress, 366–389. Berkeley: McCutchan, 1998.

Apple, M. W. *Ideology and Curriculum.* New York: Routledge, 1990.

Apple, M. W. "Constructing the Other: Rightist Reconstructions of Common Sense." In *Race Identity and Representation in Education*, edited by C. McCarthy and W. Crichlow. New York: Routledge, 1993.

Apple, M. W., and L. Weis, eds. *Ideology and Practice in Schooling.* Philadelphia: Temple University Press, 1983.

Aptheker, H. *Annotated Bibliography of the Published Writings of W. E. B. DuBois.* Millwood, N.Y.: Kraus-Thompson Organization, 1973.

Aptheker, H., ed. *The Correspondence of W .E. B. Dubois.* Amherst: University of Massachusetts Press, 1973.

Asante, M. K. *The Afrocentric Idea*. Philadelphia: Temple University Press, 1991.

Asante, M. K., and K. W. Asante. *African Culture: The Rhythms of Unity*. Trenton, N.J.: African World Press, 1990.

August, D., and K. Hakuta, eds. *Improving Schools for Language Minority Students*. Washington, D.C.: National Academy Press, 1997.

Bakhtin, M. "Discourse in the Novel." In *The Dialogic Imagination*, edited by M. Holquist, 259–422. Austin: University of Texas Press, 1935.

Bakhtin, M. M. *The Dialogic Imagination*. Edited by M. Holquist. Austin: University of Texas Press, 1981.

Banks, J. "Mulicultural Education for Young Children: Racial and Ethnic Attitudes and Their Modification." In *Handbook of Research on the Education of Young Children*, edited by B. Spodek, 236–250. New York: Macmillan, 1993.

Banks, J. A. "Multicultural Education: Historical Development, Dimensions, and Practice." In *Handbook of Research on Multicultural Education*, edited by J. A. Banks and C. M. Banks, 3–24. New York: Macmillan Publishing, 1995.

Banks, J. "The Lives and Values of Researchers: Implications for Educating Citizens in a Multicultural Society." *Educational Researcher* 27, no. 7 (1998): 4–17.

Barrera, R. "Transfer of Reading Skills in Limited-English Proficient (LEP) Children." Unpublished grant proposal submitted to OBEMLA, 1998.

Bartolomé, L. "Dancing with Bigotry: The Poisoning of Racial and Ethnic Identities." *Harvard Educational Review* 67 (1997): 222–246.

Bartolomé, L. "Beyond the Methods Fetish: Toward a Humanizing Pedagogy." In *Breaking Free: The Transformative Power of Critical Pedagogy*, edited by P. Leistyna, A. Woodrum, and S. Sherbloom, 229–252. *Harvard Educational Review*, Reprint No. 27, 1998.

Beckett, A. M. "Prekindergarten Teachers' Views About the Education of Language Minority Students." *Teacher Education and Practice* 13, no. 1 (1997): 64–75.

Behar, R. *The Vulnerable Observer: Anthropology That Breaks Your Heart*. Boston: Beacon Press, 1996.

Bellant, R. *Old Nazis, the New Right, and the Republican Party*. Boston: South End Press, 1991.

Benjamin, R. "The Maintenance of Spanish by Mexicano Bilingual Children and Its Function in Their School Lives." Ph.D. diss., University of California, Berkeley, 1993.

Benjamin, R. "The Functions of Spanish in the School Lives of Mexicano Bilingual Children." *Bilingual Research Journal* (1996): 135–164.

Benjamin, R. "*Si hablas español eres mojado*: Spanish as an Identity Marker in the Lives of Mexicano Children." *Journal of Social Justice* 24, no. 2 (1997): 26–44.

Benjamin, R., R. Pecos, and M. E. Romero. "Language Revitalization Efforts in the Pueblo de Cochiti: Becoming Literate in an Oral Society." In *Indigenous Literacies in the Americas: Language Planning from the Bottom Up*, edited by N. Hornberger, 115–136. Vol. 75 of *Contributions to the Sociology of Language*, edited by J. Fishman. Berlin/New York: Mouton, 1996.

Bennahum, D. *Extra Life: Coming of Age in Cyberspace*. New York: Basic Books, 1998.

Bering, D. "Jews and the German Language: The Concept of *Kulturnation* and Anti-semitic Propaganda." In *Identity and Intolerance: Racism and Xenophobia in Germany and the United States*, edited by D. Junker and D. Mattern. Washington, D.C.: German Historical Institute, 1998.

Bering, H. "Who's Afraid of Immigration?" *Washington Times*, 20 January 1999: A17.

Bigelow, B., eds. *Rethinking Our Classrooms: Teaching for Equity and Justice*. Milwaukee, Wisc.: Rethinking Schools, 1994.

Bigum, C. "Teachers and Computers: In Control or Being Controlled." *Australian Journal of Education* 41, no. 3 (1997): 247–261.

Bigum, C., L. Rowan, M. Knobel, C. Lankshear, and M. Doneman. "Confronting Disadvantage in Literacy Education: New Technologies, Classroom Pedagogy, and Networks of Practice." Queensland, Australia: Project for the National Language and Literacy Institute Child/ESL Node, 1999.

Bloch, M., and B. R. Tabachnick. *Increasing the School Achievement of Low-Income Minority Children Through Improved Home-School-University Collaboration*. Proposal presented to the Spencer Foundation, 1988.

Bloom, A. D. *The Closing of the American Mind: How Higher Education Has Failed Democracy and Impoverished the Souls of Today's Students*. New York: Simon and Schuster, 1987.

Bond, H. *The Education of the Negro in the American Social Order*. New York: Prentice-Hall, 1934.

Bond, H. M. *Negro Education in Alabama: A Study in Cotton and Steel*. 1939. Reprint, New York: Octagon Books, 1969.

Bounds, A. "He's Got That Teen Spirit." *Daily Times*, 24 May 1999.

Bourdieu, P. *Outline of a Theory of Practice.* New York: Cambridge University Press, 1977.

Bourdieu, P. "Language and Symbolic Power." In *WHAT BOOK NAME?*, edited by J. Thompson. Cambridge, Mass.: Harvard University Press, 1991.

Bowman, B., and F. Stott. "Understanding Development in a Cultural Context: The Challenge for Teachers." In *Diversity and Developmentally Appropriate Practices: Challenges for Early Childhood Education,* edited by B. Mallory and R. New, 119–133. New York: Teachers College Press, 1994.

Bredekamp, S., ed. *Developmentally Appropriate Practice in Early Childhood Programs Serving Children from Birth Through Age 8.* Washington, D.C.: National Association for the Education of Young Children, 1987.

Bredekamp, S., and C. Copple, eds. *Developmentally Appropriate Practice in Early Childhood Programs Serving Children from Birth Through Age 8.* Rev. ed. Washington, D.C.: National Association for the Education of Young Children, 1997.

Brice-Heath, S. *Ways With Words.* Cambridge, England: Cambridge University Press, 1983.

Brokensha, D., D. M. Warren, and O. Warren, eds. *Indigenous Knowledge Systems and Development.* Washington, D.C.: University Press of America, 1980.

Buchannan, P. "Immigration Reform." 7 April 1999. *<http://www.gopatgo. 2000.org/000-c-immigration.html>.*

Byram, M., and J. Leman. *Bicultural and Trilingual Education.* Clevedon, England: Multilingual Matters, 1990.

Cannella, G. *Deconstructing Early Childhood Education: Social Justice and Revolution.* New York: Peter Lang, 1997.

Carlson, A. *The New Agrarian Mind: The Movement Toward Decentralist Thought in Twentieth-Century America.* New Brunswick, N.d.: Transaction Publishers, 2000.

Carlson, R. A. *The Quest for Conformity: Americanization Through Education.* New York: John Wiley & Sons, 1975.

Castells, M. *The Rise of the Network Society.* Oxford, England: Blackwell, 1996.

Cazden, C. B. "Richmond Road: A Multilingual/Multicultural Primary School in Auckland." *Language and Education* 3 (1989): 143–166.

Chall, J. *Learning to Read: The Great Debate.* New York: McGraw Hill, 1967.

Chambers, R. *Rural Development: Putting the Last First*. London: Longman, 1983.

Cole, M., and S. Scribner. *Culture and Thought*. New York: John Wiley & Sons, 1974.

Colon, J. "How to Know the Puerto Ricans." In *Boricuas: Influential Puerto Rican Writings: An Anthology*, edited by R. Santiago. New York: Ballantine, 1995.

Cortés, C. "The Education of Language Minority Students: A Contextual Interaction Model." In *Beyond Language: Social and Cultural Factors in Schooling Language Minority Students*. Los Angeles: Bilingual Education Center, 1986.

Courts, P. *Multicultural Literacies: Dialect, Discourse, and Diversity*. New York: Peter Lang, 1997.

Crawford, J. *Bilingual Education: History, Politics, Theory, and Practice*. Trenton, N.J.: Crane Publishing Company, 1989.

Crawford, J. *Hold Your Tongue: Bilingualism and the Politics of English-Only*. New York: Addison-Wesley, 1992.

Crawford, J., ed. *Language Loyalties: A Source Book on the Official English Controversy*. Chicago: University of Chicago Press, 1992b.

Crawford, J. "Demographic Change and Language." 26 March 1999(a). *<http://ourworld.compuserve.com/homepages/JWCRAWFORD/canpop.htm>*.

Crawford, J. "Multilingual Government." 26 March 1999(b). *<http://ourworld.compuserve.com/homepages/JWCRAWFORD/can-mult.htm>*.

Crawford, J. "English First Founder Linked to White Supremacists." 4 April 1999. *<http://ourworld.compuserve.com/homepages/JWCRAWFORD/update3.htm>*.

Crichlow, W. "Multicultural Ways of Knowing: Implications for Practice." *Journal of Education* 172 (1990): 101–117.

Cross, W. E. "The Thomas and Cross Models on Psychological Nigrescence: A Literature Review." *Journal of Black Psychology* 4 (1978): 13–31.

Cummins, J. "Age on Arrival and Immigrant Second Language Learning in Canada: A Reassessment." *Applied Linguistics* 1 (1981): 132–149.

Cummins, J. *Empowering Minority Students*. Ontario, C.A.: California Association for Bilingual Education, 1981.

Cummins, J. "Bilingual Education and Anti-Racist Education." In *Policy and Practice in Bilingual Education: Extending the Foundations*, edited by O. García and C. Baker, 63–69. Cleveland, England: Multilingual Matters, 1995.

Cummins, J. *Negotiating Identities: Education for Empowerment in Diverse Society.* Ontario, C.A.: California Association for Bilingual Education, 1996.

Darder, A. *Culture and Power in the Classroom.* A Critical Foundation for Bicultural Education. Westport, Conn.: Bergin & Garvey, 1991.

Davidson, A. L. *Making and Molding Identity in Schools: Student Narratives on Race, Gender, and Academic Engagement.* Albany: State University of New York Press, 1996.

Davies, B., and K. Munroe. "The Perception of Order in Apparent Disorder: A Classroom Scene Observed." *Journal of Education for Teaching* 13, no. 2 (1987): 117–131.

De Alba, A., E. González-Gaudiano, C. Lankshear, and M. Peters. *Curriculum in the Postmodern Condition.* New York: Peter Lang, 2000.

De Anda, D. "Bicultural Socialization: Factors Affecting Minority Experience." *Social Work* 2 (1984): 101–107.

De Diego, J. "En la brecha." In *Lecturas Puertorriquenas: Poesia,* edited by M. Arce, L. Gallego, and L. Arrigoitia, 101. Sharon, Conn.: Troutman, 1968.

Delgado-Gaitan, C. *Literacy for Empowerment: The Role of Parents in Children's Education.* New York: The Falmer Press, 1990.

Delgado-Gaitan, C., and H. Trueba. *Crossing Cultural Borders. Education for Immigrant Families in America.* London: Falmer Press, 1991.

Delpit, L. *Other People's Children: Cultural Conflict in the Classroom.* New York: The New Press, 1995.

Department of Education, Queensland (DEQ). *English in Years 1 to 10, Queensland Syllabus Materials.* Vols. 1–6. Brisbane, Australia: Department of Education, Queensland, 1994.

Dewey, J. *Experience and Education.* New York: Teacher's College Press, 1938.

Dixon, V. and B. Foster. *Beyond Black or White.* Boston: Little Brown, 1971.

Du Bois, W. E. B. *Souls of Black Folk.* Chicago: A. C. McClurg, 1903.

Du Bois, W. E. B. *The ABC of Color.* New York: International Publishers, 1963.

Du Bois, W. E. B. *The Education of Black People. Ten Critiques, 1906–1960.* Edited by Herbert Aptheker. New York: Monthly Review Press, 1973.

Durrant, C., and B. Green. "Literacy and the New Technologies in School Education: Meeting the L(IT)eracy Challenge?" University of New England, Faculty of Education, Health and Professional Studies, Armidale, Australia, 1998. Mimeographed.

Edelsky, C. *With Literacy and Justice for All: Rethinking the Social in Language and Education*. New York: Falmer Press, 1991.

Eisenberg, Nancy. *The Roots of Prosocial Behavior in Children*. New York: Cambridge University Press, 1989.

Elley, J. W. *How in the World Do Students Read? IEA Study of Reading Literacy*. The Hague, Netherlands: The International Association for the Evaluation of Educational Achievement, 1992.

Ernst, G. "Talking Circle: Conversation and Negotiation in the ESL Classroom." *TESOL Quarterly* 28, no. 2 (1994a): 293–322.

Ernst, G. "Beyond Language: The Many Dimensions of an ESL Program." *Anthropology & Education Quarterly* 25, no. 3 (1994b): 317–335.

Ernst, G., and K. Richard. "Reading and Writing Pathways to Conversation in the ESL Classroom." *The Reading Teacher* 48, no. 4 (1994): 320–327.

Espinosa, L. *Hispanic Parent Involvement in Early Childhood Programs*. ERIC Document Reproduction Service No. ED 382 412, 1995.

Esteves, S. M. *Tropical Rains*. New York: African Caribbean Poetry Theatre, 1984.

Fanon, F. *Black Skins, White Masks*. New York: Grove Press, 1967.

Faraclas, N. "Critical Literacy and Control in the New World Order." In *Constructing Critical Literacies: Teaching and Learning Textual Practice*, edited by S. Muspratt, A. Luke, and P. Freebody, 141–172. Cresskill, N.J.: Hampton Press, 1997.

Federation for American Immigration Reform. "Immigration and Ethnic Separation." 17 March 1999. <*http://www.fairus.org/04152803.htm*>.

Fensham, P., R. Gunstone, and R. White, eds. *The Content of Science: A Constructivist Approach to Teaching and Learning*. London: The Falmer Press, 1994.

Fillmore, C. J. "A Linguist Looks at the Ebonics Debate." 1997. <http://www.cs.ncl.ac.uk/~ chris.holt/home.informal/bar/politics/ebonics>.

Fine, M. *Framing Drop-Outs: Notes on the Politics of an Urban Public High School*. Albany: State University of New York Press, 1991.

Fisher, M. "Ethnicity and the Post-Modern Arts of Memory." In *Writing Culture. The Poetics and Politics of Ethnography*, edited by J. Clifford and G. Marcus, 194–233. Berkeley: University of California Press, 1986.

Fishman, A. *Amish Literacy: What and How It Means*. Portsmouth, N.H.: Heinemann Educational Books, 1988.

Fishman, J. *Reversing Langauge Shift: Theoretical and Empirical Foundations of Assistance to Threatened Languages.* Clevedon, Philadelphia: Multilingual Matters, 1991.

Foley, D. *Learning Capitalist Culture: Deep in the Heart of Tejas.* Philadelphia: University of Pennsylvania Press, 1990.

Foorman, B. R., D. J. Francis, T. Beeler, D. Winikates, and J. M. Fletcher. "Early Interventions for Children with Reading Problems: Study Designs and Preliminary Findings." *Learning Disabilities: A Multidisciplinary Journal* 8, (1997): 63–71.

Fordham, S., and J. Ogbu. "Black Students' School Success: Coping with the Burden of Acting White." *The Urban Review* 18, no. 3 (1986): 176–206.

Francis, S. "Gray Davis' Administration Thumbs Its Nose at the People." 6 April 1999. 7 April 1999. *<http://rampages.onramp.net/~rampage/francis.htm>*.

Fránquiz, M. "Learning in the Transformational Space: Struggling with Powerful Ideas." *Journal of Classroom Interaction* 34, no. 2 (February 2000): 30–44.

Freeman, R. D. *Bilingual Education and Social Change.* Clevedon, England: Multilingual Matters, 1998.

Freire, P. *Pedagogy of the Oppressed.* Translated by M. Bergman Ramos. New York: Seabury Press, 1970.

Freire, P. *The Politics of Education: Culture, Power, and Liberation.* Translated by D. Macedo. South Hadley, M.A.: Bergin & Garvey, 1985.

Fu, D. *My Trouble Is English: Asian Students and the American Dream.* Portsmouth, N.H.: Heinemann Educational Books, 1995.

Gándara, P. *Review of Research on Instruction of Limited English Proficient Students: A Report to the California Legislature.* Santa Barbara: University of California. Linguistic Minority Research Institute, 1999.

Gee, J. P. "What Is Literacy?" In *Rewriting Literacy: Culture and the Discourse of the Other,* edited by C. Mitchell and K. Weiler, 77–102. New York: Bergin & Garvey, 1991.

Gee, J. P. *Social Linguistics and Literacies.* 2d ed. London: Falmer Press, 1996.

Gee, J. P. "The New Literacy Studies and the 'Social Turn.'" University of Wisconsin-Madison Department of Curriculum and Instruction, Madison, 1998. Mimeographed.

Gee, J. P., G. Hull, and C. Lankshear. *The New Work Order: Behind the Language of the New Capitalism.* Sydney, Australia: Allen & Unwin; Boulder, Colo.: Westview Press, 1996.

Geertz, C. *After the Fact: Two Countries, Four Decades, One Anthropologist.* Cambridge, Mass.: Harvard University Press, 1995.

Genesee, F, and E. Nicoladis. "Language Development in Bilingual Preschool Children." In *Meeting the Challenge of Linguistic and Cultural Diversity in Early Childhood Education: Yearbook in Early Childhood Education,* edited by E. Garcia and B. McLaughlin, Vol. 6, 18–33. New York: Teachers College Press, 1995.

Gerhard, U. "Integration and Fragmentation Discourses: Demanding and Supplying 'Identity' in Diverse Societies." In *Identity and Intolerance: Racism and Xenophobia in Germany and the United States,* edited by D. Junker and D. Mattern. Washington, D.C.: German Historical Institute, 1998.

Gibson, N. "Additive Acculturation as a Strategy for School Improvement." In *California's Immigrant Children: Theory, Research, and Implications for Educational Policy,* edited by R. G. Rumbaut and W. A. Cornelius, 77–105. San Diego, Calif.: Center for U.S.-Mexico Studies, 1995.

Gilbert, P., and K. Rowe. *Gender, Literacy and the Classroom.* Carlton South, Australia: Australian Reading Association, 1989.

Gingrich, N. *To Renew America.* New York: Harper Collins, 1995.

Giroux, H. *Border Crossings: Cultural Workers and the Politics of Education.* New York: Routledge, 1992.

Goldhaber, M. "The Attention Economy and the Net." 2, no. 4, April 1997. <*http://firstmonday.dk/issues/issue2_4/goldhaber/*>.

Goldhagen, D. J. *Hitler's Willing Executioners.* New York: Random House, 1996.

Goodwin, M. H. *He-Said-She-Said: Talk as Social Organization Among Black Children.* Bloomington: Indiana University Press, 1990.

Gordon, A. F., and C. Newfeld. *Mapping Multiculturalism.* Minneapolis: University of Minnesota Press, 1996.

Graue, M. *Ready for What: Constructing the Meanings of Readiness for Kindergarten.* New York: State University of New York Press, 1992.

Graves, D. *Writing: Teachers and Children at Work.* Portsmouth, N.H.: Heinemann Educational, 1983.

Green, B., and C. Bigum. "Aliens in the Classroom." *Australian Journal of Education* 37, no. 2 (1993): 119–141.

Guthrie, L., and G. P. Guthrie. "Teacher Language Use in a Chinese Bilingual Classroom." In *Becoming Literate in English as a Second Language,* edited by S. R. Goldman and H. T. Trueba, 205–231. Norwood, N.J.: Ablex Pub. Corp., 1987.

Haig-Brown, C. *Resistance and Renewal: Surviving the Indian Residential School.* Vancouver: Tillacum Library, 1991.

Hakuta, K. *Mirror of Language: The Debate on Bilingualism.* New York: Basic Books, 1986.

Hale-Benson, J. *Black Children: Their Roots, Culture, and Learning Styles.* Baltimore: Johns Hopkins University Press, 1982.

Han, J. W. "Crossing Borders: Literacy Learning for a Newly Arrived Chinese Child at School and at Home." Ph.D. diss., Washington State University, 1996.

Han, J. W., and G. Ernst-Slavit. "Come Join the Literacy Club: One Chinese ESL Child's Literacy Experience in a 1st-Grade Classroom." *Journal of Research in Childhood Education* 13, no. 2 (1999): 146–156.

Harding, V. *Hope and History: Why We Must Share the Story of the Movement.* Maryknoll, N.Y.: Orbis Books, 1990.

Hardy, A. G. *Hitler's Secret Weapon.* New York: Vantage Press, 1967.

Hassanpour, A., T. Skutnabb-Kangas, and M. Chyet. "The Non-Education of Kurds: A Kurdish Perspective." *International Review of Education* 42, no. 4 (1996): 367–379.

Hayakawa, S. I. "The Case for Official English." In *Language Loyalties: A Source Book on the Official English Controversy*, edited by J. Crawford, 94–100. Chicago: University of Chicago Press, 1992.

Haynes, D. V. "Ebonics: New Schools Want Black English as 2nd. Language: California District Seeks Federal Funds for Ebonics." 14 January 1997. <http://jan.ucc.nau.edu/~ jmw 22/*Chicago Tribune* 122096.html>.

Heath, S. B. *Language in the U.S.A.* New York: Cambridge University Press, 1981.

Heath, S. B. *Ways with Words: Language, Life and Communication in Communities and Classrooms.* Cambridge, England: Cambridge University Press, 1983.

Heath, S. B., and M. McLaughlin. "Learning for Anything Everyday." *Journal of Curriculum Studies* 26, no.5 (1994): 471–489.

Heim, M. "Transmogrification." 1999. <http://www.mheim.com/transmog/>.

Hitler, A. *Mein Kampf.* Translated by R. Manheim. Boston: 1943.

Holquist, M., ed. *The Dialogic Imagination.* Austin: University of Texas Press, 1981.

hooks, b. *YEARNING: Race, Gender, and Cultural Politics.* Boston: Houghton Mifflin, 1989.

Hoover, M. R., N. Dabney, and S. Lewis, eds. *Successful Black and Minority Schools.* San Francisco: Julian Richardson, 1990.

Hsu, F. *The Challenge of the American Dream: The Chinese in the United States.* Belmont, C.A.: Wadsworth, 1971.

Hyun, E. *Making Sense of Developmentally and Culturally Appropriate Practice (DCAP) in Early Childhood Education.* New York: Peter Lang, 1997.

Igoa, C. *The Inner World of the Immigrant Child.* New York: St. Martin Press, 1995.

"Illegal Alien Invasion." *Free Republic.* 26 April 1999. <*http://www.freerepublic.com/forum/latest.htm*>.

Ivanic, R. "I is for Interpersonal: Discoursal Construction of Writer Identities and the Teaching of Writing." *Linguistics and Education*, vol. 6, (1994): 3–15.

Jang, Y., and P. L. Mangione. *Transition Program Practices: Improving Linkages Between Early Childhood Education and Early Elementary School.* ERIC Document Reproduction Service No. ED 380 200, 1994.

Jaspaert, K. L. "Linguistic Evaluation of Dutch as a Third Language." In *Bicultural and Trilingual Education*, edited by M. Byram and J. Leman, 30–56. Clevedon, England: Multilingual Matters, 1990.

Jipson, J. "Developmentally Appropriate Practice: Culture, Curriculum, Connections." In *Intersections: Feminisms/Early Childhood*, edited by M. Hauser and J. Jipson, 221–240. New York: Peter Lang, 1998.

Jones, E., and L. Derman-Sparks. "Meeting the Challenge of Diversity." *Young Children* 47, no. 2 (1992): 12–18.

Kincheloe, J. L. *Teachers as Researchers: Qualitative Inquiry as a Path to Empowerment.* London: The Falmer Press, 1991.

Kincheloe, J. L., and S. R. Steinberg. "Who Said It Can't Happen Here?" In *Measured Lies, the Bell Curve Examined*, edited by J. L. Kincheloe, S. R. Steinberg, and A. D. Gresson, III, 3–47. New York: St. Martin's Press, 1996.

Kincheloe, J. L., and S. R. Steinberg. *Changing Multiculturalism.* Philadelphia: Open University Press, 1997.

King, E., M. Chipman, and M. Cruz-Janzen. *Educating Young Children in a Diverse Society.* Boston: Allyn and Bacon, 1994.

Kitano, H. *Japanese-Americans: The Evolution of a Subculture.* Englewood Cliffs, N.J.: Prentice-Hall, 1969.

Klesmer, H. "Assessment and Teacher Perceptions of ESL Student Achievement." *English Quarterly* 26, no. 3 (1994): 8–11.

Knobel, M. *Language and Social Practices in Four Adolescents' Everyday Lives.* Unpublished doctoral thesis, Faculty of Education, Queensland University of Technology, Brisbane, Australia, 1997.

Knobel, M. *Everyday Literacies: Students, Discourses, and Social Practice.* New York: Peter Lang, 1999.

Knoke, D., and E. O. Laumann. "The Social Organization of National Policy Domains: An Exploration of Some Structural Hypotheses." In *Social Structure and Network Analysis,* edited by P. V. Marsden and N. Lin. Beverly Hills, Calif.: Sage, 1982.

Knoke, D., F. Urban Pappi, J. Broadbent, and Y. Tsujinaka. *Comparing Policy Networks.* New York: Cambridge University Press, 1996.

Kondo, D. *Crafting Selves. Power, Gender, and Discourses of Identity in a Japanese Workplace.* Chicago: The University of Chicago Press, 1990.

Kozol, J. *Savage Inequalities; Children in America's Schools.* New York: Crown Publishers, 1991.

Krashen, S. *Principles and Practice in Second Language Acquisition.* New York: Pergamon Press, 1982.

Krashen, S., and D. Biber. *On Course: Bilingual Education's Success in California.* Sacramento, Calif.: California Association for Bilingual Education, 1988.

Krashen, S. D. *Condemned Without a Trial: Bogus Arguments Against Bilingual Education.* Portsmouth, N.H.: Heinemann Educational Books, 1999.

Kvistad, G. "Segmented Politics: Xenophobia, Citizenship, and Political Loyalty in Germany." In *Identity and Intolerance: Racism and Xenophobia in Germany and the United States,* edited by D. Junker and D. Mattern. Washington, D.C.: German Historical Institute, 1998.

Labov, W. *Language in the Inner City: Studies in the Black English Vernacular.* Philadelphia: University of Pennsylvania Press, 1972.

Labov, W. "Competing Value Systems in the Inner-City Schools." In *Children In and Out of School,* edited by P. Gilmore and A. A. Glatthorn, 148–171. Washington, D.C.: Center for Applied Linguistics, 1982.

Lacey, M. "U.S. Senate Panel Grills Officials on Ebonics Policy." <http://jan.ucc.nau.edu/~ jmw 22/LA Times 124.html>.

Ladson-Billings, G. "Like Lighting in a Bottle: Attempting to Capture the Pedagogical Excellence of Successful Teachers of Black Students." *International Journal of Qualitative Studies in Education* 3 (1990): 335–344.

Ladson-Billings, G. *The Dreamkeepers: Successful Teachers of African American Children.* San Francisco: Jossey-Bass Publications, 1994.

Lankshear, C. "Literacy and Critical Reflection." In *Critical Literacies in the Primary Classroom,* edited by M. Knobel and A. Healy. Newtown, Australia: Primary English Teaching Association, 1998.

Lankshear, C., and C. Bigum. "Literacies and New Technologies in School Settings." *Curriculum Studies* 7, no.3 (2000). Special issue on literacy, ed. E. Millard.

Lankshear, C., and I. Snyder with B. Green. *Teachers and Technoliteracies*. Sydney: Allen and Unwin, 2000.

Lareau, A. *Home Advantage*. Philadelphia: The Falmer Press, 1989.

Layton, D. "Science Education and Praxis: The Relationship of School Science to Practical Action." *Studies in Science Education* 19, (1991): 43–79.

Lave, J., and E. Wenger. *Situated Learning: Legitimate Peripheral Participation*. Cambridge: Cambridge University Press, 1991.

Lee, C. D. "Profile of an Independent Black Institution: African-Centered Education at Work." *Journal of Negro Education* 61, no. 2 (1992): 160–177.

Leistyna, P., A. Woodrum, and S. A. Sherblom. *Breaking Free: The Transformative Power of Critical Pedagogy*. Vol. 369. Cambridge, Mass.: Harvard Educational Review, 1996.

Levett, A., and C. Lankshear. "Literacies, Workplaces and the Demands of New Times." In *Literacies and the Workplace: A Collection of Original Essays*, edited by M. Brown. Geelong, Australia: Deakin University Press, 1994.

Lima, E., and M. Lima. "Identity, Cultural Diversity, and Education: Notes Toward a Pedagogy of the Excluded." In *Ethnic Identity and Power: Cultural Contexts of Political Action in School and Society*, edited by Y. Zou and E. Trueba, 321–343. Albany: State University of New York Press, 1998.

Lindfors, J. W. "The Classroom: A Good Environment for Language Learning." In *When They Don't All Speak English: Integrating the ESL Student into the Regular Classroom*, edited by P. Rigg and V. G. Allen, 55–64. Urbana, Ill.: National Council of Teachers of English, 1989.

Livingstone, I. *Caverns of the Snow Witch*. Middlesex, England: Penguin Books, 1984.

Macedo, D. *Literacies of Power: What Americans Are Not Allowed to Know*. Boulder, Colo.: Westview Press, 1994.

Macedo, D. "The Colonialism of the English-Only Movement." *Educational Researcher*, in press.

Macedo, D., and L. Bartolomé. *Dancing with Bigotry*. New York: St.Martin's Press, 1999.

Marable, M. *The Crisis of Color and Democracy: Essays on Race, Class, and Power*. Monroe, Maine: Common Courage Press, 1992.

Martin, P. L. "Illegal Immigration and the Colonization of the American Labor Market." *Center for Immigration Studies, paper 1.* Washington, D.C.: Center for Immigration Studies, 1996. ERIC, ED 300307.

Matute-Bianchi, M. E. "An Ethnographic Study of Mexican-Descent Students in a California High School." In *Social and Gender Boundaries in the United States,* edited by S. Chang and J. Currie, 81–94. Lewiston, N.Y.: Edwin Mellen Press, 1989.

May, S. *Making Multicultural Education Work.* Clevedon, England: Multilingual Matters, 1994.

McCarthy, C., and W. Chrichlow, eds. *Race, Identity, and Representation in Education.* New York: Routledge, 1993.

McFeely, W. S. *Frederick Douglass.* New York: W. W. Norton, 1991.

McLaren, P. *Life in Schools: An Introduction to Critical Pedagogy in the Foundations of Education.* New York: Longman, 1989.

McLaren, P. *Revolutionary Multiculturalism.* Boulder, Colo.: Westview Press, 1997.

McLaren, P. *Che Guevara, Paulo Freire, and the Pedagogy of Revolution.* Boulder, Colo.: Rowman and Littlefield, 2000.

McNally, D. "The Present as History: Thoughts on Capitalism at the Millennium." *Monthly Review* 51, no. 3 (July–August 1999): 135–145.

McQueen, A. "Dropout Rate of Latino Students Rises." *Daily Bruin News,* 16 March 2000: 8, 14.

Memmi, A. *The Colonizer and the Colonized.* Boston: Beacon Press, 1965.

Mendelsohn, J., ed. *The Holocaust.* Vol. 4, New York: Garland Publishing, 1982.

Mendoza-Denton, N. "Fighting Words: Latina Girls, Gangs, and Language Attitudes." In *Speaking Chicana: Voice, Power, and Identity,* edited by D. Letticia Galindo and M. Dolores Gonzáles. Tucson: The University of Arizona Press, 1999.

Meyer, L. "A Critical Look at the UNZ Initiative: English for the Children." Unpublished manuscript, San Francisco, 1988.

Millard, E. *Developing Readers in the Middle Years.* Buckingham, England: Open University Press, 1994.

Milne, R., and P. Clarke. *Bilingual Early Childhood Education in Child Care and Preschool Centres.* ERIC Document Reproduction Service No. ED 370 345, 1993.

Mohatt, G., and F. Erickson. "Cultural Differences in Teaching Styles in an Odawa School: A Sociolinguistic Approach." In *Culture and the Bilingual Classroom: Studies in Classroom Ethnography,* edited by H. Trueba,

G. Guthrie, and K. Au, 105–119. Rowley, Mass.: Newbury House, 1981.

Moll, L. C., C. Amanti, D. Neff, and N. Gonzalez. "Funds of Knowledge for Teaching. Using a Qualitative Approach to Connect Homes and Classrooms." *Theory into Practise* 32, no. 12 (1992): 132–141.

Moll, L., and J. Dworin. "Biliteracy Development in Classrooms: Social Dynamics and Cultural Possibilities." In *Discourse Learning and Schooling*, edited by D. Hicks. New York: Cambridge University Press, 1996.

Moraes, M. *Bilingual Education: A Dialogue with the Bakhtin Circle.* New York: State University of New York Press, 1996.

Morris, S. L. "Boys R Us." *LA Weekly* (March 17–23, 2000): 67.

Mosel, A. *Tikki, Tikki, Tembo.* New York: Holt, Rinehart, and Winston, 1994.

Mudimbe, V. Y. *The Invention of Africa: Gnosis, Philosophy, and the Order of Knowledge.* Bloomington: Indiana University Press, 1988.

"Multan a los Hispanos por usar Español." *El Norte* 8 February 1998: 23.

Murphy, B. "A Boy's Tale of Survival." *Denver Rocky Mountain News* 7 April 1999.

National Association for the Education of Young Children. "Responding to Linguistic and Cultural Diversity (Recommendations for Effective Early Childhood Education)." *Young Children* 51, no. 2 (1996): 4–12.

Nieto, S. "Placing Equity Front and Center: Some Thoughts on Transforming Teacher Education for a New Century." *Journal of Teacher Education* 51, no. 3 (May/June 2000): 180–187.

Noddings, N. *The Challenge to Care in Schools: An Alternative Approach to Education.* New York: Teachers College Press, 1992.

O'Donnell, J. "Engaging Students' Re-cognition of Racial Identity." In *Speaking the Unpleasant: The Politics of (Non)engagement in the Multicultural Education Terrain*, edited by R. Chávez and J. O'Donnell, 56–68. Albany: State University of New York Press, 1998.

Ogbu, J. "Understanding Cultural Diversity and Learning." In *Handbook of Research on Multicultural Education*, edited by J. A. Banks and C. A. M. Banks, 582–593. New York: Macmillan, 1995.

Ogbu, J., and M. E. Matute-Bianchi. "Understanding Sociocultural Factors: Knowledge, Identity, and School Adjustment." In *Beyond Language: Social and Cultural Factors in Schooling Language Minority Student*, 73–142. Los Angeles: Evaluation, Dissemination and Assessment Center, California State University, 1986.

Oliner, S. P., and P. M. Oliner. *The Altruistic Personality: Rescuers of Jews in Nazi Europe.* New York: The Free Press, 1988.

O'Loughlin, M. "Appropriate for Whom? A Critique of the Culture and Class Bias Underlying Developmentally Appropriate Practice in Early Childhood Education." Paper presented at the Conference on Reconceptualizing Early Childhood Education: Research, Theory, and Practice, Chicago, Ill., September 1992.

Olsen, L. M. *Crossing the Schoolhouse Border: Immigrant Students and the California Public Schools.* San Francisco: A California Tomorrow Policy Research Report, 1988.

Omni, M., and H. Winant. "By the Rivers of Babylon: Race in the United States." *Socialist Review* 13 (September/October 1986): 31–65.

Omni, M., and H. Winant. *Racial Formation in the United States: From the 1960s to the 1980s.* New York: Routledge & Kegan, 1994.

Oyster Bilingual School. *Local School Plan.* Washington, D.C.: Oyster Bilingual School, 1999.

Paley, V. G. *White Teacher.* Cambridge: Harvard University Press, 1989.

Perlmutter, P. *Divided We Fall: A History of Ethnic, Religious, and Racial Prejudice in America.* Ames: Iowa State University Press, 1992.

Perry, T., and J. W. Fraser. *Freedom's Plow: Teaching in the Multicultural Classroom.* New York: Routledge, 1993.

Perry, T., and L. Delpit. *The Real Ebonics Debate.* Boston: Beacon Press, 1998.

Petras, J. "The Third Way: Myth and Reality." *Monthly Review* 51, no. 10 (March 2000): 19–35.

Phillips, C. B. "Nurturing Diversity for Today's Children and Tomorrow's Leaders." *Young Children* 43, no. 2 (1988): 42–47.

Pica, T. "Second-Language Acquisition, Social Interaction, and the Classroom." *Applied Linguistics* 8 (1987): 3–21.

Piestrup, A. "Black Dialect, Interference, and Accomodation of Reading Instruction in First Grade." *Monographs of the Langauge Behavior Laboratory,* no. 4, University of California at Berkeley, 1973.

Popkewitz, T., ed. *Changing Patterns of Power: Social Regulation and Teacher Education Reform.* Albany: State University of New York Press, 1993.

Poplin, M., and Weeres, J. *Voices from the Inside: A Report on Schooling from Inside the Classroom.* Claremont, Calif.: The Institute for Education in Transformation at the Claremont Graduate School, 1992.

Portes, A., and R. Bach. *Latin Journey.* Berkeley: University of California Press, 1985.

Posey, J. *Exploring Indigenous Pedagogies: Why is This Knowledge Important to Today's Educators*. Ann Arbor, Mich.: University Microfilms International, 1998.

Powell, R. *Literacy as a Moral Imperative: Facing the Challenges of a Pluralistic Society*. Lanham, Maryland: Rowan & Littlefield Publishers, 1999.

Ramirez, J. D., S. D. Yuen, and D. R. Ramey. *Final Report: Longitudinal Study of Structure English Immersion Strategy, Early-Exit and Late-Exit Transitional Bilingual Education Programs for Language Minority Students*. San Mateo, Calif: Aguirre International, 1991.

Ramirez, M., and A. Castaneda. *Cultural Democracy: Bicognitive Development and Education*. New York: Academic Press, 1974.

Ramsey, P. G., and L. Derman-Sparks. "Multicultural Education Reaffirmed." *Young Children* 47, no. 2 (1992): 10–11.

Rank, H. "Patterns of Propaganda and Persuasion." Paper presented at the annual meeting of the Conference on College Composition and Communication, Denver, Colo., March 30–April 1, 1978, ERIC ED 158322.

Rashid, H. "Early Childhood Education as a Cultural Transition for African-American Children." *Educational Research Quarterly* 6 (1981): 55–63.

Rassool, N. *Literacy for Sustainable Development in the Age of Information*. Clevedon, England: Multilingual Matters, 1999.

Red Horse, J. G., R. Lewis, M. Feit, and J. Decker. "Family Behavior of Urban American Indians." In *Human Services for Cultural Minorities*, edited by R. Dana, 55–64. Baltimore: University Park Press, 1981.

Reid, E., and H. Reich. *Breaking the Boundaries: Migrant Workers' Children in the EC*. Clevedon, England: Multilingual Matters, 1992.

Reyes, M. de la Luz. "On the Threshold of Biliteracy." Paper presented at the American Educational Research Association (AERA) conference, Montreal, Canada, April 22, 1999.

Reyes, M. de la Luz. "Unleashing Possibilities: Biliteracy in the Primary Grades." In *The Best for Our Children: Critical Perspectives on Literacy for Latino Students*, edited by M. de la Luz Reyes and J. Halcon, 96–121. New York: Teachers College Press, 2001.

Rich, A. *On Lies, Secrets, and Silence: Selected Prose, 1966–1978*. New York: W. W. Norton, 1979.

Richardson, L. *Fields of Play. Constructing an Academic Life*. New Brunswick, N.J.: Rutgers University Press, 1997.

Rickford, J. R. "The Ebonics Controversy in My Backyard: A Sociolinguist's Experiences and Reflections." 20 March 1999. <http://www.stamford.edu/~ rickford/papers/Ebonics in My Backyard.html>.

Rickford, J. R. "Well-intentioned but Uninformed." S.B. 205. <http://www.stanford.edu/~ rickford/ebonics/LA-OpEd.html>.

Rogoff, B. *Apprenticeship in Thinking: Cognitive Development in a Social Context*. New York: Oxford University Press, 1990.

Rogoff, B. "Observing Sociocultural Activity on Three Planes: Participatory Appropriation, Guided Participation, Apprenticeship." In *Sociocultural Studies of Mind*, edited by J. Wertsch, P. del Rio, and A. Alvarez, 139–164. New York: Cambridge University Press, 1995.

Rotheram-Borus, M. J. "Biculturalism Among Adolescents." In *Ethnic Identity: Formation and Transmission Among Hispanics and Other Minorities*, edited by M. E. Bernal and G. P. Knight. Albany: State University of New York Press, 1993.

Rushkoff, D. *Media Virus: Hidden Agendas in Popular Culture*. 2d ed. New York: Ballantine Books, 1996(a).

Rushkoff, D. *Playing the Future: How Kids' Culture Can Teach Us to Thrive in an Age of Chaos*. New York: Harper Collins, 1996(b).

Saénz, R. Personal communication with author, January 1998.

Sando, J. *Pueblo Nations: Eight Centuries of Pueblo Indian History*. Sante Fe, N.M.: Clear Light Publishers, 1992.

Scarcella, R. *Teaching Language Minority Students in the Multicultural Classroom*. Englewood Cliffs, N.J.: Prentice-Hall Regents, 1990.

Shannon, S. "The Hegemony of English: A Case Study of One Bilingual Classroom as a Site of Resistance." *Linguistics and Education* 7 (1995): 175–200.

Shaw, J. *Meet Kirsten: An American Girl*. New York: Scholastic, 1986.

Shepherd, L., and M. Smith. *Flunking Grades: Research and Policies on Retention*. Philadelphia: The Falmer Press, 1989.

Shohat, E., and R. Stam. *Unthinking Eurocentricsm: Multiculturalism and the Media*. New York: Routledge, 1994.

Shujaa, M. J., ed. *Too Much Schooling, Too Little Education: A Paradox of Black Life in White Society*. Trenton, N.J.: Africa World Press, 1994.

Skutnabb-Kangas, T. *Linguistic Genocide in Education Or Worldwide Diversity and Human Rights*. Mawah, N.J.: Lawrence Erlbaum Associates, 2000.

Slattery, P. "Understanding Postmodern Curriculum Discourses." Paper presented at the 20th Conference of Curriculum Theory and Classroom Practice. Dayton, Ohio, 1998.

Sleeter, C. E. "How White Teachers Construct Race." In *Race Identity and Representation in Education*, edited by C. McCarthy and W. Crichlow, 157–172. New York: Routledge, 1993.

Sleeter, C. E., and C. A. Grant. *Making Choices for Multicultural Education: Five Approaches to Race, Class, and Gender.* New York: Merrill, 1988.

Sleeter, C. E., and C. A. Grant. "Race, Class, Gender, and Disability in Current Textbooks." In *The Politics of the Textbook,* edited by M. W. Apple and L. K. Christian-Smith, 78–110. New York: Routledge, 1991.

Smitherman, G. "What Go Round Come Round: King in Perspective." In *Tapping Potential,* edited by Charlotte Brooks. Urbana, Ill.: Black Caucus of the National Council of Teachers of English, 1985.

Smolicz, J. "Language as a Core Value of Culture." In *Elements of Bilingual Theory,* edited by H. B. Beardsmore. Vrije, Belgium: Universiteit Brussel, 1989.

Smrekar, J. L. "Asian Preschool Children's Second Language Learning in Relation to Play and Social Behavior." Ph.D. diss., Penn State University, 1994.

Soto, L. D. *Families as a Learning Environment: Reflections on Critical Factors Affecting Differential Achievements.* University Park: The Pennsylvania State University Press, 1988.

Soto, L. D. "Boricuas in America: The Struggle for Identity, Language, and Power." *The Review of Education/Pedagogy/Cultural Studies* 19, no. 3 (1997): 349–365.

Soto, L. D. *Language, Culture, and Power. Bilingual Families and the Struggle for Quality Education.* Albany, N.Y.: State University of New York Press, 1997.

Soto, L. D. "Bilingual Education in America: In Search of Equity and Social Justice." In *Unauthorized Methods: Strategies for Critical Teaching,* edited by J. Kincheloe and S. Steinberg. New York: Routledge, 1998.

Soto, L. D. "Growing Up Bilingual/Biliterate in America." Paper presented at the American Educational Research Association, Montreal, Canada, 1999.

Soto, L. D. "The Multicultural Worlds of Childhood in Postmodern America." In *The Early Childhood Curriculum: Current Findings in Theory and Practice,* edited by C. Seefeldt, 3rd ed., 218–242. New York: Teachers College Press, 1999.

Soto, L. D., J. L. Smrekar, and D. L. Nekovei. "Preserving Home Languages and Cultures in the Classroom: Challenges and Opportunities." *Directions in Language & Education,* no. 13 (1999): National Clearinghouse for Bilingual Education, May 13, 1999. <*http://www.ncbe.gwu.edu/ncbepubs/directions/13.htm*>.

Spindler, G., ed. *Doing the Ethnography of Schooling: Educational Anthropology in Action.* New York: Holt, Rinehart, and Winston, 1982.

Spindler, G., and L. Spindler. "Cultural Politics of the White Ethniclass in the Mid-Nineties." In *Ethnic Identity and Power: Cultural Contexts of Political Action in School and Society*, edited by Y. Zou and E. Trueba, 27–42. Albany, N.Y.: State University of New York Press, 1998.

Spring, J. *The American School, 1492–1996*. New York: McGraw-Hill, 1997.

Ssekamwa, J. C. *History and Development of Education in Uganda*. Kampala, Uganda: Fountain Publishers, 1997.

Steven, R. *The Way Things Aren't: Rush Limbaugh's Reign of Error*. New York: The New Press, 1995.

Stotsky, S. *Losing Our Language: How Multicultural Classroom Instruction Is Undermining Our Children's Ability to Read, Write, and Reason*. New York: The Free Press, 1999.

Suarez-Orozco, M. "Minority Status and Education: A Theoretical Framework Comparison." Paper presented at the AERA Annual Conference, San Francisco, 1992.

Sue, S., and D. W. Sue. "Chinese-American Personality and Mental Health." *Amerasia Journal* (1978): 36–49.

Suina, J. "Secrecy and Knowledge in the Pueblo Organization." In *The Head of the Rio Grande: A Reader*, edited by J. Williams. Albuquerque, N.M.: Southwest Institute, 1990.

Swartz, E. "Multicultural Education: From a Compensatory to a Scholarly Foundation." In *Research and Multicultural Education: From the Margins to the Mainstream*, edited by C. A. Grant, 32–43. Washington, D.C.: The Falmer Press, 1992.

Tabachnick, R., and K. Zeichner, eds. *Issues and Practices in Inquiry-Oriented Teacher Education*. New York: The Falmer Press, 1991.

Tabors, P. *One Child, Two Languages: A Guide for Preschool Educators of Children Learning English as a Second Language*. Baltimore: Paul H. Brookes Publishing, 1997.

Taylor, D., and C. Dorsey-Gaines. *Growing Up Literate*. London: Heinemann Educational Books, 1988.

*Testimonial Letter of Professor John Rickford, Dept. of Linguistics, Stanford University, to Sen. Arlen Specter, Chairman, Subcommittee on Labor, Health and Human Services and Education, Committee on Appropriations* [Ebonics Panel]. January 22, 1997. <http://www.stanford.edu/~rickford/ebonics/Specter Letter.html>.

The Longmont Hispanic Study. *We Too, Came to Stay*. Longmont, Colo.: The Longmont Hispanic Study and El Comité, 1988.

Thomas, J. *Doing Critical Ethnography*. Newbury Park, Calif.: Sage Publications, 1993.

Thomas, W. P., and V. P. Collier. *School Effectiveness for Language Minority Students*. Washington, D.C.: National Clearinghouse for Bilingual Education, 1997.

Trueba, E., and Y. Zou. "Introduction." In *Ethnic Identity and Power: Cultural Contexts of Political Action in School and Society*," edited by Y. Zou and E. Trueba, 1–26. Albany: State University of New York Press, 1998.

United States Census of Population and Housing. "Summary Social, Economic, and Housing Characteristics." New Mexico 1990 (CPH-5-33) Final Report. Washington, D.C.: Government Printing Office, 1992.

U.S. Department of Education. *What Works: Research About Teaching and Learning*. 2nd ed. Washington, D.C.: U.S. Department of Education, 1987.

U.S. Department of Education. *Condition of Bilingual Education in the Nation Report: A Report to Congress and the President*. Washington, D.C.: U.S. Government Printing Office, 1992.

U.S. English. "Common Language Quotes." 26 March 1999(a). 26 March 1999. <*http://www.us-english.org/foundation/quotes.htm*>.

U.S. English. "Opponents of Official English." 26 March 1999(b). 26 March 1999. <*http://www.us-english.org/anti-english.htm*>.

U.S. English. "Supporters of Official English." 26 March 1999(c). <*http://www.us-english.org/coalition.htm*>.

Valdés, G. *Con Respeto: Bridging the Distances Between Culturally Diverse Families and Schools*. New York: Teachers College Press, 1996.

Vale, D., A. Scarino, and P. McKay. *Pocket ALL: A Users' Guide to the Teaching of Languages and ESL*. Carlton South, Australia: Curriculum Corporation, 1991.

Valencia, R. *Chicano School Failure and Success*. Philadelphia: The Falmer Press, 1991.

Valentine, C. "Deficit Difference and Bicultural Models of Afro-American Behavior." *Harvard Educational Review* 41 (1971): 137–157.

Valenzuela, A. *Subtractive Schooling: U.S.-Mexican Youth and the Politics of Caring*. Albany: State University of New York Press, 1999.

van Dijk, T. *Ideology: A Multidisciplinary Approach*. London: Sage Publications, 1998.

Vasquez, O. "Connecting Oral Language Strategies to Literacy: An Ethnographic Study Among Four Mexican Immigrant Families." Ph.D. diss., Stanford University, 1990.

Vernon-Feagans, L. *Children's Talk in Communities and Classrooms*. Malden, Mass.: Blackwell Publishers, 1996.

Villenas, S. "The Colonizer/Colonized Chicana Ethnographer: Identity, Marginalization and Co-option in the Field." *Harvard Educational Review* 66, no. 4 (1996): 711–730.

Voloshinov, V. N. *Marxism and the Philosophy of Language.* New York: Seminar Press, 1973.

Vygotsky, L. *Thought and Language.* Cambridge: The MIT Press, 1962.

Vygotsky, L. *Mind in Society: The Development of Higher Psychological Processes.* Edited by M. Cole, V. John-Steiner, S. Scribner, and E. Souberman. Cambridge: Harvard University Press, 1978.

Wallace, C. "Participatory Approaches to Literacy with Bilingual Adult Learners." *Language Issues* (1989): 6–11.

Warren, D. M., L. J. Slikkerveer, and D. Brokensha. *The Cultural Dimension of Development: Indigenous Knowledge Systems.* London: Intermediate Technology Publications, 1995.

Weinberg, S. "Where the Streets Cross the Classroom: A Study of Latino Students' Perspectives on Cultural Indentity in City Schools and Neighborhood Gangs." Ph.D. diss., University of California, Berkeley, 1994.

Weis, L. "Schooling and Cultural Production: A Comparison of Black and White Lived Culture." In *Ideology and Practice in Schooling,* edited by M. Apple and L. Weis, 253–261. Phildelphia: Temple University Press, 1983.

Welch, O. M., and C. R. Hodges. *Standing Outside on the Inside: Black Adolescents and the Construction of Academic Identity.* Albany: State University of New York Press, 1997.

Wiley, T., and M. Lukes. "English-only and Standard English Ideologies in the US" *TESOL Quarterly* 30 (1996): 511–535.

Willet, J. "Becoming First Graders in an L2: An Ethnographic Study of L2 Socialization." *TESOL Quarterly* 29, no. 3 (1995): 73–503.

Williams, P. *The Alchemy of Race and Rights.* Cambridge, Mass.: Harvard University Press, 1991.

Willie, C. V., A. M. Garibaldi, and W. L. Reed, eds. *The Education of African-Americans.* New York: Auburn House, 1991.

Winterson, J. *Art Objects: Essays on Ecstasy and Effrontery.* New York: Vintage Books, 1995.

Wong Fillmore, L. "Instructional Language as Linguistic Input: Second Language Learning in the Classroom." In *Communicating in the Classroom,* edited by L. C. Wilkinson, 283–296. New York: Academic Press, 1982.

Wong Fillmore, L. "When Learning a Second Language Means Losing the First." *Early Childhood Research Quarterly* 6, no. 3 (1991): 323–346.

Woodson, C. *The Mis-Education of the Negro*. Washington, D.C.: The Associated Publishers, 1933.

Wright, R. N. *The Outsider*. New York: Harper & Row, 1953.

Yeo, F. L. *Inner-City Schools, Multiculturalism, and Teacher Education*. New York: Garland Publishing, 1997.

Zentella, A. C. "The Language Situation of Puerto Ricans." In *Language Diversity: Problem or Resource?*, edited by S. L. McKay. Rowley, Mass.: Newbury House, 1988.

Zentella, A. C. *Growing Up Bilingual*. Boston: Blackwell Publishers, 1997.

Zinn, H. *A People's History of the United States, 1492–Present*. 1980. Revised and updated. New York: Harper Perennial, 1995.

# CONTRIBUTORS

REBECCA BLUM-MARTÍNEZ is an Associate Professor in Bilingual and ESL Education in the Division of Language, Literacy, and Sociocultural Studies, in the College of Education, at the University of New Mexico. She received her Ph.D. from the University of California, Berkeley, in 1994. An immigrant from Mexico, she has focused her research on issues of language retention in both immigrant and indigenous communities. Her dissertation (Benjamin, 1993) won the 1995 National Association for Bilingual Education dissertation contest.

LYUDMILA BRYZZHEVA is a doctoral student at The Pennsylvania State University, Department of Curriculum and Instruction, with an emphasis in bilingual education. Born and raised in Tula, Russia, she received her bachelor's degree in teaching English/German as a foreign language at Leo Tolstoy State Pedagogical University of Tula, Russia. While in Russia, she taught English to children, ages 5–14, for three years. That became the reason for developing an interest in bilingual education, and application of Lev Vygotsky's and Mikhail Bakhtin's theories to teaching practice.

LISA COSTANZO is a second-year doctoral student in the Social, Multicultural, and Bilingual Foundations department at The University of Colorado-Boulder. Her specific area of focus is literacy in Bilingual Special Education. Ms. Costanzo assists Dr. Reyes in data collection and analysis in her longitudinal study of biliteracy in the primary grades. She has worked with Dr. Reyes since February 1999. Before coming to CU, Lisa was a teacher of bilingual special education in Syracuse, New York for six years. Prior to that she was a Peace Corps volunteer in Costa Rica. She is a certified teacher in Special Education (B.S., Syracuse University), Elementary Education (M.S., SUNY-Oswego), and Bilingual Education (endorsement, SUNY-Brockport).

JIM CUMMINS teaches in the Department of Curriculum, Teaching, and Learning at the University of Toronto. He has published widely in the areas of language learning, bilingual education, educational reform, and the implications of technological innovation for education. Among his publications are *Brave New Schools: Challenging Cultural Illiteracy through Global Learning Networks* (with Dennis Sayers, St. Martin's Press, 1995), *Negotiating Identities: Education for Empowerment in a Diverse Society* (California Association for Bilingual Education, 1996), and *Language, Power, and Pedagogy* (Multilingual Matters, 2000).

RICHARD DE GOURVILLE began his teaching career as a Spanish teacher on the island of Trinidad, working in both public and private denominational schools. He has also taught ESL in the Republic of Korea and worked as a Spanish teacher in the School District of Philadelphia. He holds a B.A. from the University of The West Indies, St. Augustine, Trinidad; an M.Ed. degree in Multicultural Education from Eastern College; and is currently pursuing a Ph.D. degree in Curriculum and Instruction with a major emphasis in Bilingual Education as a Title 7 Fellow.

GISELA ERNST-SLAVIT (Ph.D. University of Florida) is an Associate Professor at Washington State University-Vancouver. Her research interests include teacher education, oracy and literacy development, bilingual and ESL education, and the use of ethnographic and sociolinguistic perspectives in the study of classrooms. She is a past president of the Washington Association for the Education of Speakers of Other Languages (WAESOL) and has published in the *Anthropology and Education Quarterly, Linguistics & Education, TESOL Quarterly, TESOL Journal, Qualitative Studies in Education, Hispania, The Journal of Classroom Interaction, The Foreign Language Annals, The Reading Teacher, Journal of Research in Childhood Education,* among others.

MIRYAM ESPINOSA-DULANTO is an Assistant Professor at The Pennsylvania State University in the Curriculum and Instruction Department. Her Ph.D. is from the University of Wisconsin-Madison with a concentration on Multicultural Education and Curriculum Theory and Research. Her master's was also from Wisconsin-Madison, in Educational Policy Studies. Her undergraduate work was in Lima, Peru, and she has extensive teaching experience in rural and urban settings.

MARÍA E. FRÁNQUIZ is an Assistant Professor at the University of Colorado at Boulder. Her teaching and research focus on access to educational opportunities, best practices for second language learners, identity struggles between and among Latino/Mexicano/Chicano students. She teaches in the areas of Literacy and Bilingual/Multicultural Foundations of Education. Her dissertation, *Transformations in Bilingual Classrooms: Understanding Opportunity to Learn within the Change Process*, won the Outstanding Dissertation Award from the National Association of Bilingual Educators in 1997. She has published articles in *Language Arts, Primary Voices, TESOL*, and the *Journal of Classroom Interaction*. The National Academy of Education Spencer Fellowship Program funded the research project she reports about in this book.

CATHY GUTIERREZ-GOMEZ is an Assistant Professor for the Early Childhood Multicultural Education program at the University of New Mexico. Her research interests include emergent literacy and multicultural teacher preparation. Dr. Gutierrez-Gomez serves on the local early childhood community council and participates in various collaborative efforts between UNM and the public school system. She is also presently serving as a commissioner for the National Head Start Fellowships Program and serves on the ATE Commission on Racism.

HAROON KHAREM is an Assistant Professor at Brooklyn College. He completed his Ph.D. from The Pennsylvania State University where he taught courses in the Department of African-American Studies. His dissertation was titled "The Hidden Curriculum: A Pedagogy of White Supremacy and Its Maintenance in America." His research focus is in the history of race relations in the United States, especially in education.

MICHELE KNOBEL is an adjunct Associate Professor for Central Queensland University in Australia, and a freelance education researcher who lives happily in Mexico. Her current research interests are school students' in-school and out-of-school literacy practices, technological literacies, and Mexican history. Her recent books include: *Everyday Literacies: Students, Discourse and Social Practice; Critical Literacies; and Ways of Knowing: Researching Literacy* (with Colin Lankshear). Her dream is to one day become a fluent Spanish speaker.

COLIN LANKSHEAR is a freelance educational researcher and writer living in Mexico. He is currently a Heritage Fellow of Excellence (Catedrático Patrimonial) of the Mexican Council for Science and Technology in the Center for University Studies at the National Autonomous University of Mexico. He also works as an Adjunct Professor for Central Queensland University in Australia. His recent books include *Changing Literacies* (Open University Press), *Ways of Knowing: Researching Literacy* (with Michele Knobel), *Teachers and Technoliteracy* (with Ilana Snyder), and *Curriculum in the Postmod-*

*ern Condition* (with Alicia de Alba, Edgar González Gaudiano, and Michael Peters).

PETER McLAREN, a former elementary school teacher and union journalist, is a Professor at the Graduate School of Education and Information Studies, University of California, Los Angeles. Active as a critical social theorist and in local, national, and international political reform efforts, Professor McLaren has published over thirty books and monographs in a variety of fields including anthropology, cultural studies, critical literacy, sociology, critical pedagogy, and multicultural education. His books and articles have been translated into twelve languages. Professor McLaren lectures worldwide on the politics of liberation. His most recent books include *Critical Pedagogy and Predatory Culture* (Routledge), *Revolutionary Multiculturalism* (Westview Press), *Schooling as a Ritual Performance* (3rd edition, Rowman and Littlefield), *Life in Schools* (3rd edition, Longman), and *Che Guevara, Paulo Freire*, and the *Pedagogy of Revolution* (Rowman and Littlefield).

RYAN MOSER has a B.A. in Spanish from the University of Richmond. He is currently completing a master's in Bilingual Education at The Pennsylvania State University. He has worked for Pennsylvania Migrant Education, and has taught high school Spanish and ceramics classes. Ryan has lived in Spain and The Netherlands. He now lives in Pennsylvania where he spends his time with his friends, trying to be a decent and caring human being.

IRENE PABON is a doctoral student and Bilingual Education Title 7 Fellow in the College of Education at The Pennsylvania State University. She was born and raised in Puerto Rico. Ms. Pabon is married and has three children, Craig, Carol, and Chiedza. She has taught in the Puerto Rico Public Educational System as well as in California, Connecticut, and Pennsylvania. She holds a master's of science in Human Services from Springfield College in Massachusetts and a Sixth-Year Diploma in Professional Education from The University of Connecticut in Bilingual Education.

MARÍA DE LA LUZ REYES is an Associate Professor in the School of Education at the University of Colorado-Boulder. Her research includes literacy for second language learners, biliteracy, and racism in the academe. Dr. Reyes has published extensively, including *The Best for our Children: Critical Perspectives for Literacy for Latino Students* (Teachers College Press with J. Halcon) and in the *Harvard Educational Review*.

LADISLAUS M. SEMALI, Associate Professor of Education at The Pennsylvania State University, Curriculum and Instruction Department, specializing in Language, Media, and Literacy Education, is the author of *The Age of Democracy* (Austin & Winfield) and editor of *Intermediality: The Teachers' Handbook of Critical Media Literacy* with Ann Pailliotet (Westview Press). Contact: *lms11@psu.edu*

JOCELYNN SMREKAR is Assistant Professor of Education at Clarion University of Pennsylvania, where she teaches undergraduate early childhood courses. Prior to this she was an Associate Professor of Education at Texas A&M University—Kingsville. While at TAMUK she was coordinator of the King Ranch Family Trust, coordinator of the early childhood graduate program, and taught graduate and undergraduate early childhood courses. She has published articles on early childhood and early bilingual education.

LOURDES DÍAZ SOTO is Visiting Professor at Teachers College, Columbia University and Professor of Education at The Pennsylvania State University's Department of Curriculum and Instruction. She has published widely in the areas of bilingual and early childhood education. Among her publications are *Language, Culture, and Power* (SUNY Press) and *The Politics of Early Childhood Education* (Peter Lang Publishing). Contact: soto@exchange.tc.columbia.edu.

LEILA E. VILLAVERDE, Ph.D., Assistant Professor, Curriculum Studies at DePaul University. She teaches curriculum theory, history, and design, multiculturalism, and teacher education. She is the co-editor of *Rethinking Intelligence* with Joe L. Kincheloe and Shirley Steinberg and *Dismantling White Privilege* with Nelson Rodriguez. She also lectures on art education and creativity.

JOFEN WU HAN obtained her M. A. in Comparative Literature and her Ph.D. in Language/Literacy Teaching and Learning. Her teaching and research interests include composition theory and pedagogy, second language teaching and learning, and ethnographic educational research. Currently, she serves as an adjunct faculty teaching informational writing at Western Michigan University.

LYNUS YAMUNA teaches at The University of Goroka, Papua New Guinea. His research interests include school resistance in Papua New Guinea English-only learning contexts, bilingual and multicultural teacher education, and the use of phenomenological and ethnographical perspectives in the study of students' school experiences. He chaired the Department of Language and Literature at Goroka from 1991–1994. He also has eight years' secondary teaching experience in Papua New Guinea secondary schools.

# Studies in the Postmodern Theory of Education

*General Editors*
*Joe L. Kincheloe & Shirley R. Steinberg*

Counterpoints publishes the most compelling and imaginative books being written in education today. Grounded on the theoretical advances in criticalism, feminism, and postmodernism in the last two decades of the twentieth century, Counterpoints engages the meaning of these innovations in various forms of educational expression. Committed to the proposition that theoretical literature should be accessible to a variety of audiences, the series insists that its authors avoid esoteric and jargonistic languages that transform educational scholarship into an elite discourse for the initiated. Scholarly work matters only to the degree it affects consciousness and practice at multiple sites. Counterpoints' editorial policy is based on these principles and the ability of scholars to break new ground, to open new conversations, to go where educators have never gone before.

For additional information about this series or for the submission of manuscripts, please contact:

> Joe L. Kincheloe & Shirley R. Steinberg
> c/o Peter Lang Publishing, Inc.
> 275 Seventh Avenue, 28th floor
> New York, New York 10001

To order other books in this series, please contact our Customer Service Department:

> (800) 770-LANG (within the U.S.)
> (212) 647-7706 (outside the U.S.)
> (212) 647-7707 FAX

Or browse online by series:

> www.peterlangusa.com